The Constitution of the United States

HARPERCOLLINS COLLEGE OUTLINE

The Constitution of the United States

13th Edition

Harold J. Spaeth, Ph.D., J.D.
Michigan State University

Edward Conrad Smith

HarperPerennial

A Division of HarperCollins*Publishers*

An American BookWorks Corporation Production

Project Manager: Judith A.V. Harlan
Editor: Robert A. Weinstein

Library of Congress Cataloging-in-Publication Data

Spaeth, Harold J.
   Constitution of the United States / Harold J. Spaeth, Edward Conrad Smith. — 13th ed.
      p.   cm. — (HarperCollins college outline series)
   Rev. ed. of: The Constitution of the United States, with case summaries / edited by Edward Conrad Smith and Harold J. Spaeth.
Bicentennial (12th) ed. c1987.
   "An American BookWorks Corporation production"—T.p. verso.
   Includes bibliographical references and index.
   ISBN 0-06-467105-4 (pbk.)
   1. United States—Constitutional law—Digests.   I. Smith, Edward Conrad, 1891-
II. Smith, Edward Conrad, 1891-   Constitution of the United States, with case summaries.   III. Title.   IV. Series.
KF4547.8.S6 1991
342.73'029—dc20
[347.30229]   90-56021

---

91 92 93 94 95 ABW/RRD 10 9 8 7 6 5 4 3 2 1

Contents

Preface

This book is intended to explain the Constitution of the United States: why the document is what it is, and how it remains able to form the fundamental law of a nation more than two centuries after it was drafted. A nation, moreover, that bears only a passing resemblance to what it was in 1787.

My objective is to make the Constitution understandable, to strip away the mystique and the mythology that permeates and surrounds it. I have attempted to do so plainly and clearly and, in the process, focus on the reality of the workings of the constitutional system and the place of the Supreme Court and its decisions within the constitutional scheme of things.

This book had its beginning in 1936 as a small paperback that contained the annotated text of the Declaration of Independence and the Constitution. It was a time of unusual interest in the Constitution because of the clash of the rising New Deal with the laissez-faire economic policies that had dominated public policy since the last decades of the nineteenth century. As of 1936, a conservative majority on the Supreme Court was rather systematically declaring important New Deal legislation, which was intended to combat the effects of the Great Depression, unconstitutional.

In the more than fifty years that have elapsed since the book first appeared, interest in the Constitution and the Supreme Court have remained keen, whetted by the Red Scare of the 1950s, the civil rights movement of the 1960s and revolution in criminal procedure that the Warren Court engineered during the same decade, and contemporary concerns about pornography, sex discrimination, abortion, affirmative action, sexual orientation, the right to die, and the end of the Cold War.

During this period, knowledge about the Court and the Constitution has developed apace. This edition, the Thirteenth, not only includes the most important of the Supreme Court's decisions through 1990, it presents a wealth of new material that integrates the character of the American constitutional system and the freedoms that the Constitution guarantees with the decision making of the Supreme Court. New chapters have been added on the democratic character of the Constitution, the Supreme Court's jurisdiction, legal rights and entitlements, the relationship between the state and federal courts, and the selection of the justices. These chapters incorporate the most recent scholarly knowledge and insight.

The book also includes for the first time a chronology of important events in the history of the Constitution. Some 358 leading Supreme Court decisions have been summarized. For easy reference, they are topically organized into 72 categories that are divided among nine chapters.

The idea for expanding the book's contents and reorganizing them into a more coherent and explanatory whole originated with Fred Grayson, president of the American BookWorks Corporation. His creative touch has transformed the book into a markedly better one. He assigned Judith A.V. Harlan to be manager of the project, which, from my standpoint, was a most happy choice. An experienced editor in her own right, Judy's work with chief justices in two different states provided a welcome supplement to my purely academic orientation.

I wish to acknowledge the assistance of Robert A. Weinstein who reviewed the manuscript in a thoroughly professional fashion. As an author, I have come to value highly the reviewer who suggests, as he did, alternative language for that which is found wanting. Finally, and by no means least, I thank Susan McCloskey who copy edited the manuscript carefully, competently, and unobtrusively. I have learned to appreciate editors such as she who do not tamper with words and phrases unnecessarily but only object to those instances where one's style or syntax is undebatably flawed.

Harold J. Spaeth
East Lansing, MI
December 24, 1990

1

The Origins of the Constitution

The Constitution of 1787 was the product of seven centuries of development in England and the United States. The Magna Charta (1215) is as much the heritage of Americans as of the English. So is the common law that limited the authority of the Crown's ministers and governed the Crown's subjects. Colonial legislatures claimed the rights and privileges of Parliament against royal governors. From their experience in living under charters in some of the colonies, Americans learned the value of written documents that specified the rights of the people and the powers of government. They frequently made efforts to adapt English institutions to the conditions of a new continent and a relatively classless society.

Disagreement among Americans about the political relationship of the colonies to the mother country produced a breach between them. King George III, his ministers, and the majority party in Parliament regarded the colonies as subordinate to England. Americans believed each colony to be a coequal part of the Crown's dominions and as such entitled to self-government and exempt from parliamentary taxation, legislation, and administrative regulation. They sought to redress their grievances by protests, petitions, nonimportation agreements, and, finally, by resort to arms.

In May 1775, three weeks after the Revolutionary War began at Lexington and Concord, the Second Continental Congress met in Philadelphia. Its members, delegates of patriotic organizations in each of the colonies, were to coordinate measures for the common defense. The Congress assumed many of the powers of government: it created an army and navy, appointed officers, borrowed money, issued paper currency, and appealed to Europe for help. It adopted the Declaration of Independence, recommended the creation of state constitutions, and drew up the Articles of Confederation, all highly important documents in American constitutional development.

REVOLUTION AND INDEPENDENCE

Though a few radical leaders advocated independence from the beginning, most Americans hoped for reconciliation with Great Britain. On July 6, 1775, the Congress issued the lengthy "Declaration of the Causes and Necessity of Taking Up Arms," which detailed American grievances while explicitly denying any intention to separate from Great Britain and establish independent states. King George replied by proclaiming a state of rebellion in the colonies, and Parliament dutifully passed an act that cut off trade with the colonies. Moderate leaders now became convinced that independence was the only alternative to submission. Thomas Paine's emotionally charged pamphlet *Common Sense* was widely circulated throughout the colonies and drew thousands of ordinary Americans to the cause of independence. On June 7, 1776, Richard Henry Lee of Virginia proposed the following resolution to the Continental Congress:

Resolved, That these United Colonies are, and of right ought to be, free and independent States, that they are absolved from all allegiance to the British Crown, and that all political connection between them and the State of Great Britain is, and ought to be, totally dissolved.

Drafting the Declaration

On June 10 the Congress selected five of its ablest members—John Adams, Benjamin Franklin, Thomas Jefferson, Robert R. Livingston, and Roger Sherman—to draft a declaration of independence. Jefferson was the chief author of the draft submitted to the Congress on June 23. The Congress made two or three changes and voted for independence on July 2. On July 4 John Hancock, president of the Congress, signed the final draft copy. All but one of the other signatures were appended on August 2.

Contents of the Declaration

The philosophy underlying the Declaration of Independence derives from John Locke's second treatise, *On Civil Government* (1690), which he had written for the avowed purpose of justifying the English revolution of 1688. According to Locke, people had once lived isolated lives in a state of nature. At a certain stage of development they entered into social contracts with one another, thereby creating a society as well as a government. By the terms of the contract individuals surrendered part of their natural rights and in return received protection against other people and other advantages of government. Governmental actions were to correspond with moral principles, with the will of the majority determining what was right or wrong. If a government seriously threatened the interests of society, the people might overthrow it and substitute it with another. Jefferson omitted specific references to the imaginary state of nature and social contracts, asserting instead that the equality of people and their natural rights were "self-evident."

The Declaration indicted the king and Parliament for usurping power and for tyrannical actions, such as "abolishing our most valuable laws" and "waging war against us." For these and other reasons, the United Colonies declared themselves free and independent states with all the powers rightfully belonging to sovereign states.

Effects of the Declaration

The Declaration of Independence powerfully stimulated the patriots' cause. It persuasively justified a resort to arms and implied that American governments would rest on the will of the people. Though it did not immediately result in the emancipation of slaves or in universal suffrage, abolitionists and suffragettes effectively used the egalitarian principles of the Declaration to advance their causes. The Declaration continues to prod the American conscience today to improve the conditions of various minorities.

STATE CONSTITUTIONS

Beginning in 1776, revolutionary assemblies in most states formulated written constitutions, using colonial charters as models. All of them had certain common features.

Popular Sovereignty

The people were declared to be the source of governmental authority. In the words of the Georgia constitution of 1777: "We, therefore, the representatives of the people, from whom all power originates and for whose benefit all government is intended, by virtue of the power delegated to us, do ordain...that the following rules and regulations be adopted for the future government of this state." The Massachusetts constitution of 1780 expressed the same idea in the form of an original social contract: "The whole people covenants with each citizen, and each citizen with the whole people, that all shall be governed by certain laws for the common good."

Eclipse of the Executive

Executive power in the states entered an eclipse that lasted until the adoption of the Constitution of the United States. Pennsylvania's first constitution did not even provide for a governor. In ten states the governor's term was just one year, and his administrative powers were few. Only New York gave the governor sufficient power and a long enough term (three years) to enable him to be an effective chief executive.

Legislative Supremacy

In a majority of the states, the legislature elected the governor, judges, and other officers and determined the policies of government. It possessed lawmaking, financial, and supervisory powers. As the successor of Parliament, the legislature was considered to hold general residual authority: it could exercise any power not granted to another governmental body. Except in Pennsylvania and Georgia, the legislature comprised two houses. In most states, its members were chosen by voters who owned considerable property.

Limited Government

The most remarkable state document of this period was the bill of rights prefixed to the Virginia constitution of 1776. George Mason wrote the first fifteen articles; Patrick Henry wrote the sixteenth article, on religious freedom. The Virginia Bill of Rights states the principles on which all branches of government, including the legislature, should operate and guarantees individual liberties. It influenced the writing of later constitutions both in the United States and in Europe.

THE CONFEDERATION OF THE STATES

The same Virginia resolution that proposed independence called on Congress to prepare a plan for a confederation of the states. On July 12, 1776, debate began on a draft written by John Dickinson; it continued whenever time could be spared from urgent military matters. Unfortunately, the concerns of the individual states outweighed considerations of national interest. States with claims to western lands refused to grant Congress power to settle boundary disputes. The small states insisted on amendments to ensure their sovereignty, while the large states tried (in vain) to apportion voting strength in Congress according to population or the amount that each state contributed to the common fund. The southern states insisted on apportioning expenses of the Confederation according to the value of land in private hands rather than on the basis of total population including slaves. Not until November 1, 1777, did Congress submit the Articles to the states for ratification.

Most of the states ratified them fairly promptly, but Maryland, expressing fears for its future among powerful neighbors, held out until other states agreed to cede their western lands to the United States. The Articles became effective on March 1, 1781.

Structure of the Confederation

The Articles variously described the new arrangement as a "confederacy," a "firm league of friendship," and a "perpetual Union." It was less a government than an agency that enabled cooperation among the state governments. Each state retained its sovereignty, freedom, and independence. To amend the Articles required unanimous approval of the state legislatures. No article provided for an executive or for a permanent judiciary. The chief organ of government was a congress composed of delegates annually chosen from each state. Each state paid its own delegates and could recall them at will. Each delegation cast one vote, and any important action required the approval of nine states. The Articles did provide, however, for cooperation among the states, including a full faith and credit clause and a privileges and immunities clause. Several limitations on state action that were expressed in Article VI were later carried over into the Constitution of the United States, as were many of the powers granted to Congress in Article IX. The fatal defects of the Articles were in their omissions. They did not provide for a vigorous executive or empower Congress to control commerce among the states and with foreign countries. Rather than enabling Congress to tax, they only permitted it to "requisition" the states to provide necessary revenue by levying appropriate taxes and remitting the proceeds. Finally, they did not permit Congress to exert any of its limited powers over individuals.

The Confederation Period

Unsettled economic conditions at the close of the Revolution severely tested both the state governments and Congress. In some states the legislatures yielded to the demands of debtors and issued large quantities of paper money or enacted "stay laws" postponing the dates when debtors were legally obliged to pay their creditors. In violation of the Articles, some states imposed tariffs or other trade barriers that prevented the free flow of commerce from other states. In varying degrees, states failed to meet their financial obligations to the Confederation. Of a total of $10 million requisitioned by Congress, only $1.5 million was actually paid; one state paid nothing at all. Largely because of Congress's inability to meet interest payments, the public debt increased after the Revolution ended. The Confederation maintained only a small army, 750 officers and men, for the defense of the United States against Indians and other potential enemies. With the Ordinances of 1785 and 1787, Congress established fundamental and durable policies for the survey of public lands and the government of territories, but it was unable to promote much settlement in the Northwest Territory. Though the country's ablest leaders engaged in diplomacy, they were singularly unsuccessful in negotiating commercial treaties, in part because foreign nations feared that the states would not fulfill the treaty obligations of the United States.

Failure of the Amending Process

In 1781 Congress proposed an amendment to the Articles that would enable it to levy a duty of 5 percent on all imported goods. All the states ratified the amendment except Rhode Island. Twelve states ratified a second amendment aimed at meeting Rhode Island's objections, but this time New York refused to give its approval despite Congress's warning that without revenues the Confederation would disintegrate. Both Rhode Island and New York possessed fine harbors that served as ports of entry for the trade of nearby states, and both were unwilling to surrender part of their tariff duties for the common good. The position of Rhode Island and New York made it plain that if the Union were to be strengthened, other means would have to be employed than the cumbersome procedure in the Articles.

THE MOVEMENT FOR A NEW CONSTITUTION

A number of groups combined to create the Constitution of the United States. Among the most important were former officers of the Continental Army and former members of Congress who, in the course of their service, had developed national loyalties; leaders from the large states of Virginia, Pennsylvania, and Massachusetts who believed that the power of one state to prevent change endangered the future of all the states; leaders from the small states of Connecticut, New Jersey, and Delaware who sought to overcome the commercial restrictions of New York and Pennsylvania; Georgians who wanted national help against an Indian war that threatened them; and merchants and shipowners in all the states. Leaders included Alexander Hamilton of New York, who as military secretary to George Washington had observed the weakness and incapacity of Congress, and James Madison, an associate of Thomas Jefferson and opponent of Patrick Henry in Virginia politics.

Call for the Convention

In 1785 commissioners from Virginia and Maryland amicably settled boundary disputes, navigation rights on Chesapeake Bay, and tariff duties. When the Maryland commissioners proposed a larger conference, which would include Delaware and Pennsylvania, the Virginia legislature seized the opportunity to call a meeting of delegates from all the states at Annapolis in September 1786. Nine states responded by appointing delegates, but only five states were represented when the conference convened because the delegates from four states failed to reach the convention site in time to participate. Those present adopted a strongly worded report, supposedly written by Hamilton, stressing the deficiencies in the existing government and calling for a convention of delegates from all the states to meet in Philadelphia on May 14, 1787, for the purpose of "digesting a Plan" to remedy the defects in the Articles of Confederation. After several states had chosen delegates, Congress issued a formal call for a Convention "for the sole and express purpose of revising the Articles of Confederation."

Selection of Delegates

The Virginia legislature chose an able delegation, including Washington, who was persuaded to come out of retirement, James Madison, George Mason, and Governor Edmund Randolph. Pennsylvania sent the largest delegation: it included Benjamin Franklin, whose reputation only Washington's surpassed; James Wilson, who consistently asserted that Americans were one people, who became an original member of the Supreme Court, and who died in debt and disgrace before the end of the century; and Gouverneur Morris, a brilliant New Yorker temporarily residing in Philadelphia. Morris, in addition to penning the Constitution's most famous phrase, "We the People of the United States," holds the record for most frequently addressing his fellow delegates—173 times.

Although the New York legislature designated Hamilton as a delegate, it also took care to send with him John Lansing and Robert Yates, members of the state's dominant antifederalist party. The New Hampshire legislature chose delegates but neglected to provide for their expenses; they arrived in late July—after Lansing and Yates of the New York delegation had left the convention. Only Rhode Island appointed no delegates. Other outstanding members included Rufus King and Elbridge Gerry of Massachusetts, Roger Sherman and William Samuel Johnson of Connecticut, and John Rutledge and the two Pinckneys of South Carolina.

Of the fifty-five delegates who attended, thirty-nine had served in Congress, and all were experienced in the politics of their states. Eight had signed the Declaration of Independence and at least thirty were veterans of the Revolutionary War. One, Robert Morris, helped finance it. A large number were young men, in their early thirties; the average age was about forty-three. Among those not in attendance were Jefferson and John Adams, who were serving abroad as ministers to France and Great Britain, respectively. Henry and a number of other leaders who were primarily interested in state politics declined to participate. Interestingly, no more than thirty of the fifty-five attendees were ever present at any session of the Convention.

THE CONVENTION OF 1787

Only the Virginia and Pennsylvania delegations arrived in Philadelphia at the appointed time; because of transportation problems, not until May 25 could the Convention be convened. The delegates unanimously elected Washington as presiding officer. Rules of procedure provided each state delegation with one vote. The delegates agreed to keep their deliberations secret, an action that is partly responsible for the view—technically accurate—that they engaged in an undemocratic conspiracy to undo the work of the Revolution by replacing the Articles with a centralized government that would undermine state sovereignty. The closed sessions enabled the participants to express opinions freely, to advance tentative proposals, to reconsider decisions without being publicly chastised for inconsistency, and to negotiate, bargain, and compromise. The delegates determined to prepare a comprehensive document and to be judged on their work as a whole.

Records of the Convention

Although the delegates decided to keep the public ignorant of their deliberations, Madison, sensing the historical importance of the Convention, obtained its permission to take notes of the debates. Other members sometimes helped by giving him copies or outlines of their remarks. Madison's notes, which were not published until 1840, four years after his death, constitute practically the only dependable source of information concerning the debates. The recollections of other delegates, written after the Convention had adjourned, supplement them in part.

The Virginia Plan

After arriving in Philadelphia, the Virginia delegation proposed a series of resolutions that provided for the supremacy of the legislative branch, a national executive, and a system of national courts. The legislature would consist of two houses, one of which would be elected by popular vote and the other selected by the first house from persons nominated by the state legislatures. A state's voting strength in each house would be proportionate to the taxes paid by the state or to the number of its free inhabitants. The legislature would have the power to enact laws on all matters in which the separate states were incompetent, to void state laws contravening the Constitution, to use the military forces of the Union against any recalcitrant state, and to elect the national executive and the judges of national courts.

The delegates debated the Virginia plan for two weeks, making a number of changes. They agreed that representatives in the lower house should be apportioned according to population and—by a margin of one vote—that the same apportionment should apply to the second house. The delegation from New Jersey requested an adjournment in order to prepare a different plan.

The New Jersey Plan

On June 15 William Paterson of New Jersey introduced another series of resolutions. The Convention would propose amendments to the Articles of Confederation only as Congress had specified. Congress would have the power to levy duties on goods imported into the United States, to impose a tax on documents, and to regulate the collection of both. If additional revenues were needed, Congress would not only requisition the states but also collect taxes in noncomplying states. Congress would have the power to regulate foreign and interstate commerce. All laws of Congress and all treaties made under the authority of the United States would be the supreme law of the respective states. Congress would choose a plural executive, with general authority to execute federal acts, appoint federal officers, and direct all military operations. A supreme court appointed by the executive with jurisdiction on appeal over cases arising from the construction of treaties, the regulation of trade, and the collection of revenue was also proposed.

If the New Jersey plan had been formulated before the Convention met, it would have been satisfactory to all but the most dedicated nationalists. But only New York and Delaware supported it. Furthermore, many provisions of the Virginia plan, especially the one determining apportionment of the upper house according to population, required alteration before they would gain support from the smaller states.

The Great Compromise

At this point the lines between the large and small states became tightly drawn and talk of adjourning the Convention was heard. Apart from slavery, no subject more sorely divided the delegates than the matter of representation in the national legislature. Large-state delegates insisted that representation be based on population; the small states feared to enter a union dominated by the large states. Besides, they argued, their residents would never accept a constitution that did not recognize the principle of state equality. After an initial rejection and three weeks of recrimination, the delegates agreed to the Great (sometimes called the Connecticut) Compromise: a lower house chosen according to population and with the sole authority to originate revenue bills, and an upper house in which each state would have an equal vote.

Compromise of Sectional Interests

Northern commercial interests wanted Congress to have the power to regulate interstate commerce, while the South opposed duties on exports. In addition to free exportation of their commodities, southern delegates also demanded that Congress have no power to interfere with the slave trade. The compromise finally reached provided, in return for congressional power over interstate commerce, that exports would not be taxed and that the slave trade could continue until 1808. The formula for apportioning representatives and direct taxes counted a slave as three-fifths of a free person.

Powers of Congress

Most of the delegates considered impractical the broad grant of federal powers in the Virginia plan. To disallow state laws would cause resentment, and the use of military force would amount to making war on a state. Instead, the delegates decided to enumerate the specific powers that Congress might exercise. The Committee on Detail compiled a list, taking most of the powers—some of them verbatim—from the Articles of Confederation and adding others from various state constitutions. The tax power remained broadly stated except concerning direct taxes. Congress received a choice of means to carry out its enumerated powers at the end of Article I, section 8 of the Constitution in the "necessary and proper" clause.

The Executive Article

Nothing gave the Convention more trouble than the creation of an adequately empowered executive who would be accountable to the electorate. The delegates debated the merits of a plural as opposed to a single executive. They considered tenure for life and for a single seven-year term before settling on a four-year term with the opportunity for reelection. In provisions borrowed from the constitution of New York, the Convention created a strong executive, but they made him subject to impeachment and trial by Congress. As to presidential selection, the Convention discarded legislative election, because it would make the president subservient to Congress, and also popular election, because it would give excessive weight to the populous states. The result was an electoral college weighted in favor of the small states. The least populous state would have three electors, while a state with ten times as many people would have only four times as many electors. If no candidate received a majority of the votes of the electoral college, the House of Representatives, voting by states and with each state having one vote, would select from among the five highest ranking candidates. Washington was expected to be the first president, serving as many terms as he desired. After his administration, the delegates thought, the electoral vote would be divided among many candidates, which would throw the election into the House, where the small states, being in the majority, would choose the president.

The Judiciary Article

The Convention agreed early on to create a supreme court and to provide federal judges with tenure. Sharp differences did arise over whether to create a separate set of lower federal courts or to provide for the trial of federal cases in courts of the various states. The delegates astutely resolved the issue by authorizing Congress to create inferior federal courts if it so desired. The Supreme Court received original jurisdiction to decide cases involving foreign diplomatic and consular officers and to resolve disputes between states. Federal judges were to be appointed by the president with the consent of the Senate.

The Supremacy Clause

Article VI of the Constitution, a provision that first appeared in the New Jersey plan, declared that laws made in accordance with the Constitution and treaties would be the supreme law of the land. State judges were bound to uphold the supremacy of federal law even if it conflicted with state constitutions or laws. Another clause aimed at strengthening the Union required state legislative, executive, and judicial officers to take an oath to support the Constitution of the United States.

Position of the States under the Constitution

The federal government guarantees to each state a republican form of government, protection from invasion, and, at its request, protection from domestic violence. No state can be divided, merged with another state, or be deprived of its equal vote in the Senate without its own consent. The Constitution says nothing about state sovereignty. The states may not coin money, issue paper money, make anything but gold and silver coin a legal tender in payment of debts, pass any law impairing the obligation of contracts, levy taxes on imports or exports, or, without the consent of Congress, enter into a compact with another state, i.e., come to a treatylike agreement. These prohibitions addressed concerns of financial and business interests about laws enacted by various states during the confederation period. In order to promote harmonious relations with one another, the states must give full faith and credit to the public acts, records, and judicial decisions of other states; treat citizens of other states as they do their own residents; and return fugitives from justice and runaway slaves to the states from which they had fled.

The Source of the Constitution's Authority

The preamble of the Articles of Confederation named the states in order from north to south. But how was the Convention to enumerate the participating states without knowing which would ratify? In a brilliant flash of inspiration, the delegates began the Constitution with the words "We the people of the United States . . . do ordain and establish this Constitution . . ."

Method of Ratification

The members of the Constitutional Convention considered ratification by state conventions composed of specially elected delegates more likely than ratification by the state legislatures. The legislatures would not view kindly an instrument of government that would reduce their own powers. Given the opposition of New York and Rhode Island, the Convention abandoned all thought of requiring every state to ratify it. Because of antifederalist sentiment, the delegates decided that the Constitution should go into effect when nine states ratified it.

Amending Procedure

The delegates recognized that changing circumstances and conditions might flaw the Constitution after it took effect; they therefore determined not to continue the disastrous amending procedure of the Articles of Confederation. They first voted to permit Congress to call a convention to propose amendments at the request of two-thirds of the states. This method has never been used, but in 1911 the vote of one more state would have opened the door. The goal then was the direct election of senators. The foreboding prospect of a second constitutional convention prodded enough reluctant senators to use the alternative method for proposing amendments provided by the Framers: a two-thirds vote of both houses of Congress. The means of ratification the Constitution provides parallels the choice of methods for proposing amendments: the legislatures of or conventions in three-fourths of the states.

Guarantees of Rights

The original Constitution contains several important guarantees of individual rights: the writ of habeas corpus and prohibition of bills of attainder and ex post facto laws (see the Glossary of Constitutional Words and Phrases) in Article I, section 9; trial by jury and a narrow definition of treason in Article III; and a prohibition of religious tests as a condition for holding federal office in Article VI. A formal list of other rights was considered either too difficult to specify or unnecessary. A proposal late in the session to appoint a committee to draft a bill of rights failed badly.

End of the Session

A committee on style arranged in logical order the provisions previously approved. Gouverneur Morris apparently wrote the final draft. Only thirty-nine of the fifty-five members who attended at least some of the sessions signed the Constitution; for various reasons such major participants as Eldridge Gerry of Massachusetts and George Mason and Edmund Randolph of Virginia refused to sign. Randolph, however, made amends by casting a crucial vote for ratification at the Virginia ratifying convention. On September 17 the Convention adjourned after nearly four months in virtually continuous session.

Political Theory of the Constitution

Although Madison and others had studied the history of previous federations, they had formulated no hard-and-fast theories on the subject. Their attitude was pragmatic. Every constitutional provision was based on experience in the states, the colonies, or Britain. The powers delegated to the federal government were determined by what was needed and what the state conventions might accept. For theoretical inspiration the delegates relied on John Locke and on Montesquieu's *Spirit of the Laws*. Both writers had insisted on the need to separate powers in order to prevent tyranny; in Montesquieu's view even the people's representatives in the legislature could not be trusted. The delegates therefore specified the powers of each branch in a separate article and devised ingenious checks and balances to make cooperation among the legislative, executive, and judicial branches even more difficult. Although the Constitution makes no mention of Locke's state of nature or his original contract, it derives its authority from the will of the people—as the Preamble and Article VII indicate. To people familiar with Locke's theories, the Constitution created a latter-day social contract.

THE CONTEST OVER RATIFICATION

The convention sent copies of the Constitution to Congress, which transmitted them without comment to the states. More or less promptly (except in Rhode Island) the legislatures arranged for the selection of delegates to conventions. In the contest over ratification, the federalists, though a minority, had the advantage of unity, initiative, and a novel and interesting proposal. The opposition was divided, overconfident, and badly led.

Discussions in the Press

The text of the Constitution and arguments for and against its adoption occupied much of the space in U.S. newspapers during the ensuing months. The most noteworthy series of articles supporting ratification was written by Hamilton, Madison, and John Jay for New York newspapers. Their masterful essays formulated a theory of maximum liberty and governmental effectiveness through federalism and refuted the objections of the antifederalists on theoretical and practical grounds. *The Federalist Papers* (as the collected articles were later called) remains the best theoretical justification of the U.S. constitutional system.

Richard Henry Lee's series, "Letters of the Federal Farmer," perhaps best exemplified the antifederalist position. He characterized the new system of government as "calculated ultimately to make the states one consolidated government." He warned that adoption of the Constitution might result in abolition of the laws, customs, and constitutions of the states. He argued that the proposed House of Representatives would not be sufficiently responsive to the wishes of the people and objected to the absence of a bill of rights to protect individual liberties. Other antifederalists, taking a narrow, legalistic approach, argued that the Convention had exceeded its authority, since it had been called only to propose amendments to the Articles of Confederation. They demanded to know by what authority the Convention had used the phrase "We the people," since the states were the parties to the agreement that had created the Articles of Confederation. On practical grounds some antifederalists asserted that a federal government could not effectively exert power over so large a territory as the United States; others feared that its capital would become, as London had, a center of concentrated power. Few clauses in the proposed Constitution escaped criticism.

Ratification of the Constitution

By mid-January 1788, five state conventions had ratified the Constitution—Delaware, New Jersey, and Georgia unanimously, Connecticut and Pennsylvania by votes of two or three to one. Maryland approved it on April 28 and South Carolina on May 23 by overwhelming majorities. Intense opposition was encountered in the other six states. When the Massachusetts convention met in January, preliminary votes showed a majority of the delegates opposed to the Constitution; they were led by Gerry, Samuel Adams, and John Hancock. After heated discussion, the opposition yielded when supporters agreed to recommend antifederalist amendments to the Constitution. Massachusetts ratified it by a narrow vote on February 6. In New Hampshire the federalists avoided defeat in January by procuring a long adjournment. After a bitter struggle, they won out on June 21, and New Hampshire became the ninth state to ratify. Four days later the Virginia federalists, under the leadership of Madison and John Marshall, overcame an early disadvantage, despite the efforts of Mason, Henry, and Lee. In New York the antifederalists had a two-to-one advantage, but news of New Hampshire's and Virginia's ratification turned the tide. By a margin of three votes, New York ratified the Constitution on July 26, 1788. The new government commenced operations on April 30, 1789. North Carolina entered the Union the following November and Rhode Island more than a year later.

In the state conventions, the federalists' main strength came from representatives of shipowners, merchants, and artisans in the towns near the Atlantic coast and from frontiersmen. These groups felt the need for more adequate foreign and military policies and for an end to interstate trade barriers. Opposition to the Constitution was strongest in up-country agricultural areas where the principal needs were for better roads and courthouse services, both of which state and local governments could supply. In varying degrees, antifederalist attitudes were determined by state and local political alignments, vague fears of a federal colossus, and the conviction, held especially in New York and Rhode Island, that establishment of the federal government would increase taxes on land and other property. In the debates over ratification, the most criticized feature of the Constitution was the lack of a bill of rights. The federalists mollified the opposition by promising to add a bill of rights through the amendment process. They were not obliged to yield on any other point.

CHANGES IN THE CONSTITUTION BY AMENDMENT

On June 8, 1789, in accordance with federalist promises, Madison introduced a number of proposed amendments in the House of Representatives. He intended them to be inserted at appropriate places in the text of the Constitution, but Roger Sherman of Connecticut persuaded Congress to add them at the end, so that each amendment would stand or fall on its own merits when submitted to the states for ratification. Congress decided that the president's signature to a proposed amendment was not required. As noted above, never have two-thirds of the states asked Congress to call a constitutional convention. Congress has proposed all amendments, of which some ten thousand have been introduced, determined their exact phraseology, and sometimes fixed a limit of seven years within which to ratify the amendment. Except for the Twenty-First Amendment, which repealed Prohibition, state legislatures ratified all the others. Once a legislature has ratified an amendment, neither it nor the voters of the state in a referendum may rescind the ratification. But the same or a later legislature may ratify an amendment after previous failures to ratify. The Twenty-First Amendment was referred to state conventions in order to obtain the opinion of bodies especially chosen for the purpose of determining whether or not to retain Prohibition.

The Bill of Rights

The first ten amendments are called the Bill of Rights. Their contents derive from English and colonial experience and from the political thought and experience of the Revolutionary and Confederation periods.

The First Amendment is actually the third of seventeen proposed amendments that Madison pushed through the House of Representatives. (The Senate subsequently refused to approve the last five.) It prohibits the establishment of a state-supported church, requires the separation of church and state, and guarantees freedom of worship, of speech, and of the press and the right to peaceably assemble and petition the government. On occasion, the Supreme Court has treated the provisions of the First Amendment as more fundamental than other parts of the Constitution. Indeed, a few justices have considered them to be virtually absolute, construing the amendment's language literally: "Congress shall make no law . . ." On the other hand, the Court has upheld substantial limitations on the exercise of the First Amendment during wartime and when the public has feared subversion.

The Second and Third amendments reflect the Framers' concerns about a standing army and soldiers billeted in private households.

The Fourth to the Eighth amendments pertain to the protection of life, liberty, and property. Most of their provisions are aimed at protecting citizens from improper conduct by the police and at establishing fair procedures in collecting evidence and in the arrest, indictment, and trial of individuals. These amendments prohibit unreasonable searches and seizures, the use of illegally obtained evidence, compelling individuals to incriminate themselves, involuntary confessions, denial of reasonable bail, double jeopardy, unduly delayed or unfair trials, and cruel or unusual punishment. Accused persons have the right to be informed of the charges against them, to confront their accusers in open court, and to have the court's help in compelling the attendance of witnesses to testify on their behalf. The requirement of due process of law (equivalent to the English "law of the land") governs the interpretation of these and other matters, including the judge's fairness in conducting the trial and instructing the jury. The due process clause also protects property rights against impairment by legislation in excess of Congress's powers as well as from unfair acts and procedures by executive and administrative officers, quasi-legislative commissions, and courts of law.

The Ninth Amendment assures the public that the enumeration of rights in the Constitution is not exhaustive and does not preclude the existence and enforcement of others.

The Tenth Amendment limits the centralizing tendencies of government. When it was proposed, antifederalists made a determined but unsuccessful effort to confine the federal government to expressly granted powers and to reserve all other powers to the states or to the people thereof. As adopted, the amendment leaves the principle of implied federal powers intact and acknowledges the existence of undefined powers belonging to the public at large.

Later Amendments

The Eleventh Amendment prohibits a nonresident from suing a state in the federal courts. It was adopted in response to states' rights sentiments after the Supreme Court took jurisdiction of a case (*Chisholm v. Georgia*, 1793) in which South Carolina creditors sued Georgia to recover confiscated property.

The Twelfth Amendment recognizes the effect of political parties on the political process. In the election of 1800, all the Republican members of the electoral college—each of whom could cast two votes for president—gave one vote to Jefferson and the other to Aaron Burr, the party's nominees for president and vice-president, respectively. The resulting tie caused the election to be decided in the House of Representatives, which the federalists controlled. Before Jefferson was finally chosen, much partisan maneuvering to elect Burr president had transpired. To prevent a similar situation from recurring, the Twelfth Amendment requires each elector to designate separately his or her choice for president and vice-president.

The Thirteenth Amendment constitutionalized Lincoln's Emancipation Proclamation and freed all slaves (mostly those in border states) who had not been included in the Proclamation. The phrase "involuntary servitude" outlaws peonage or forced labor under contract.

The Fourteenth Amendment rejected southern doctrines of state sovereignty and secession and overrode the Supreme Court's decision in *Scott v. Sandford* (1857), which held that no black person could be a U.S. citizen. The due process and equal protection clauses safeguard civil rights and liberties from state impairment. For many years the Supreme Court used the language in the due process clause that prohibits states from depriving "any person of . . . property" to insulate business from state regulation. But beginning with *Gitlow v. New York* (1925), the Court gradually expanded its definition of due process to include most of the noneconomic guarantees in the Bill of Rights and thereby protect them from state impairment. A similar development occurred with respect to the equal protection clause. In *Plessy v. Ferguson* (1896), the Court upheld the constitutionality of "separate but equal" public facilities. Subsequently, the Court held governmentally mandated segregation to be inherently unequal in *Brown v. Board of Education* (1954).

The Fifteenth Amendment forbids the states to deny a person the right to vote because of race, color or previous condition of servitude. Southern states, however, used the failure to pay a poll tax and unfairly administered literacy tests to prevent blacks from voting until the mid-1960s.

The Sixteenth Amendment overrides the Supreme Court's decision in *Pollock v. Farmers' Loan & Trust Co.* (1895), which held that a tax on incomes derived from property was a direct tax, and empowers Congress to impose an income tax in violation of Article I, section 9 of the Constitution.

The Seventeenth Amendment requires that U.S. senators be popularly elected instead of chosen by the legislatures of the various states.

The Eighteenth Amendment prohibited the manufacture, sale, or transportation of intoxicating liquors and gave Congress and the state legislatures concurrent power to enforce the amendment.

The Nineteenth Amendment forbids a state to deny suffrage because of sex.

The Twentieth Amendment moves the beginning of congressional sessions from March 4 to January 3 and of presidential terms to January 20 of the year following the election at which the president was chosen. A newly elected Congress must meet January 3, two months after its election, instead of thirteen months afterward.

The Twenty-First Amendment repeals the Eighteenth.

The Twenty-Second Amendment limits the president to two terms in office, thereby constitutionalizing the customary limitation that had existed from the end of Washington's second term until the election of Franklin D. Roosevelt to a third and fourth term.

The Twenty-Third Amendment enables the voters of the District of Columbia to elect as many presidential electors as the District would be entitled to if it were a state, but not more than the least populous state.

The Twenty-Fourth Amendment forbids denying a person the right to vote in any federal election because of failure to pay a poll or any other tax. (The Supreme Court subsequently declared the poll tax requirement in state elections unconstitutional in *Harper v. Virginia State Board of Elections* [1966]).

The Twenty-Fifth Amendment provides that the vice-president shall become acting president whenever the president states that he is unable to perform his duties or a similar statement is made by a body authorized by Congress to determine if the president is unable to perform his duties. If the president asserts his competence, Congress must decide the matter within twenty-one days and, by a two-thirds vote of both houses, may declare the president unable to perform his duties.

The Twenty-Sixth Amendment extends suffrage in both state and national elections to all citizens who are eighteen years of age. It was adopted after the Supreme Court, in *Oregon v. Mitchell* (1970), declared the provisions of the Voting Rights Act of 1965 unconstitutional insofar as they related to state elections.

This chapter has traced the origins of the Constitution from the colonial period, through the Declaration of Independence and the Articles of Confederation, to the convention that adopted the Constitution in 1787. The deficiencies in the Articles of Confederation are noted, as are the efforts the Framers made to overcome them. The chapter concludes with a summary of the contents of each of the twenty-six amendments that have been added to the Constitution.

2

Democracy and the Constitutional System

*F*rom the standpoint of public involvement, what sort of government did the Framers establish? That is the question that this chapter poses. Largely as a result of constitutional amendments, the opportunities for public participation are much greater today than they were when the Constitution was adopted. Nonetheless, the legacy of the Framers' work continues to characterize the operation of the constitutional system.

THE NONDEMOCRATIC CHARACTER OF THE CONSTITUTIONAL SYSTEM

Popular belief to the contrary, the Framers of the Constitution did not establish a democratic system of government. The most that can be said is that they established a government of, by, and for white males who owned a fairly substantial amount of property. Blacks and Indians were excluded from participation, as were all women. Not until the reforms of the Jacksonian Era, during the 1820s and 1830s, did the states remove property qualifications for voting and holding public office. In 1870 the Fifteenth Amendment barred the state and federal governments from denying persons the right to vote on the basis of race, while in 1920 the Nineteenth Amendment prohibited women from being denied the right to vote.

Limitations on the Exercise of Power

What the Framers did establish was a governmental system whose powers were severely limited substantively and procedurally. As even a cursory reading of the Constitution reveals, the document is loaded with statements of that which government shall not do. (See sections 9 and 10 of Article I for examples.)

Even where the Constitution permits power to be exercised, it typically specifies the manner in which that power is to be used. Thus, section 7 of Article I details the procedure that Congress must follow to enact a law, while section 2 of Article III requires that all federal crimes except impeachment be tried by jury. The consequence is that we live under a negative, do-nothing system of government, one in which it is very difficult for government to act. For example, the discord between the House and Senate that prevents efficient legislative action and the inherent conflict between president and Congress that blocks resolution of acknowledged governmental issues are not necessari ly the fault of corrupt or self-serving politicians. Instead, they result from separation of powers, checks and balances, and a bicameral (two-body) legislature, to say nothing of the further division of power between the federal government and the states.

Simply stated, the Framers viewed governmental conflict and inefficiency as essential in a constitutional structure whose overriding purpose is to promote individual liberty—to leave people alone to the greatest possible extent. In the Framers' eyes, majority rule—the essence of democracy— would merely replace monarchy with a mob. In either case, tyranny would result. From their perspective, that government is best that governs least.

The Constitutional Irrelevance of Public Opinion

Consequently, public opinion and popular desires have no constitutional mandate. The Supreme Court, in its opinions interpreting the Constitution, regularly says as much:

> . . . government's interest cannot justify its infringement on First Amendment rights. We decline the Government's invitation to reassess this conclusion in light of Congress's recent recognition of a purported "national consensus" favoring a prohibition on flag-burning. . . . Even assuming such a consensus exists, any suggestion that the Government's interest in suppressing speech becomes more weighty as popular opposition to that speech grows is foreign to the First Amendment.

Three days after a majority of the justices used the foregoing language to declare Congress's Flag Protection Act unconstitutional in *United States v. Eichman* (1990), a minority of the justices also noted that public sentiment does not justify infringing on the Fourth Amendment's ban on unreasonable searches and seizures:

> . . . I do not dispute the immense social cost caused by drunken drivers, nor do I slight the government's efforts to prevent such

tragic losses. Indeed, I would hazard a guess that today's opinion will be received favorably by a majority of our society, who would willingly suffer the minimal intrusion of a sobriety checkpoint stop in order to prevent drunken driving. But consensus that a particular law enforcement technique serves a laudable purpose has never been the touchstone of constitutional analysis.

SOCIAL RIGHTS

Apart from the irrelevance of public opinion or majority rule as bases for constitutional interpretation is the total absence of any so-called "social" rights in the Constitution—certain claims of a positive sort that individuals may make on government, such as the right to an education, to a job, to adequate housing, health care, and disability and retirement benefits. The lack of any such affirmative rights accords with the negative, liberty-oriented character of the constitutional system. To the extent that these rights exist, they derive from state action or federal legislation, not from the Constitution.

The Right to Vote

One may argue, however, that because the right to vote has effectively become universal, it amounts to an affirmative right. A close inspection of constitutional language suggests that this is not the case. In the first place, nowhere does the Constitution guarantee anyone the right to vote. Article I, section 2 only says that persons may vote in a federal election if they are qualified to vote for the more populous house of the legislature of the state in which they reside. Secondly, the states are free to qualify whom they wish so long as in doing so they do not violate the Fourteenth, Fifteenth, Nineteenth or Twenty-Sixth amendment. But because the Supreme Court has construed the equal protection clause of the Fourteenth Amendment quite broadly where voting is concerned, the states are now forbidden to condition voting on substantial residency require ments or on any sort of a tax. As a result, it appears that the Court will void any state restriction other than those aimed at deterring election fraud and those based on section 2 of the Fourteenth Amendment that allow for the disenfranchisement of convicted felons.

Indigency

The constitutional requirement that indigent persons accused of crime must be provided an attorney before they may be sentenced to jail may also appear to have transformed the right to counsel into an affirmative right. But here also, the Court's rationale belies what seems to be the case. The right to a fair trial when a person's liberty is at stake is a fundamental right that government may not deprive persons of. So also are marital and family rights. Fairness decrees that government may not condi tion these rights on persons' ability to pay. Hence, indigents must be provided an attorney and may not be required to pay filing or transcript fees to appeal a conviction or obtain a divorce.

An Example

Though an extreme situation, the facts of *DeShaney v. Win nebago County Department of Social Services* (1989) well illustrate the negative character of our constitutional rights. A four-year-old boy's father beat him so severely that the resulting brain damage left the child profoundly retarded. The child and his mother sued the county and its officials for depriving the child of his liberty without due process of law by failing to protect him against his father's abuse. The county had first learned of the child's suspicious injuries two years earlier. He was subsequently hospitalized three times for bruises and abrasions; a home-visiting caseworker recorded her suspicions of ongoing child abuse; and a child-protection team was formed. Nonetheless, the county took no action; the child remained in the father's custody, notwithstanding evidence that the father was failing to cooperate with juvenile authorities as he had promised.

By a 6 to 3 vote, the Supreme Court affirmed the decision of the lower federal courts that nothing in the Constitution required the county to help the boy. The language invoked while in the father's, rather than the county's, custody had made the child vulnerable; nor had it done anything to

Constitution divides powers bestowed on gov't between fed. & state systems

THE SUPREME COURT AS GUARDIAN OF

All gov't actions must accord w/ Constitution..."

Though the preceding discussion documents the fact that our constitutional rights limit rather than compel positive govern mental action, we still need to explain why the Supreme Court is ultimately responsible for protecting our liberties from govern mental abridgment.

First, the Constitution is the fundamental law of the land. All governmental actions must accord with its provisions. Any action incompatible with its strictures is without force or effect; it is simply unconstitutional.

Second, as the negative phrases of the Constitution indicate, Americans do not trust government. We view politics as a dirty business, and politicians are regarded as the moral equivalent of thieves and charlatans.

Third, the Constitution divides the limited powers bestowed on government between the federal and state governmental systems. In doing so, the Framers did not define with any precision the scope of the powers each might exercise. Although Article VI of the Constitution specifies that federal law is supreme over that of the states, some body must authoritatively document the exis tence of a conflict in the first place before the supremacy clause comes into play.

Fourth, the Framers further divided the powers delegated to the federal government among three autonomous branches: executive, legislative, and judicial. The checks and balances produced by this separation of powers left the federal judiciary largely apart from the inherent conflict that characterizes the relationship between president and Congress. From this flow two results. One, judges are not considered mere politicians, but, rather, principled decision makers whose only guide is the Constitution. Two, because Congress and president are usually at loggerheads, each thwarting the desires of the other, policy making becomes difficult. The executive and legislative branches are much too divided and much too weak to resolve many public policy issues. Because the political branches are unable to resolve society's major social, economic, political, and cultural issues, resolution falls on the remaining decision maker: the courts, and ultimately the Supreme Court.

Fifth, the interaction of the four preceding factors enabled the Supreme Court to justify its policy-making role by formulating the doctrine of judicial review. This John Marshall did in 1803 in the case of *Marbury v. Madison.*

The Constitutional system that governs inhabitants of the United States does little governing compared to what people in the rest of the world experience. The substantive and procedural limits that the Framers imposed on government created a negative, largely do-nothing system. Such social rights as U.S. citizens possess are provided by the state and federal governments, not by the Constitution. Constitutional rights, by contrast, guarantee individuals liberty from governmental action, and are exemplified by the various provisions in the Bill of Rights.

In other words, the Constitution specifies what government may not do to people, not what government must do for people. Ultimate responsibility for protecting constitutional rights and liberties rests with the Supreme Court.

3

The Supreme Court and the Constitution

Because of the Supreme Court's position at the apex of the judicial system, Chief Justice Hughes once remarked that the Constitution means what the Supreme Court says it means, and Woodrow Wilson said that the Supreme Court resembles a constitutional convention in continuous session. As the court of last resort, the Supreme Court authoritatively interprets the Constitution. The buck stops here. Only the adoption of a constitutional amendment can override its decisions, and this has happened only four times in history: the Eleventh Amendment in 1798 reversed the 1793 decision in Chisholm v. Georgia, *which permitted an individual to sue a state in federal court; the Fourteenth Amendment in 1868 reversed the 1857 decision in* Scott v. Sandford, *which held blacks not to be American citizens; the Sixteenth Amendment in 1913 reversed the 1895 decision in* Pollock v. Farmers' Loan and Trust Co., *which prohibited a federal income tax; and the Twenty-Sixth Amendment in 1971 reversed part of the 1970 decision in* Oregon v. Mitchell, *which denied Congress's power to enfranchise eighteen- to twenty-year-olds in state elections.*

THE BACKGROUND OF JUDICIAL REVIEW

One searches the Constitution in vain for a statement granting the Supreme Court the power of judicial review. Article III does not list it among the subjects to which judicial power extends, while in Article VI, it is "the Judges in every State" whom the supremacy clause binds, with no mention of a federal court to review and make uniform the state courts' decisions. In the Constitutional Convention, the Framers did debate the need for an authority with power to veto legislative actions, but the proposal was voted down. How, then, was it possible for judicial review to become one of the most significant features of the American constitutional system?

The Impact of the Common Law

An important influence was the Anglo-American legal system. The common law of England, which one commentator described as "the fruit of reason ripened by precedent," originated and developed in decisions of the courts, with the latest decision forming a precedent for the decision of similar cases that followed. The colonists brought the common law with them to America, where it became the everyday law for all the colonies. Another predisposing influence was the written charters and other documents that granted and limited the powers of colonial governments. The English privy council could disallow the acts of colonial legislatures and, through its judicial committee, it heard appeals from colonial courts. Theories of John Locke and Montesquieu on the desirability of limiting governmental powers, including those of the legislature, formed another important influence.

In Number 78 of "The Federalist Papers," Alexander Hamilton argued forcefully for judicial review, on the ground that the Constitution is superior to ordinary legislation and can be preserved only if the judiciary may void all legislative acts in conflict with its provisions. In 1798 Thomas Jefferson and James Madison advanced a different means of reviewing acts of Congress. Through the Kentucky and Virginia Resolutions, they called on the other states to declare the Alien and Sedition Acts unconstitutional. The Alien Act authorized the president to deport dangerous aliens; the Sedition Act made it a crime to bring the federal government into disrepute—its objective was to repress political opposition to the Federalist party. Although many states agreed that these laws did violate the Constitution, those north of Maryland also maintained that the federal courts, and not the states, are the proper organ to interpret the Constitution.

JOHN MARSHALL

The establishment of judicial review was largely the work of John Marshall, who was appointed chief justice by President John Adams in 1801, just before Jefferson became president and his party took control of Congress. In *Marbury v. Madison* (1803), Marshall wrote the opinion declaring unconstitutional a minor provision of the Judiciary Act of 1789 and thereby created a precedent for review of federal legislation. In *Fletcher v. Peck* (1810), the Court for the first time declared unconstitutional an act of a state legislature.

In the cases that followed, the Supreme Court sustained the exercise of federal power in some and invalidated state encroachments on the federal sphere in others. Among the most important were *M'Culloch v. Maryland* (1816), where Marshall exploited the language of the "necessary and proper" clause of Article I, section 8 to create the doctrine of implied federal powers, which substantially expanded the matters on which Congress might legislate; and *Gibbons v. Ogden* (1824), where Marshall defined extremely broadly the commerce that Congress could regulate. Both of these decisions are among the most important ever handed down by the Court.

THE TANEY COURT

The next chief justice, Roger B. Taney, who served from 1836 to 1864, had been President Andrew Jackson's attorney general and reflected Jacksonian attitudes toward states' rights and private property. During his tenure, the Court halted and in some respects reversed its stream of decisions strengthening and expanding federal authority. The Taney Court loosened the bonds of national supremacy, thereby permitting the states greater freedom of action. Neither the power given Congress to regulate interstate commerce nor the clause prohibiting states from making laws impairing the obligation of contracts precluded the states from regulating economic activities in a manner beneficial to their own residents. Taney's most famous—or infamous—decision, *Scott v. Sandford* (1857), unsuccessfully attempted to settle the slavery controversy and, by declaring the Missouri Compromise unconstitutional, confirmed the precedent for judicial review that *Marbury v. Madison* had established.

THE POST–CIVIL WAR COURT

During the Civil War, the Supreme Court lost prestige because military considerations tended to override judicial determinations of constitutional rights. During Reconstruction, the Court found itself in the middle of the constitutional struggle between the Radical Republicans, who controlled Congress, and President Andrew Johnson. The Court's size and jurisdiction were altered for partisan political purposes. As the Civil War receded, the Court began to follow a laissez-faire course. Through the use of the due process clause of the Fourteenth Amendment, state efforts to regulate business and economic activities were declared unconstitutional. The Court, narrowly confining the scope of the interstate commerce clause, treated federal legislation similarly.

The Rise of Laissez-Faire

None of the chief justices possessed the leadership qualities that had made Marshall and Taney great. Some associate justices, however, were first-rate, including Samuel Miller, Stephen Field, and the first Justice Harlan, but they were a minority among others who had been attorneys for railroads and other business interests. These, along with Justice Field, brought to the Court their proclivities for laissez-faire economics. The demands of reformist elements, such as the Greenbackers and Populists, for political and social change affected the Court scarcely at all.

Before the end of the nineteenth century, the Court had invalidated the federal income tax, defined the word "commerce" so as to prevent effective enforcement of the Sherman Antitrust Act, and washed its hands of racial matters. As far as a majority of the justices was concerned, the business of America was business and the purpose of the Court was to keep it that way.

THE EARLY-TWENTIETH-CENTURY COURT

The Court continued its probusiness stance into the twentieth century by formulating two constitutional doctrines that have since been overruled. Under "freedom of contract," the Court invalidated state and federal attempts to regulate wages and hours of work on the ground that they violated individuals' rights to contract with their employers for the sale of their labor. Under "business affected with a public interest," it struck down legislation regulating businesses other than those that had traditionally been subject to public regulation, such as inns and public utilities.

In its interpretations of the constitutional commerce and taxing powers, the Court upheld laws benefiting business and agricultural interests, but was strangely unable to find a constitutional basis for outlawing child labor. (Compare *McCray v. United States* [1904] with *Bailey v. Drexel Furniture Co.* [1922].) Such able and forward-looking justices as Oliver Wendell Holmes and Louis Brandeis protested such interpretations and, by their dissenting opinions, prepared the way for new directions in constitutional law.

THE NEW DEAL

During the Depression of the 1930s, President Franklin Roosevelt proposed and Congress enacted bold new legislation regulating many phases of American industry. It was inevitable that such legislation would come before the Supreme Court for review. The Court was then nearly equally divided in its disposition toward governmental regulation of the economy. Four justices—Willis Van Devanter, James McReynolds, George Sutherland, and Pierce Butler—staunchly supported laissez-faire economics. Three justices—Brandeis, Harlan Stone, and Benjamin Cardozo— believed that the Constitution should be interpreted in the light of existing economic conditions. Chief Justice Hughes usually sided with these three. Justice Owen Roberts initially sided with the four conservatives to make a majority that declared unconstitutional most of the early New Deal legislation.

The Court-Packing Scheme

After the Democratic landslide in the 1936 election, President Roosevelt proposed to increase the size of the Court by adding one new justice for each of the sitting justices who was over seventy years old, on the ground that the aged justices could not keep up with their work. The Chief Justice, however, presented convincing evidence that the Court's calendar was current.

Notwithstanding presidential pressure, Congress refused to enact this Court-packing plan, in large part because in the midst of the debate the Court began to uphold the more carefully considered and better drafted New Deal measures that Congress had passed to replace those the Court had previously voided.

Court packing then became moot when, in the spring of 1937, Justice Roberts switched sides. By a margin of 5 to 4, the Court upheld several important New Deal statutes, among them the Social Security Act and legislation permitting labor to organize and bargain collectively. In the process, the meaning of interstate commerce was expanded to include all but purely local production and trade. Intrastate commerce and the Tenth Amendment lost nearly all significance in constitutional law. Although his Court-packing plan failed, Roosevelt cemented the New Deal by filling seven vacancies on the High Bench in the next four years, in addition to promoting Justice Stone to the chief justiceship.

THE WARREN COURT

The appointment of Earl Warren as chief justice in 1953 proved to be an event of special significance. Though he did not dominate the Court in the manner of Marshall, he exercised a steady and consistent influence. His most famous decision was *Brown v. Board of Education* (1954, 1955), in which a unanimous Court declared compulsory racial segregation in public schools unconstitutional.

During Warren's sixteen-year tenure, the Court made the Bill of Rights more explicit than ever before. In numerous cases it expanded the meaning of freedom of speech and the press, required the states to observe nearly all the procedural guarantees in the Fourth through the Eighth amendments, and mandated that members of the House of Representatives and the two houses of the state legislatures be elected from districts of equal size.

Judicial Activism

Commentators have described the Warren Court as activist because of its willingness to create new precedents to protect the rights of individuals. The activist label also fits the Marshall, Taney, post–Civil War, and other Courts equally well. They also created precedents to justify the policies they espoused. The fact that they did not particularly concern themselves with noneconomic civil rights and liberties does not make them less activist than the Warren Court. What the post–Civil War and the early-twentieth-century Courts did for business, the Warren Court did for individual freedom.

THE BURGER COURT

With the end of the Warren Court in 1969, membership changes caused the Court to turn in a conservative direction. The four justices nominated by President Nixon (Warren Burger, Harry Blackmun, Lewis Powell, and William Rehnquist) tended to vote together and to be joined by Byron White or Potter Stewart in numerous 5-to-4 decisions that differed from the positions of the Warren Court. With the retirement of William Douglas in 1975 and his replacement by John Stevens, the liberal majority of the 1960s was reduced to two: William Brennan and Thurgood Marshall. Opposite them sat the Chief Justice and Rehnquist. The other five justices occupied moderate to conservative positions.

A Conservative Orientation

On balance, the Burger Court weighed the balance between society as a whole and the rights of individuals a little more heavily on the side of society. It opposed gender discrimination more than the Warren Court, however; a woman's right to an abortion and many rights afforded welfare recipients also resulted from decisions of the Burger Court. With regard to First Amendment freedoms, commercial advertising received constitutional protection, and parochial school efforts to gain governmental funding were defeated.

Although the constitutionality of some forms of affirmative action was upheld, the Burger Court maintained the status quo generally on racial issues. Practical problems of law enforcement received substantial support, contrary to the behavior of the Warren Court majority.

THE REHNQUIST COURT

With the retirement of Chief Justice Burger at the end of the 1985–86 term, President Reagan nominated Justice Rehnquist, the Court's most conservative member, as Burger's replacement. To replace Rehnquist as associate justice the President selected Antonin Scalia, whom he had previously nominated to be a judge on the federal court of appeals for the District of Columbia.

*Further
Rightward
Tendencies*

Inasmuch as Justice Scalia had established a track record similar to that of Burger, his appointment did not appreciably alter the course of the Court's decisions. But the replacement of Justice Powell with Anthony Kennedy at the end of the first term of the Rehnquist Court has made the Court somewhat more conservative.

The most striking evidence of this rightward movement occurred in a series of affirmative action and employment discrimination cases decided during the first half of 1989. Kennedy's vote determined the outcome in three of the four, including one that overturned a unanimously decided liberal Burger Court decision.

Justice Souter

President Bush nominated little-known David Souter to replace Justice Brennan at the beginning of the 1990 term. His selection will probably provide the conservatives with a comfortable majority on virtually all issues. The youth of the new nominees and the reduction of the liberals to a single justice, Thurgood Marshall, insure conservative domination of the Court well into the twenty-first century.

Since the time of John Marshall the Supreme Court has confronted and resolved most of the major controversies that have convulsed American society. Aided and abetted by the doctrine of judicial review, the Court's policy-making capacity has cycled between the poles of liberalism and conservativism depending on the orientation of its membership.

4

The Jurisdiction of the Supreme Court

Although losing litigants commonly pledge to take their cases all the way to the U.S. Supreme Court, such action does not depend on the persistence of parties who have lost their cases. The Court may only decide such cases as the Constitution and Congress authorize it to hear. Vast areas of the law are the exclusive purview of the state courts: most criminal offenses, personal injuries, commercial activities, and property disputes. Moreover, only a handful of the cases that are grist for the federal courts are decided by the Supreme Court because the justices are free to pick and choose among the cases that proper ly land on the doorstep of its marble palace.

HOW CASES REACH THE SUPREME COURT

Except for a handful of cases between states or between a state and the federal government (in which the Supreme Court functions as a trial court), the Court hears cases under its appellate jurisdiction after they have been decided either by a lower federal court (usually a circuit court of appeals) or by the highest court in a state that has jurisdiction to try the particular case. The justices strictly limit access to the Court, accepting for review no more than 1 to 2 percent of the cases losing litigants bring to their attention.

Federal Questions

With a few relatively unimportant exceptions, the federal courts may decide only "federal questions"—those that pertain to the meaning of an act of Congress, a treaty of the United States, or a provision of the Constitution. Disputes about property, contracts, or personal injuries rarely have such a component. Hence, judicial resolution of these commonplace matters is the province of the state courts.

**Writ of
Certiorari**

Most cases come to the Supreme Court on a writ of certiorari, which Congress authorized in 1925. It is a petition that a losing litigant files with the clerk of the Court requesting the justices to review the lower court's decision. If four justices vote to grant the petition, the Court will hear and decide the case. The usual grounds for granting the writ are the presence of a fundamental constitutional issue, an issue of general importance, an important private right, a federal statute not previously interpreted by the Court or conflicting decisions by lower federal or state courts on a particular federal question.

HOW THE COURT OPERATES

The justices examine lower court records of the case, study the briefs of the attorneys who represent the litigants, and, if the petition to review the case is granted, hear oral arguments. A majority vote determines the outcome of the case. If because of nonparticipation a tie vote results, the decision of the lower court stands. When he votes with the majority, the chief justice assigns the writing of the Court's opinion. Otherwise, the senior associate justice who voted with the majority makes the assignment. A justice who disagrees with the decision of the court may write a dissenting opinion. If a justice agrees with the decision but not with the reasons given in the opinion of the court, he or she may write an opinion concurring in the result. Such opinions, especially dissents, sometimes foreshadow changing interpretations of constitutional law.

THE EFFECT OF PRECEDENTS

Constitutional precedents set by the Supreme Court bind all lower courts, state and federal. The Supreme Court, interestingly enough, need not follow its own precedents, but it usually does so. Frequent overruling of precedents would make the law uncertain and the outcome of later cases unpredictable.

On the other hand, slavish adherence to a specific line of precedent may retard adaptation of the law to changing circumstances and conditions. The

Court has several options. It may follow precedent. It may distinguish the case before it from earlier cases and apply a different set of precedents to its resolution. It may specifically overrule the precedent. It may ignore the precedent, in effect overruling it sub silentio. It may label an issue a "political question" to be decided by Congress or the executive branch. Whatever it chooses to do, the Court's decision becomes the law of the land.

Formal Alteration of Precedent

During the thirty-six terms from the beginning of the Warren Court in 1953 through the end of the 1988 term, the Court over ruled or otherwise formally altered precedents in ninety-five opinions, an average of less than three per term. The total number of precedents these ninety-five cases overturned (eighty) or formally altered (fifteen) cannot be specified with precision because the Court does not always indicate how many precedents its opinion has voided. The vast majority, however, only per tained to a single precedent.

During these same thirty-six terms, the Court declared 396 state laws and local ordinances unconstitutional—356 of the former and forty of the latter, along with 55 acts of Congress. The Court, therefore, was more than four times as likely to overturn a statute as it was to formally alter a precedent. The Court voided an average of 11 state and local laws on constitutional grounds per term, along with an average of 3 acts of Congress every two years.

FEDERAL COURT JURISDICTION

Notwithstanding the authoritative character of its decisions and its policy-making capabilities, the Supreme Court does not sit to right every wrong—popular belief to the contrary. The often- heard vow of losing litigants that they will take their cases all the way to the Supreme Court may represent their sense of injus tice, but it most assuredly does not reflect reality. The Supreme Court, along with the other federal courts, are courts of limited jurisdiction in the sense that they may not hear any case or controversy unless it falls within the grant of power contained in Article III, section 2 of the Constitution. Moreover, as section 2 also makes clear, with a few minor exceptions, Congress must enact legislation authorizing the Court to hear various types of cases. This dependence of the federal courts on Con gress for their jurisdiction is the major control that Congress has over the judiciary. Although Congress has rarely used this power to check

Supreme Court policy making (the last major instance occurred in 1932 when Congress forbade the federal courts to issue injunctions at management's request in labor disputes), its exercise can deprive the courts of their ability to resolve disputes in sensitive areas.

Federal Questions

Federal questions are the heart of federal court jurisdiction. Article III defines them as "all cases . . . arising under this Constitution, the Laws of the United States, and treaties." To invoke federal-question jurisdiction, a plaintiff must demonstrate to the court's satisfaction that the case substantially involves a constitutional provision, an act of Congress or administrative action pursuant thereto, or a treaty of the United States.

Other Subjects of Federal Jurisdiction

Of lesser importance are disputes to which the United States is party, those between states, admiralty and maritime matters, cases concerning foreign diplomatic personnel accredited to the United States, and those between residents of different states. Virtually all cases to which the United States is party contain a federal question. Except for an occasional interstate controversy, which usually concerns a boundary dispute or water rights, these other types of cases rarely reach the Supreme Court.

ACCESS TO THE FEDERAL COURTS

The mere fact that parties seeking access to the federal courts can show a federal question does not guarantee that their cases will be heard. Plaintiffs must also meet a set of constitutional and Court created criteria known as "standing to sue." An actual dispute must exist between two or more persons. Federal courts will not decide hypothetical cases or render an advisory opinion. Neither will they hear a case in which the parties' interests do not conflict; e.g., a stockholder suing a corpora tion to prevent the payment of a tax.

Elements of Standing to Sue

The dispute, moreover, must concern a legal injury—rights and interests that have statutory or constitutional protection. Ordinary commercial competition, for example, does not have such protection. The injury that plaintiffs allege must be one they personally suffer. Unless the injured person is incapable by reason of death or incompetence, a third party may not initiate litigation in the federal courts except for prosecutors and others charged with enforcing federal law.

Cases that otherwise lie within the jurisdiction of the federal courts will not be decided if they are "political questions." While the short definition of a political question is whatever the Supreme Court says it is, such cases concern matters that the Court prefers the other branches of government resolve. Examples include the ratification of a constitutional amendment, the legitimacy of competing state governments, and the occupation of enemy territory.

The Supreme Court has instructed the federal courts to refuse to resolve issues if the judicial decision lacks "finality"; if the matter is one Congress has authorized a nonjudicial official or agency to authoritatively decide. The classic example concerns the eligibility of veterans for pension and disability benefits. Federal courts will not touch this matter because any action they take can be overturned by the Veterans Administration, whose decision is final and binding. In other words, if a court's decision is susceptible to review by a bureaucrat or by an administrative agency, it lacks finality.

With rare exceptions, courts also refuse to rehear a case they have decided. In short, litigants are entitled to only one bite of the apple. Once a court has entered a final judgment on the merits of a controversy, res judicata bars the same parties from relitigating the same claim in a second lawsuit. Similarly, collateral estoppel prevents a party from relitigating an issue that was actually decided in an earlier proceeding, as long as that issue had to be decided in order to resolve the original dispute. Thus, if a competent court authoritatively establishes that the negligence of Airline X caused a plane crash, Airline X may not deny its negligence in a lawsuit brought by another victim of the same crash.

Finally, if Congress has prescribed administrative procedures for resolving certain kinds of disputes—such as unfair labor practices, sex discrimination, the amount of taxes owed—litigants must exhaust these remedies before accessing the federal courts.

This chapter outlined the procedure whereby cases reach the Supreme Court. Most such cases contain a federal question. If four or more of the justices vote to hear the case, the Court will decide the matter. Very few cases pass through this screen. By and large, only those that raise an important unresolved question that concerns an act of Congress or a provision of the Constitution.

Apart from the foregoing factors, the federal courts will not hear a case unless the plaintiff—the party who seeks access to the court—who initiates the lawsuit—has standing to sue. By determining whether a litigant is a proper party the federal courts limit the types of disputes that they will hear. They do so in order to avoid hypothetical and redundant controversies, and to avoid unnecessary conflict with other decision makers.

5

The Relationship Between the State and Federal Judicial Systems

*A*lthough the Supreme Court regularly resolves conflicts between the executive and legislative branches of the federal government, the same cannot be said of disputes between the federal government and the states. The Court, for example, has not hesitated to resolve such bitter president-Congress conflicts as the ones involving the one-house legislative veto (Immigration and Naturalization Service v. Chadha [1983]) and the reduction in the federal fiscal deficit (Bowsher v. Synar [1986]). But federal-state relations are another matter. The difference is that federal-state disputes involve a conflict of laws whereas those that concern separation of powers pertain to the exercise of power.

Exacerbating federal-state conflicts is the fact that they pit the Supreme Court against the state courts, which, under the Constitution, possess considerable autonomy. Moreover, the Framers allowed for overlapping, or concurrent, jurisdiction between the federal and state courts. Federal questions frequently arise in the course of state court proceedings. A state court, for example, may authorize local officials to take a person's property without payment of just compensation; a justice of the peace may admit illegally seized evidence or compel persons to incriminate themselves; or a local judge may rule obscene communication protected by the First Amendment.

WHO SHALL DECIDE?

Prior to the Civil War, state court judges correctly argued that nothing in the Constitution decreed the Supreme Court to be the authoritative interpreter of the fundamental law. They pointed out that, like federal judges, they also took an oath to support and maintain the Constitution, and that they were as competent as their federal counterparts to do so. Hence, they argued, when a federal question arose in the course of state proceedings, the decision of the state supreme court should be final. The action by Congress purporting to authorize Supreme Court review of state court decisions, they continued, invaded state sovereignty and demeaned the integrity of the state courts; and was therefore unconstitutional.

In a landmark decision, *Martin v. Hunter's Lessee* (1816), the Supreme Court rejected the state's position and affirmed the constitutionality of the pertinent provision of the Judiciary Act of 1789. A contrary outcome would, of course, allow each state's supreme court to determine for itself the meaning of the Constitution, acts of Congress, and treaties of the United States. For example, the meaning of the First Amendment, due process, and the Civil Rights acts would vary from one state to another. Uniformity of federal law would be nonexistent. Each provision of the Constitution and federal statutes would mean something different, depending in which state one happened to be.

COMITY

The decision in *Martin v. Hunter's Lessee* did not make the state courts superfluous where federal questions were concerned. Mindful of the tender sensibilities of the states and their judges, the Supreme Court has devised a system of comity for the purpose of minimizing conflict between the two judicial systems. The chief feature of comity is its statement of the Supreme Court's refusal to intrude into ongoing state court proceedings. The justices described it in *Younger v. Harris* (1971) as follows:

> . . . a proper respect for state functions, a recognition of the fact that the entire country is made up of a Union of separate state governments, and a continuance of the belief that the National Government will fare best if the States and their institutions are left free to perform their separate functions in their separate ways.

This, perhaps for lack of a better and clearer way to describe it, is referred to by many as "Our Federalism," and one familiar with the profound debates that ushered our Federal Constitution into existence is bound to respect those who remain loyal to the ideals and dreams of "Our Federalism." The concept does not mean blind deference to "States' Rights" any more than it means centralization of control over every important issue in our National Government and its courts. The Framers rejected both these courses. What the concept does represent is a system in which there is sensitivity to the legitimate interests of both State and National Governments, and in which the National Government, anxious though it may be to vindicate and protect federal rights and federal interests, always endeavors to do so in ways that will not unduly interfere with the legitimate activities of the States. It should never be forgotten that this slogan, "Our Federalism," born in the early struggling days of our Union of States, occupies a highly important place in our Nation's history and its future.

The Abstention Doctrine

The vehicle whereby the Court manifests its sensitivity to legitimate state interests is the abstention doctrine, "whereby the federal courts, 'exercising a wise discretion,' restrain their authority because of' scrupulous regard for the rightful independence of the state governments' and for the smooth working of the federal judiciary." The abstention doctrine requires the federal courts to avoid intruding themselves into ongoing state judicial proceedings or otherwise duplicating litigation already begun in a state court. Litigants must exhaust state administrative and judicial remedies before they take their federal questions into a federal court. Determination of the constitutionality of state laws and regulations rests initially with the state courts themselves. If the state courts resolve the federal questions their cases contain compatibly with federal law, there will be no need for the Supreme Court to review them.

ADEQUATE AND INDEPENDENT STATE GROUNDS FOR DECISION

The Supreme Court had traditionally supplemented the abstention doctrine by assuming that state court decisions containing federal questions rested "on an adequate and independent state ground." In other words, if the state court did not clearly indicate that its decision was based on state, as opposed to federal, law, and if the party petitioning the Supreme Court for review could not persuade the justices to the contrary, the Court assumed that the state court based its decision on its own law and that that law was sufficient to support the state court's decision.

In 1983, in *Michigan v. Long*, the Burger Court reversed its policy of deference and ruled that when

> ... A state court decision fairly appears to rest primarily on federal law, or to be interwoven with the federal law, and when the adequacy and independence of any possible state law ground is not clear from the face of the opinion, we will accept . . . that the state court decided the case the way it did because it believed that federal law required it to do so.

The Effect of the Long Decision

To overcome this new—and contradictory—presumption, the state court bore the burden of demonstrating that the federal cases and authorities that it cited in its opinion did "not themselves compel the result that the [state] court has reached," but were used only for "guidance." How might the state court meet this burden? "If the state court decision indicates clearly and expressly that it is alternatively based on *bona fide separate*, adequate, and independent grounds, we, of course, will not undertake to review the decision." (Italics added.) Not only must state courts apparently issue a plain statement denying reliance on federal law, but they must also persuade the justices that this reliance is genuine. The addition of the word "separate" to "bona fide," "adequate," and "independent" should enable the justices to review any state court decision they wish so long as it makes reference to some federal authority.

Why did the conservative Burger Court, with a reputation of deference to the states, suddenly change its tune?

Analysis of decisions in which the majority used *Michigan v. Long* to review state court decisions shows it to be a means to overturn liberal state decisions upholding the rights of persons accused or convicted of crime, particularly those involving unreasonable searches and seizures.

The Subordination of Considerations of Federalism

The willingness of the Court's conservative majority to subordinate considerations of federalism to its substantive policy preferences should occasion no surprise. Matters of procedure, such as considerations of federalism, are regularly invoked when the majority supports the merits of the lower court's decision. The justices, of course, do defer, but they never do so blindly. Justices who are conservative on criminal procedure (Rehnquist, Burger, O'Connor, Powell, White, and Blackmun) apparently thought the Court's traditional standard of review unduly hindered them from reversing liberal state court decisions. They therefore changed the rules of the game so that their substantively conservative policy preferences could continue to be accommodated.

Other procedural rules that many view as guides for judicial decision making are judicial restraint and strict construction.

JUDICIAL RESTRAINT

Judicial restraint asserts that because federal judges are electorally unaccountable and serve lifetime terms, they ought to defer to publicly accountable decision makers, state and federal. Judicial restraint accordingly posits that judges in general, and Supreme Court justices in particular, should uphold congressional legislation and the actions of state and local governments. Furthermore, many issues, especially those involving economic regulation, are exceedingly technical and complex. Hence, advocates of judicial restraint maintain that federal judges should defer to the decision making of the experts in the bureaucracy and in the various federal regulatory commissions and agencies.

Judicial Restraint as Rationalization

Judicial restraint is a useful and convenient basis for appellate court judges to rationalize their decisions. It supports liberal and conservative decisions equally well. If the court or judge approves of the decision previously made in the case, judicial restraint may be used to justify it. If, however, the court or judge wishes to overturn the previous decision, judicial restraint will not work.

At the Supreme Court level, judicial restraint is issue-specific. The individual justices do not defer blindly. They only defer the actions and decisions of which they approve. They do not defer to those with which they disagree. Systematic analyses show that liberal justices defer when the decisions they review were themselves liberally decided, and conservatives to those that produced a conservative outcome. Judicial restraint thus serves only to cloak the political character of the judicial process, to help preserve the notion that judges merely find and do not make the law.

The Court's overruling of precedents and its declarations of unconstitutionality help evidence the subjective use to which judicial restraint is put. To the extent to which judicial restraint is considered a conservative doctrine, a conservative Court should manifest its restraint by adhering to precedent and by deferring to the actions of Congress and those of state and local governments. Such, however, is not the case.

With regard to precedent, the liberal Warren Court and the moderately conservative Burger Court each formally altered precedent an average of 2.5 times per term. The conservative Rehnquist Court, by contrast, has averaged 4.3 alterations per term. One should note that the Rehnquist Court's average may be less valid because these data are drawn from only its first three terms, whereas those for the Warren and Burger Courts span sixteen and seventeen years, respectively.

Judicially Activist Courts

In recent years, many conservatives have criticized the Warren Court for its judicial activism—which is the antithesis of judicial restraint—often referring to Justice Brennan as the most notable example of judicial activism. Ironically, evidence—in the form of declarations of unconstitutionality—indicates that the more conservative Burger and Rehnquist courts are more inclined to judicial activism than the liberal Warren Court. The Burger and Rehnquist courts have voided on constitutional grounds an average of 13.24 and 10.67 state and local laws per term. The Warren Court—although considered to be especially active because of its hostility to the states in matters of race relations and law enforcement—averaged only 8.69. At the federal level, the Warren Court declared actions of Congress unconstitutional an average of 1.38 times per term, while the Burger Court average is 1.71. In its first three terms, the Rehnquist Court declared 4 acts of Congress unconstitutional, an average of 1.33 per term.

STRICT CONSTRUCTION

Unlike judicial restraint, strict construction is a recognized rule of law. Its legal meaning, however, bears no relationship to the meaning recent presidents and their supporters have given it.

Legally, strict construction has two meanings. It can mean a literal interpretation of the Constitution. The First Amendment, for example, states that Congress shall make no law concerning speech and press. To the strict constructionist, this language means that any and all efforts by Congress to curb communication are unconstitutional; the fact that the speech is obscene, libelous or subversive is irrelevant. The other legal meaning of strict construction pertains to the construction of criminal laws. Because of the historic severity of criminal punishment and the stigma that attached to persons convicted of crime, any ambiguity in the wording of a criminal law was to be construed in the defendant's favor. Thus, if two meanings of the statutory language are equally plausible, the strict constructionist opts for the one that benefits the accused.

Strict Construction as a Political Term

The political meaning of strict construction is an entirely different matter, however. Beginning with former President Nixon, who used the phrase to characterize federal judges who emphasized law and order and did not support further expansion of civil rights and liberties, the political meaning has come to characterize judges and judicial candidates who are thought to interpret the Constitution in a limited, noninnovative fashion. Presidents Reagan and Bush promoted their nominees for Supreme Court vacancies on the basis that they were strict con structionists. From the standpoint of public and Senate consumption, the label "strict constructionist" has become a substitute phrase for "politically conservative."

This chapter has surveyed the essence of the relationship between the federal and state judicial systems, as well as the use of judicial restraint and strict construction in the Court's decisions.

The supremacy clause of the Constitution gives primacy to federal law. Notwithstanding, by creating a system of comity implemented by the abstention doctrine, the Supreme Court has deferred to the state courts' resolution of cases containing federal questions. As a result of its decision in Michigan v. Long, however, the Court has created a precedent that a majority may use to narrowly confine the scope of adequate and independent state grounds for decision.

Neither judicial restraint nor strict construction is used by the justices as substantive guides for their decisions. Instead, they serve only to rationalize the justices' policy preferences thereby enabling them to appear deferential to Congress, federal bureaucrats, and state decision makers. Data show the liberal Warren Court to have exercised judicial restraint to a greater extent than the Burger Court did or the Rehnquist Court has done to date.

6

Legal Rights and Entitlements

As described in chapter 2, the rights provided by the Constitution are negative: they exist to prevent or limit government from unduly interfering with individuals' freedom of action. They are meant to protect liberty, to ensure that government leaves people alone. This does not mean, however, that Americans lack affirmative—or social—rights; e.g., education, job security, health and welfare benefits. Although the Constitution sets a floor below which government may not go insofar as individual freedom and liberty are concerned, nothing in the Constitution prevents Congress or the state and local governments from providing individuals more rights than the Constitution specifies.

At the federal level, Congress does precisely that when it passes legislation that provides eligible individuals with "entitlements": affirmative rights beyond those decreed by the Constitution. State and local governments have also done so, arguably to a greater extent than the federal government. These rights concern such matters as unemployment compensation, veterans benefits, social security, Medicare, occupational licenses, jobs, government contracts, a vast range of subsidies and franchises, use of public facilities, and the provision of an extremely wide variety of governmental services.

DIFFERENCES BETWEEN ENTITLEMENT AND CONSTITUTIONAL RIGHTS

These rights differ from those contained in the Constitution in several respects. First, they are legal, not constitutional, rights. Their source is federal law, or the action of state and local governments. Consequently, they do not rest on as permanent a basis as constitutional rights.

Second, they may impose duties and responsibilities on private persons or entities, such as businesses. By contrast, constitutional rights concern and limit only governmental action, with but few exceptions—e.g., the Thirteenth Amendment outlaws governmentally mandated as well as privately established slavery.

Third, for all practical purposes the Constitution is concerned with these affirmative rights—these entitlements—only to a limited extent; i.e., that government may not define who is eligible in a way that denies persons the equal protection of the law. Nor may government deprive any person who possesses such a right without due process of law.

Equal Protection

This means that government may not classify people for the purpose of granting them an entitlement on an unreasonably discriminatory basis. Equal protection does not mean equal treatment. All legislation treats some people differently from other people. People who earn a lot of money generally pay more income tax than those who earn only a minimum wage. Most people must be sixty-five to receive Medicare benefits. In most colleges and universities, a minimum of 128 semester credits, not 127, gets one a degree. All the equal protection clause requires is that there be no unreasonable discrimination. Hence, conditioning entitlements on the basis of race, sex, religion, or national origin generally violates equal protection.

Due Process

Due process, on the other hand, prohibits government from taking away a statutorily or state-provided right without notice and hearing. What kind of notice and what kind of hearing—a full-blown adversarial-type trial hearing, before or after deprivation, or a brief, informal one—depends on the importance of the right to the individual and the likelihood that government's decision to terminate the entitlement may erroneously deprive persons of their rights.

Not all nonconstitutionally based rights are affirmative ones. Nothing prevents a state from restraining itself or its local governments beyond the limit that the Constitution mandates. For example, a number of states' definition of unreasonable search is more broad than the Supreme Court's interpretation of the Fourth Amendment. In *Michigan v. Sitz* (1990), the

Court ruled that briefly stopping motorists at highway sobriety checkpoints does not violate the Constitution. But nothing prevents Michigan, or any other state, from construing its own constitutional provision against unreasonable searches and seizures to include such stops. Thus, though the U.S. Constitution permits sobriety checkpoints, Michigan may rule that its constitution does not. In other words, the U.S. Constitution establishes a floor under our rights—a bottom level—not a ceiling.

THE SCOPE OF CONSTITUTIONAL RIGHTS

Whereas constitutional rights generally apply only to governmental action, those based on statutes need not be so limited. The equal protection clause, for example, prohibits government from engaging in job discrimination while the civil rights laws prohibit private employers from doing so. This distinction results because the scope of the constitutional provisions that address private discrimination—chiefly the interstate commerce clause—extends beyond governmental action.

Constitutional Bases for Regulating Private Activity

The language of Article I, section 8, in which the powers of Congress are enumerated, allows for the regulation of private activity. Beginning with *Wickard v. Filburn* (1942) and extending through *Katzenbach v. McClung* (1964), the Supreme Court construed the scope of the interstate commerce clause very broadly. Intrastate activities that may affect interstate commerce are covered just as much as commodities that physically cross a state line. Hence, growing twenty-three acres of wheat on a farm for on-farm consumption constituted interstate commerce even though no state line was crossed, as did running a rib joint not patronized by interstate travelers, because it sold locally some beef procured from out of state.

PURPOSE VERSUS EFFECT

Coupled with the scope of the Constitution's provisions and the use of statutory authority to create affirmative rights are the criteria the Supreme Court uses to interpret actions that allegedly violate individual freedom.

Action challenged as violating the First Amendment, and most other constitutional provisions, may be ruled unconstitutional because either its purpose or its effect is bad. The same is true if Congress indicates that a law may be violated either deliberately or inadvertently. Not so, however, where the due process and equal protection clauses are concerned. Here governmental action may be voided only on a showing of bad purpose or motive. Thus, in the area of school segregation, with but a handful of exceptions, only southern schools purposefully separated students on the basis of their race (de jure segregation).

In the North, racial segregation in the public schools, according to the Supreme Court, occurred without governmental action or only as the effect of governmental action (de facto segregation).

The landmark case of *Washington v. Davis* (1976) well illustrates this point. Two blacks who sought to become police officers in the District of Columbia claimed that the personnel test that all applicants had to take was racially discriminatory because a higher percentage of blacks than whites failed it. The Court ruled that a disproportionate racial impact does not, in and of itself, violate the Constitution. Though the effect of the policy discriminates, a constitutional violation requires a showing that the test was deliberately designed to thwart black applicants.

The Court's use of purpose rather than effect enables it to exercise considerably more discretion than if effect were the criterion. The reason somebody does something is a highly subjective matter, whereas the effect of somebody's action is an empirical question, one that can be quantitatively measured. Not so purpose or intent. Here judgment becomes fully subjective. Purpose, like beauty, lies in the eye of the beholder. Unless the lawmaking body speaks with a single unequivocal voice, which for all practical purposes it never does, courts may plausibly read into a statute or regulation almost any objective they desire.

*T*he affirmative rights—entitlements—that Americans have they receive from government, not from the Constitution. As chapter 2 indicates, constitutional rights are negative in the sense that they protect persons from governmental action. They do not allow individuals to demand that government do things for them.

Entitlements are constrained by the Constitution to only a limited extent. Government may not take them away without affording those who have them due process of law. Nor may government distribute entitlements in an unreasonably discriminatory manner. Apart from these considerations, Congress, as well as the state and local governments, are largely free to grant, condition, or revoke these affirmative rights as they see fit.

7

The Selection of Justices

*B*etween September 26, 1789, and the seating of David Souter on October 9, 1990, 105 persons had taken the oath of office as members of the United States Supreme Court. One additional person died before he could take his seat: Edwin M. Stanton, whom Grant nominated in 1868, died four days after the Senate confirmed him. All but one of the justices have been males.

Each of these persons, compatibly with the Constitution's provisions, was nominated by the president and confirmed by a majority vote of the Senate. Another seven individuals, having been nominated and confirmed, declined to accept the position. Five of these instances occurred early in our history: in 1789, 1796, 1800, and two in 1811; the other two in 1837 and 1882.

FAILED NOMINATIONS

An additional twenty-nine persons were nominated by a president but failed to be confirmed. These are persons the Senate either rejected or refused to consider or nominations that were postponed or withdrawn by the president. Three of these twenty-nine were subsequently confirmed after being nominated a second time: William Paterson in 1793, Roger Taney in 1836, and Stanley Matthews in 1881. In addition to these twenty-nine, seven others—as noted in the preceding paragraph—declined the position for which they were chosen. One nominee, Edward King, twice failed to be confirmed: the Senate postponed action in 1844, and a year later President Tyler withdrew his second nomination. Virtually half of the failed nominations —fourteen—occurred between 1844 and 1874. By contrast, only one nominee failed to be confirmed in the seventy-four years between 1894 and 1968: John J. Parker in 1930.

Analysis of the failed nominations indicates three distinguishable sets of circumstances explaining their outcome: lack of nominee qualifications, conflict between the presidents and a majority of the senators, and the presidents' lame-duck status. This last factor pertains to the last months of the term of office of a president who is not a candidate for re-election.

Lack of Qualifications

Although the particular qualities of a nominee can enable the Senate to rationalize rejection, more often than not failure to confirm occurs when purely political reasons make disapproval feasible. For example, the matter of qualifications was raised against Nixon's first two nominees to the Fortas vacancy in 1969 and 1970, Clement Haynsworth and G. Harrold Carswell. The former had participated in cases in which he held a litigant's stock, while the major argument that Carswell supporters made in favor of their candidate was that mediocrities also deserved representation on the Court. Furthermore, both were suspected of being deficient in their support for civil rights. Yet it was Democratic control of the Senate that occasioned their defeat. Both of them received only forty-five supporting votes, which largely fell along party lines.

Lack of qualifications also explains three other rejections: John Rutledge's in 1795, Alexander Wolcott's in 1811, and Douglas Ginsberg's in 1987. President Reagan withdrew Ginsberg's nomination following the revelation that he had smoked marijuana while an undergraduate student at Cornell University and as a faculty member at Harvard Law School.

Control of the Senate

In all likelihood, the Carswell and Haynsworth nominations would not have been defeated if the same party had controlled the Senate and occupied the White House. This variable is important for at least two reasons. First, ideological antagonism is more likely from the opposition party than from the president's own party. Second, partisanship is a strong cue in congressional voting and is likely to occur independently of ideological considerations. Of the nominations made when the president's party controlled the Senate, 90 percent were confirmed, as opposed to only 58 percent when the opposition party had a majority.

Of the persons failing to be confirmed because of political differences, five failed during the post–Civil War period, three of whom were nominated by Grant and two by Cleveland. Holding the record for number of candidates rejected is Tyler, who had four nominees spurned a total of five times in 1844 and 1845. Political differences between president and Senate also accounted for the most one-sided defeat of a nominee: Robert Bork by a vote of 58 to 42 in 1987.

The Timing of Nominations

The timing of an appointment affects the success of a presidential nomination even more than Senate control. The Senate's incentive to block Supreme Court nominees becomes especially pronounced in a president's final year in office. Rules governing debate enable the Senate to block nominations regardless of whether the president's party controls it. In 1968, for example, Lyndon Johnson sought to promote Abe Fortas to the chief justiceship to replace Earl Warren, and Homer Thornberry to fill Fortas's slot. The Republicans and some southern Democrats, sensing a Republican victory in the November election, engineered a filibuster, forcing Johnson to withdraw the nomination. As a second result, the Senate took no action on Thornberry.

The Fortas-Thornberry situation was not an isolated event. Almost 90 percent of the nominations made during the first three years of a president's term have been confirmed, as compared with but 54 percent of fourth-year nominations. The record for futility as a lame duck belongs to Millard Fillmore, who had three successive nominees rejected in a six-month period between August of 1852 and February of 1853.

If the opposition party's control of the Senate is added to the fourth year of a president's term, the probability of confirmation declines still more precipitously. When the president's party controlled the Senate, ten of twelve lame-duck nominations were approved (83 percent), as compared with only four of fifteen when the opposition party comprised a majority (27 percent). The Senate's rejection of Bork and Ginsberg late in 1987, as well as the confirmation of Anthony Kennedy in early 1988, are included in these figures.

WHOM PRESIDENTS CHOOSE

As a general rule, presidents desire to appoint to the Court individuals who share their own personal policy preferences. This normally means that active membership in the president's political party will be a necessary, but not sufficient, condition for nomination. Presidents and their advisers correctly view party affiliation as an accurate indicator of a potential nominee's ideological orientation. There have been exceptions, however. President Taft divided his six nominations equally between Democrats and Republicans. But his three Democratic nominees were all southern Democrats and, then as now, the ideological difference between most southern Democrats and conservative Republicans is slight. Taft, incidentally, saw more of his nominees confirmed than any other president except Washington, Andrew Jackson, and Franklin Roosevelt. Taft, moreover, served only a single term as president.

Presidents have sometimes selected persons to serve on the Supreme Court for reasons other than ideological affinity. Eisenhower, for example, apparently chose Earl Warren, the then governor of California, to be chief justice because Warren played the key role in helping Eisenhower secure the necessary votes at the Republican convention in 1952. Four years later,

Eisenhower's advisers, concerned about his re-election, persuaded him to nominate a Catholic New Jersey Democrat, William Brennan. Eisenhower had not done particularly well in the East or among Catholics in 1952, and Brennan's nomination was an effort to increase his support among these groups. Truman was another president who paid little heed to whether his policy views were compatible with those of his nominees, preferring to nominate associates from his days in the Senate.

The failure of a president to nominate ideological clones to the High Bench is clearly shortsighted. President Truman admitted as much when he characterized his selection of Tom Clark as his "biggest mistake." The best insurance that a president has that his administration will live after his term of office is the careful filling of Supreme Court vacancies with persons who share his vision and support his policies. Franklin Roosevelt's populating the Court with New Dealers ensured the success of his policies, while the astute selections of Nixon, Reagan, and Bush ensure that conservative policies will continue to emanate from the Supreme Court well into the twenty-first century.

In seeking to appoint persons who share their public policy views, presidents sometimes guess wrongly. The liberal Woodrow Wilson, for example, nominated James McReynolds, whom many scholars view as the most reactionary individual ever to sit on the Supreme Court. It is also likely that Eisenhower was less than pleased with many of the decisions of his chief justice, Earl Warren.

THE JUSTICES' CHARACTERISTICS

The individuals who have served on the Supreme Court have a limited range of characteristics. Only one has been a woman, Sandra Day O'Connor, and only one a black, Thurgood Marshall. The great majority have been Anglo-Saxon Protestants, middle class or above, socially prominent, with professional training and background. With three exceptions, they have all been active in partisan politics, and all have practiced law at some stage of their careers. No person of Slavic ancestry has sat on the Court, and only one of Italian extraction, Antonin Scalia. Eight Catholics have served, including two chief justices, Taney and Edward White. From the appointment of Anthony Kennedy in 1988 until the resignation of William Brennan in 1990, the Court was one-third Catholic. Five Jews have also served. The first was Louis Brandeis in 1916. The last Jew, Abe Fortas, left the Court in 1969. Reagan nominated Douglas Ginsberg in 1987, but his name was withdrawn without Senate action.

Geographical considerations played a part in the selection process during the nineteenth century; they have been an incidental factor since. Republican presidents prefer to select persons with previous judicial experience. Lower court judges tend to be conservative and thus attractive to Republican presidents. Among the sitting justices, six of the seven who were nominated by Republican presidents had previous judicial experience; Chief Justice Rehnquist did not. Of the two Democrats, Marshall had previous experience, Byron White did not.

LENGTH OF SERVICE

Once appointed, a justice, according to the Constitution, serves for life "during good behavior." Vacancies, accordingly, seldom occur—only on an average of once every twenty-three months. The longest period without a change in personnel covered the twelve years between 1811 and 1823. Indeed, during a fifteen-year period ending in 1826, only one change occurred. More recently, from the nominations of Lewis Powell and William Rehnquist in December 1971 until the resignation of Chief Justice Burger in July 1986, only two changes occurred: John Paul Stevens replaced William Douglas in 1975 and Sandra Day O'Connor replaced Potter Stewart in 1981.

Impeachment Efforts

No justice has ever been successfully impeached. The closest a member of the Court has come to impeachment was in 1804, when the House of Representatives voted to impeach Samuel Chase. (The Senate acquitted him.) On the other hand, impeachment resolutions have been introduced against a number of justices, but the resolution involving Chase is the only one the House has ever approved. The most recent attempt to unseat a Supreme Court justice occurred in the spring of 1970, when fifty-two conservative Republicans and an equal number of Democrats, mostly southerners, introduced a resolution calling for the impeachment of Justice Douglas because excerpts from one of his books appeared in an issue of a sexually explicit magazine. This was not the first time such a resolution had been introduced against Douglas. His three divorces, off-the-bench activities, and liberal voting record had made him a target of conservatives for the preceding twenty years.

Although presidents have seen the majority of their nominees to the Supreme Court confirmed by the Senate, a number have not been. Three reasons explain the Senate's failure to confirm: lack of nominee qualifications, partisan conflict between the president and a majority of the senators, and the lame-duck status of the nominating president.

Wise presidents who wish their policies to have life beyond their term of office take pains to select nominees whose views reflect their own. Most presidents have attempted to follow this course, even at considerable political cost—e.g., Nixon's selection of Carswell and Haynsworth in 1969 and 1970. Other presidents have behaved markedly less astutely—among them Truman and Eisenhower.

The 105 persons who have sat on the Supreme Court have displayed a very limited set of personal characteristics. With but two exceptions they have been white males. They are overwhelmingly Anglo-Saxon in ancestry, Protestant, from socially privileged and economically well-off families. They themselves have graduated from prestigious educational institutions, been professionally successful, and highly active in partisan politics.

8

Chronology of Events in U.S. Constitutional History

This chapter contains a chronological listing of important events affecting the Constitution and the Supreme Court of the United States. It begins with the Revolutionary War and ends with the retirement of Justice William Brennan and his replacement with David Souter in 1990.

1775   The Revolutionary War begins with battles at Lexington and Concord.

1776   The Virginia Bill of Rights is adopted.

      The Declaration of Independence is proclaimed.

1781   The Articles of Confederation are ratified.

1783   The Revolutionary War ends with the signing of a peace treaty between England and the United States.

1787   The Continental Congress enacts the Northwest Ordinance for governing the territory north of the Ohio River and east of the Mississippi. Freedom of religion, trial by jury, and public support of education are guaranteed. Slavery is outlawed.

      The Constitutional Convention convenes.

1789   The Constitution is ratified.

1790   The Supreme Court convenes its first session in New York City.

1791   The Bill of Rights becomes part of the Constitution.

1793   The Court announces its first major decision, *Chisholm v. Georgia*, which authorizes citizens of one state to sue another state in the Supreme Court. Ironically, the Eleventh Amendment, ratified in 1798, nullifies the Court's decision.

1795   The first chief justice, John Jay, resigns to become governor of New York. Washington nominates John Rutledge of South Carolina as Jay's successor, but for the first time the Senate refuses to confirm a Supreme Court nominee.

1796   John Marshall makes his only appearance as an attorney before the Supreme Court when he argues the case of *Ware v. Hylton*. In stark contrast to the nationalist position he espoused as chief justice, here he alleges the supremacy of state laws that conflict with federal treaties. He loses the case.

1798   The Eleventh Amendment, prohibiting a nonresident from suing a state in federal court, is ratified.

1800   Thomas Jefferson is elected president.

1801   John Marshall is appointed chief justice by the lame-duck president John Adams shortly before Jefferson takes office.

1803   *Marbury v. Madison*, which enunciates the doctrine of judicial review, is decided.

1804   The House of Representatives, for the only time in history, votes to impeach a Supreme Court justice, Samuel Chase. The Senate, however, one year later, fails to muster the two-thirds vote required to convict Chase on charges of partisan political behavior.

The Twelfth Amendment, governing the election of the president and vice-president, is ratified.

1810   The Supreme Court declares a state law unconstitu tional for the first time in *Fletcher v. Peck*.

1812   Congress declares war on Great Britain.

1814   British troops capture and burn Washington, including the Capitol and White House.

1815   The treaty ending the War of 1812 is signed.

1816   The Court rules that it, rather than the state courts, has final authority to determine the meaning of constitutional provisions and acts of Congress.

1819   The doctrine of implied powers is formulated in *M'Culloch v. Maryland*.

The contract clause is construed to prevent states from abridging corporate charters as well as public grants.

1820   Congress enacts the Missouri Compromise, which outlaws slavery north of the 36th parallel. The Supreme Court declares the law unconstitutional thirty-seven years later in *Scott v. Sandford*.

1823   The longest period in the Court's history without a change of personnel (twelve years) ends with the death of Justice Livingston.

The Monroe Doctrine declares the Western Hemisphere off limits to further European colonization and commits the United States to noninvolvement in European affairs.

1824 With no candidate receiving a majority of the electoral votes, the presidential election is thrown into the House of Representatives, which chooses John Quincy Adams over Andrew Jackson.

1828 Jackson defeats Adams for the presidency. Democratizing features of American government intensify: property-holding and tax-paying qualifications for voting largely disappear, as do religious qualifications for holding public office. Public offices themselves, including state judgeships, become elective rather than appointive.

1832 An attempt by Georgia to subject Cherokee Indians to its authority, notwithstanding Supreme Court decision to the contrary, ends when President Jackson reverses his pro-state position and supports expanded federal judicial power.

1833 *Barron v. Baltimore*, Chief Justice Marshall's last major constitutional opinion, holds that the Bill of Rights applies only to the federal government, not to the states.

1835 John Marshall dies.

1836 Because of Senate opposition to the nomination of Roger Taney as Marshall's successor, the Supreme Court, for the only term in its history, is without a chief justice.

Abolitionist sentiment begins to wrack Congress.

1837 Taney is finally confirmed by the Senate, notwithstanding the opposition of two giants of American constitutional law, Daniel Webster and Henry Clay.

Three major decisions, *Charles River Bridge v. Warren Bridge*, *New York v. Miln*, and *Briscoe v. Bank of Kentucky*, portend an increase in the rights of the states vis-à-vis the national government by limiting the scope of the contracts clause and upholding state regulations affecting interstate commerce.

1842 *Prigg v. Pennsylvania* holds that the federal government, not the states, has authority over fugitive slaves.

1844 The longest vacancy in Supreme Court history begins with the death of Justice Baldwin. Because of partisan conflict between President Tyler—the first non-elected president—and the Senate, Baldwin's seat remains vacant for twenty-seven months. No other president comes close to matching Tyler's record of futility in trying to secure Senate confirmation of his Supreme Court nominees: one of six.

1845 Texas is annexed, which leads one year later to war with Mexico.

1848 Gold is discovered in California.

1850 The Compromise of 1850 takes effect. Unsuccessful, it proves to be the final effort to resolve the slavery controversy. California is admitted as a free state; slavery in the territories of Utah and New Mexico is left to their inhabitants; slave trading is abolished in the District of Columbia; and a fugitive slave law protective of southern interests is enacted.

1854 The Republican party is founded.

1857 The Dred Scott decision rules the Constitution to be a white man's document: no black may be a citizen; slaves are property with which Congress may not interfere. The decision splits the Democratic party and opens the door for Republican electoral successes.

1860 Lincoln is elected president. South Carolina secedes from the Union.

1861 Ten other states follow South Carolina into secession. The Civil War begins with the Confederate attack on Fort Sumter.

1863 The Emancipation Proclamation declares southern slaves free.

1864 Chief Justice Taney dies and is succeeded by Salmon P. Chase.

1865 Lee surrenders at Appomattox ending the Civil War. Five days later John Wilkes Booth assassinates President Lincoln.

The Thirteenth Amendment, abolishing slavery, is ratified.

1866 The Ku Klux Klan is founded in Pulaski, Tennessee.

The Radical Republicans gain control of Congress and mount a program of Reconstruction to govern the South.

The Supreme Court rules that military tribunals have no jurisdiction over civilians where the regular courts are open and operating.

1868 The Fourteenth Amendment, prohibiting the states from depriving persons due process or denying them equal protection of the law, is ratified.

President Andrew Johnson is impeached.

Ulysses Grant is elected President.

1869 Congress increases the size of the Supreme Court to nine, where it has remained ever since.

In its first Fourteenth Amendment case, *Paul v. Virginia*, the justices rule that corporations are not citizens and therefore cannot invoke the amendment's privileges and immunities clause.

1870 The last of the Civil War amendments, the Fifteenth, is ratified, prohibiting the states or the United States from denying anyone the right to vote because of race.

By a 4-to-3 vote, the Supreme Court rules that Con gress has no power to authorize paper money as legal payment of debts, the method used to finance the Civil War. President Grant carefully fills the Court's two vacancies with individuals sym pathetic to the use of paper money, and, fifteen months after the initial decision, the Court reverses itself and rules that the Legal Tender Acts were a proper exercise of congressional power.

1873 By a 5-to-4 vote, the Court holds in the Slaughterhouse cases that nothing in the Fourteenth Amendment expands the scope of individual rights against state action.

With only Chief Justice Chase dissenting, the Court rules in *Bradwell v. Illinois* that a state violates no constitutional provision in denying a woman a license to practice law because of her sex.

Chief Justice Chase dies unexpectedly.

1874 After two unsuccessful attempts to fill the chief justiceship—the most in history—Grant nominates Morrison Waite, a little-known Ohio attorney without judicial experience who has never argued a case before the Supreme Court.

1877 Five members of the Supreme Court serve on the electoral commission that resolves the disputed election of 1876. In return for southern Democratic support of the Republican nominee, Rutherford B. Hayes, the GOP promises to withdraw federal troops from the South and end further efforts at Reconstruction.

The Court reaffirms its 1873 decision in the Granger cases that the Fourteenth Amendment does not prevent states from regulating the use of private property.

1883 In the Civil Rights cases, the Court narrowly defines what constitutes state action under the due process and equal protection clauses of the Fourteenth Amendment, and in the process declares the Civil Rights Act of 1875 unconstitutional. Not until after World War II would the Court with any regularity support civil rights claims.

1886 Although corporations are not citizens entitled to the protections afforded by the Fourteenth Amendment, they are "persons" who cannot be deprived of liberty or property without due process of law. With its decision in this case, *Santa Clara County v. Southern Pacific Railway*, the Court begins to write the doctrines of laissez-faire economics into the Constitution.

1887 The Interstate Commerce Act is passed, creating the first regulatory commission in United States history. Supreme Court decisions, however, sap the strength from its provisions, making it impotent to regulate the railroads, who are the focus of the Act.

1888 L.Q.C. Lamar of Mississippi is appointed to the Supreme Court. He is the first Democratic court justice in a quarter century.

Chief Justice Waite dies. He is replaced by Melville Fuller, a Chicago railroad attorney.

1890   Congress enacts the Sherman Antitrust Act. Because of lax enforcement and hostile court decisions, the law does little to curb the growth of concentrated economic power.

1895   The Supreme Court rules that the Sherman Antitrust Act, which is based on Congress's power to regulate interstate commerce, does not apply to manufacturing because manufacturing is not commerce.

Overruling a 100-year-old precedent, the Court declares the income tax unconstitutional, necessitating the adoption of the Sixteenth Amendment eighteen years later.

A unanimous Court approves the use of federal judicial power to stop strikes through the use of the labor injunction.

1896   The Court formulates the separate but equal doctrine in *Plessy v. Ferguson*, thereby relegitimating the racist society that the Civil War and the Civil War amendments sought to terminate.

1897   The "liberty" that the Fourteenth Amendment protects includes freedom of contract: i.e., the right of individuals to sell their labor without governmental regulation of hours, wages, or working conditions—with some very limited exceptions.

1898   In *Smyth v. Ames*, the Court further extends its probusiness judicial activism, holding that if states set the rates railroads may charge, those rates must provide a fair return on investment, and that the federal courts will determine what is and is not fair.

The Spanish-American War begins, as a result of which the United States acquires Puerto Rico, Hawaii, and the Philippine Islands.

1902   Theodore Roosevelt appoints Oliver Wendell Holmes to the Supreme Court.

1905   *Lochner v. New York* is decided: freedom of contract precludes a state from restricting bakers to a ten-hour day and a sixty-hour week.

1908   Freedom of contract also invalidates the act of Congress outlawing yellow-dog contracts which allow employers to fire employees because they join a labor union; hence, employers may fire employees who join a union.

Although the Sherman Act does not particularly restrain business activity, the Court construes it to ban secondary boycotts by labor unions in *Loewe v. Lawlor*.

As a result of the advocacy of Louis D. Brandeis, who would join the Supreme Court eight years later, the Court accepts limitations on freedom of contract where women are con cerned. Accordingly, a state may restrict laundresses to a ten- hour day.

1909   William Howard Taft takes the oath of office as president. During his tenure, six of his nominees take seats on the Supreme Court, more than those of any other single-term president. Only Washington's ten successful nominees and Franklin Roosevelt's nine exceed his number.

1910   Chief Justice Fuller dies and, for the first time, an associate justice, Edward D. White, is promoted to the chief justiceship.

1911   In *Standard Oil Co. v. United States*, the Court says that the Sherman Act outlaws only unreasonable restraints of trade even though the Act contains no such qualification. The federal courts, of course, determine what is and is not reasonable.

1913   The Sixteenth (income tax) and Seventeenth (popular election of senators) amendments are ratified.

1914   World War I begins.

The Clayton Antitrust Act, which supplements and strengthens the Sherman Act, is passed.

1916   President Wilson nominates the first Jew, Louis Brandeis, to the Supreme Court. Over the opposition of former President—and soon-to-be Chief Justice—Taft and of various bar and business leaders, he is confirmed after four months of acrimonious hear ings. Although his opponents describe him as a trouble-making radical, anti-Semitism fuels much of the opposition.

1917   The United States declares war on Germany.

1918   By a 5-to-4 vote in *Hammer v. Dagenhart*, the Court declares unconstitutional Congress's effort to outlaw child labor.

The armistice ending World War I is signed.

1919   The "noble experiment"—Prohibition—spearheaded by the Women's Christian Temperance Union and the Anti-Saloon League, is written into the Constitution as the Eighteenth Amendment.

1920   Women get the right to vote with the ratification of the Nineteenth Amendment.

1921   Chief Justice White dies. President Warren Harding chooses former President Taft as his successor.

1922   Congress's second effort to ban child labor—based this time on the power to tax rather than the interstate commerce clause—meets the same fate as in 1918.

1923   The Supreme Court rules that a federal minimum wage law for women violates freedom of contract.

1925   In the course of upholding the conviction of a left-winger for distributing a pamphlet urging the overthrow of the government, the Court casually notes that freedoms of speech and of the press are among the fundamental rights and liberties that the Fourteenth Amendment protects from state abridgement.

From this beginning, over the next forty years, the Court incorporates virtually all the provisions in the Bill of Rights into the due process clause of the Fourteenth Amendment. As a result, state and local governments, just like the federal government, may not deprive individuals of the liberties that the Bill of Rights guarantees.

1929 The stock market crashes; the Great Depression begins.

1930 President Hoover replaces Chief Justice Taft, who resigned, with Charles Evans Hughes, who had left the Supreme Court in 1916 to accept the Republican nomination for president.

1931 For the first time the Court strikes down a state law that violates the First Amendment: California's law that prohibits the display of a red flag as a symbol of opposition to government. Two weeks later, in *Near v. Minnesota*, the Court rules that a state law prohibiting publication of a scandal sheet violates the First Amendment's guarantee of freedom of the press.

1932 The Norris-LaGuardia Act forbids the federal courts to issue injunctions in labor disputes to prevent strikes, boycotts, or picketing.

1933 Franklin Roosevelt takes office. The New Deal begins. Major regulatory legislation is enacted, including the Agricultural Adjustment Act and the National Industrial Recovery Act. Congress creates the Civilian Conservation Corps to provide outdoor work for unemployed males between the ages of eighteen and twenty-five and establishes the Tennessee Valley Authority to construct dams and power plants in especially depressed parts of Appalachia.

The Twentieth Amendment, which ends the practice of congressional lame-duck sessions, is ratified.

The Twenty-First Amendment is ratified, repealing Prohibition.

1934 Major federal regulatory commissions are created: the Securities and Exchange Commission, the Federal Communications Commission, the National Labor Relations Board, and the Federal Housing Administration.

In *Nebbia v. New York*, the Court rules that the Fourteenth Amendment does not prevent a state from fixing the maximum and minimum prices of milk.

1935 Congress enacts the National Labor Relations Act, which gives labor the legal right to bargain collectively, and the Social Security Act, which provides unemployment compensation, old-age pension benefits, aid to blind and disabled persons, and aid to families with dependent children.

The Court declares the National Industrial Recovery Act unconstitutional and also the Railroad Retirement Act, which established a comprehensive pension system for railroad workers.

1936 The Court continues to strike down major portions of the New Deal: the Agricultural Adjustment Act and the Bituminous Coal Conservation Act. Additionally, the Court declares that all state minimum wage laws—including those that apply to women and children—violate due process.

1937 The Court unanimously rules in *DeJonge v. Oregon* that the due process clause of the Fourteenth Amendment makes binding on the states the First Amendment's guarantee of freedom of assembly.

Following his landslide re-election in 1936, President Roosevelt submits to Congress a so-called Court-packing plan that will allow him to appoint additional justices to the Supreme Court for the unexpressed purpose of preventing further invalidation of New Deal legislation. But Justice Roberts's switch in vote—described as "the switch in time that saved nine"—produces a pro–New Deal majority and makes Roosevelt's Court packing scheme a moot issue as the decisions below indicate.

West Coast Hotel Co. v. Parrish overrules the 1923 decision *Adkins v. Children's Hospital* and the 1936 decision *Morehead v. New York ex rel. Tipaldo*, and upholds the State of Washington's minimum wage law. As the justices earlier read freedom of contract into the Constitution, they now read it out.

In *National Labor Relations Board v. Jones & Laughlin Steel Corp.*, the Court finally accepts reality and recognizes that manufacturing is a part of commerce that Congress has power to regulate. As a result, the National Labor Relations Act is ruled to be constitutional.

Steward Machine Co. v. Davis upholds the unemployment compensation provisions of the Social Security Act. *Helvering v. Davis* upholds its old-age pension benefits.

As the coup de grâce to the battle over Court packing and the constitutionality of the New Deal, Justice Van Devanter announces his retirement, thus giving Roosevelt his first opportunity to fill a seat on the Supreme Court and thereby increase judicial support for the New Deal. His selection, Hugo Black, is confirmed five days after nomination.

1938 Justice Sutherland becomes the second member of the Old Guard to resign. By the middle of 1941, Roosevelt fills five additional Court vacancies.

The Fair Labor Standards Act prohibits child labor and establishes a nationwide minimum wage and maximum hour law. The Court upholds its constitutionality three years later in *United States v. Darby*.

1939 World War II begins with the Nazi invasion of Poland.

1940   In an opinion by Justice Frankfurter, the Court holds that public school children may be compelled to salute the flag, notwithstanding their religious objections.

1941   Chief Justice Hughes resigns. For the second and last time in history, a president crosses party lines to select a chief justice when Roosevelt nominates Harlan Fiske Stone. (Taft was the first to do so when he promoted Edward D. White in 1910.)

The Japanese attack Pearl Harbor.

1942   In *Wickard v. Filburn*, the justices unanimously assert that Congress's power to regulate interstate commerce gives it control over activities that are neither commercial nor interstate.

1943   The Court overrules its compulsory flag salute decision of 1940.

1944   Unsubstantiated "military necessity" permits citizens to be summarily imprisoned solely because of their race. This decision, *Korematsu v. United States*, remains the law.

1945   President Franklin Roosevelt dies; Harry Truman succeeds him. World War II ends and the Cold War begins.

1946   Fred Vinson becomes chief justice on the death of Stone.

1947   The First Amendment's clause establishing freedom of religion is made binding on the states.

1948   The Supreme Court rules that state courts may not constitutionally enforce racially restrictive housing covenants.

1949   The Fourth Amendment's ban on unreasonable searches and seizures is held to apply to the states.

1950–1952   A series of decisions upholds federal and state legislation curbing alleged subversive activity.

1950   The Korean War begins.

1951   The Twenty-Second Amendment, limiting presidential terms, is ratified.

1952   The Court rules motion pictures to be a significant medium of expression protected by the First Amendment.

The Court curbs presidential power by ruling that Truman's seizure of the steel mills to avoid a strike that would disrupt Korean military actions exceeds constitutional limitations.

1953   Earl Warren becomes chief justice.

1954   The separate but equal doctrine is overruled in *Brown v. Board of Education*, paving the way for southern school desegregation.

1957   The Court makes the conviction of alleged subversives more difficult by requiring prosecutors to show that the accused took some action to forcibly overthrow the U.S. government.

The Supreme Court declares obscenity to be without constitutional protection.

1961–1969 The Warren Court begins to expand the rights of persons accused of crime by using various provisions in the Fourth to Eighth amendments to restrict state and local law enforcement activities.

1961 *Mapp v. Ohio* holds that the judicially created exclusionary rule prohibits the use of illegally seized evidence in state, as well as federal, trials.

1962 The Twenty-Third Amendment is ratified, allowing the District of Columbia to participate in presidential elections.

The Court rules that redistricting malapportioned legislative bodies is a judicial, not a political, question. Within the next twenty-seven months, the Supreme Court will formulate a "one person, one vote" rule and apply it to the House of Representatives and both houses of the states' legislatures. These decisions break the historical rural domination of legislative politics and shift power to cities and their suburbs.

The Court rules that officially sanctioned prayer in the public schools violates the Constitution's establishment of religion clause.

1963 The Sixth Amendment requiring that all person accused of serious crime be provided an attorney is ratified.

President Kennedy is assassinated.

1964 The Twenty-Fourth Amendment, prohibiting poll and other voting taxes, is ratified.

The Court determines that the First Amendment prevents public officials and celebrities from collecting damages for libelous media statements unless they prove the statement was made "with knowledge that is was false or with reckless disregard of whether it was false or not."

The Court holds that the Fifth Amendment's protection against self-incrimination applies to state defendants.

The Court unanimously upholds the constitutionality of the Civil Rights Act of 1964 and its ban on discrimination in places of public accommodations.

1965 The Court makes defendants' Sixth Amendment right to confront and cross-examine their accusers binding on the state, as well as the federal, governments.

The Court rules that the Ninth Amendment guarantees a right to personal privacy, which prohibits a state from criminalizing the use of contraceptives.

1966 *South Carolina v. Katzenbach* upholds the constitutionality of the Voting Rights Act of 1965. As a result, southern blacks, for the first time since Reconstruction, are able to vote with relative ease.

In *Miranda v. Arizona* the Court decides that suspects must be read their rights before police questioning. The collapse of law enforcement is widely forecast, and efforts to impeach Earl Warren gain additional steam.

1967 The Twenty-Fifth Amendment, governing presidential incompetence, is ratified.

A unanimous Court rules that criminalizing the most pathological of America's racial fears—interracial marriage—violates due process as well as equal protection.

The Court rules that defendants in state courts have as much right to obtain favorable witnesses as does the prosecution.

Thurgood Marshall, the first black nominated for the Supreme Court, takes his seat.

1968 Because of opposition to the Vietnamese War, President Johnson withdraws from the presidential race.

The court decides that the due process clause of the Fourteenth Amendment requires states to provide a trial by jury to persons accused of serious crimes.

A unanimous Court terminates the "with all deliberate speed" formula for desegregating southern schools under the mandate of *Brown v. Board of Education* and orders desegregation "now."

The court held that the First Amendment does not protect draft card burning.

Robert Kennedy is assassinated in Los Angeles while campaigning for the presidency.

Richard Nixon defeats Hubert Humphrey in the presidential election.

1969 The Court rules that the First Amendment protects symbolic speech and applies to children as well as adults. Hence, students may wear armbands to protest the Vietnam War.

Under investigation for his dealings with a convicted felon, Justice Fortas, the last Jewish person to sit on the Supreme Court, resigns. He is the only justice to resign under threat of impeachment.

The Court rules that the due process clause prohibits the states from denying individuals protection from double jeopardy.

President Nixon nominates Warren Burger to succeed Chief Justice Warren, who has announced his intention to resign at the end of the Court's term.

1969–1970 Nixon's efforts to fill the Fortas vacancy prove problematic. The Senate rejects his first two nominees, Clement Haynsworth and Harrold Carswell. Not since 1894 have two successive nominees been rejected.

The Senate, however, does confirm his third choice, Harry Blackmun, by a vote of 94 to 0.

1970   The Court determines that like adult defendants, juveniles are entitled to the same evidentiary standard: beyond a reasonable doubt.

The Court rules that Congress has power to lower the voting age to eighteen only for federal, not for state and local, elections. As a consequence, the Twenty-Sixth Amendment is proposed and ratified one year later.

1971   The Court holds that cross-district busing, racial quotas, and redrawn school district boundaries are permissible means of ending southern school segregation.

With each justice writing an opinion, the Court denies the government's request for an injunction prohibiting the publication of the "Pentagon Papers," classified documents pertaining to American involvement in Vietnam.

In *Reed v. Reed*, the Court, for the first time, voids a law because it discriminates against women.

1972   White House aides break into Democratic headquarters in the Watergate Office Building in Washington.

The Court rules that the right to counsel applies to all cases in which jail is a possible sentence.

With each justice again writing an opinion, the Court voids all death penalty statutes in the United States.

1973   *Roe v. Wade* is decided. The due process clause entitles women to an abortion "without undue governmental interference."

The Court decides that because the Constitution nowhere mentions education, it is not a fundamental right insofar as the equal protection clause is concerned. Hence, states are free to finance their schools by local property taxes even though the dollars available vary widely from district to district.

1974   By an 8-to-0 vote, the Court requires President Nixon to comply with a subpoena of certain White House tapes dealing with the Watergate affair. Seventeen days later Nixon resigns.

The Court rules that a multi-district remedy for school desegregation may involve only districts that have themselves discriminated. Hence, suburban Detroit districts cannot constitutionally be required to participate in the desegregation of the Detroit schools.

1975   American troops withdraw from Vietnam.

The justices unanimously agree that the guarantee of liberty in the due process clause prevents involuntary confinement in mental hospitals of persons dangerous to no one and capable of surviving in the outside world.

Justice Douglas resigns after thirty-six years on the Court, more than any justice in history.

1976 The Court determines that carefully crafted statutes authorizing the death penalty for first degree murder do not necessarily violate the Eighth Amendment.

1977 In a series of three decisions, the Court rules that neither the Constitution nor the Social Security Act requires states to pay for nontherapeutic abortions. Furthermore, public hospitals may, as a matter of policy, refuse to perform abortions. Such actions do not constitute unreasonable governmental interference with a woman's right to an abortion.

1978 The Supreme Court decides the Bakke case, the first major decision involving affirmative action. Numerical quotas are illegal, but goals are not. Furthermore, race may not be the sole criterion for such programs, but may be one of several.

1980 Ronald Reagan is elected President.

1981 Sandra Day O'Connor becomes the first woman to sit on the Supreme Court.

1982 The Court rules that a state may ban media coverage of the testimony of child sex victims in criminal trials only on a case-by-case basis.

1983 The one-house legislative veto is ruled unconstitutional.

Michigan v. Long, posing a major threat to the autonomy of state courts, is decided. The Court overturns its traditional presumption that state court decisions containing a mixture of state and federal issues rest "on an adequate and independent state ground." Since *Long*, if the basis for the state court's decision is unclear, the Supreme Court assumes it to be based on federal grounds.

1984 The Court rules that the inclusion of a nativity scene in a city's secular Christmas display does not violate the Constitution's establishment clause.

1985 The Court determines that although the privileges and immunities clause of Article IV of the Constitution allows states to discriminate against nonresidents for "substantial" reasons, New Hampshire's denial of a license to a Vermont lawyer is not such.

The Court holds that a legislatively mandated moment of silence for meditation or voluntary prayer in the public schools violates the establishment clause.

1986 According to the Court, the Constitution confers no right on consenting adult homosexuals to engage in oral or anal sex.

The Court decides that affirmative action plans need not be "victim specific," but that racial preferences in hiring and promotion are constitutionally preferable to layoffs.

President Reagan promotes Justice Rehnquist to replace Chief Justice Burger. Antonin Scalia occupies Rehnquist's seat.

1987 The Court unanimously rules in *St. Francis College v. Al-Khazraji* that members of white ethnic groups are also protected from employment, housing, and other forms of discrimination.

The Court decides that Louisiana law requiring schools that teach evolution to also teach "creation science" violates the establishment of religion clause.

1989 In a set of three decisions involving affirmative action, the Court holds that (1) state and local governments must narrowly tailor their minority hiring and contract programs to remedy documented policies of official discrimination; (2) employees must bear the burden of proving job discrimination; and (3) the federal law banning race discrimination in private employment contracts governs only hiring, not harassment while on the job.

The Court rules that mentally retarded persons and those as young as sixteen may constitutionally be sentenced to death.

1990 The Court decides that for persons making their wishes clearly known, the Constitution recognizes a right to die.

Justice Brennan resigns after thirty-three years on the Supreme Court. President Bush nominates, and the Senate confirms, David Souter as his replacement.

Supreme Court Decisions

The next nine chapters contain a selection of important United States Supreme Court decisions. The chapters more or less follow the ordering of the major provisions of the Constitution, with each chapter organized around one or more of the articles of the Constitution or around one or more of the amendments to the Constitution. The initial chapters address the structure and powers of the federal judiciary, Congress, and the president. The powers of the states and their relationship to the federal government are considered next. A chapter on the freedoms guaranteed by the First Amendment is followed by one that considers the other major provisions of the Bill of Rights. Two chapters treat the Fourteenth Amendment—the most litigated portion of the Constitution. One deals with a number of privacy issues, the other with myriad manifestations of discrimination. This portion of the book concludes with a chapter on citizenship.

Without ignoring decisions of historical importance, this set of chapters gives emphasis to cases of current significance. The cases in each chapter are arranged in chronological order so that the reader can follow the evolution of judicial policy making and constitutional doctrine. A number of cases pertain to more than a single topic; in such instances, the case is cross-referenced to the chapter and the heading under which it is summarized.

9

Judicial Power and Authority

*T*his chapter contains the important decisions that have enabled the Supreme Court to establish itself as an authoritative policy- making body. The most important of these decisions articulated the doctrine of judicial review, which holds that the courts in general and the Supreme Court in particular determine the constitutionality of the actions of the other branches of government.

The Constitution's Framers also divided the powers delegated to the federal government among the legislative, executive, and judicial branches. The Framers further intended Congress and the president to be at odds with one another. When such conflicts cannot be resolved through the normal political process, the Supreme Court, relying on the principle of separation of powers, may be called upon to resolve them.

The Framers of the Constitution also provided for the supremacy of federal law when it conflicts with that of the states. Relying on its position as the authoritative interpreter of the fundamental law—the Constitution—the Court also resolves these matters, thereby determining the degree of centralization or decentralization that will prevail at any given point in time.

The last sections of this chapter specify the jurisdiction of the federal courts, their organization, and the relationship that governs the state and federal court systems.

JUDICIAL REVIEW

Marbury v. Madison(1803)

This decision was the Court's first elaboration of the principle of judicial review. William Marbury had been appointed justice of the peace for the

District of Columbia by President John Adams and confirmed by the Senate in 1801 shortly before the incoming administration of Thomas Jefferson took office. At the time, Adams's newly appointed chief justice, John Marshall, was also serving as secretary of state. As secretary of state, Marshall was to deliver to Marbury the commission that would authorize him to begin his job as justice of the peace. For unknown reasons, Marshall failed to give Marbury his commission before he—Marshall—turned over his duties as secretary of state to his successor, James Madison.

When Marbury requested Madison to give him his commission, Madison refused. Marbury thereupon applied directly to the Supreme Court, as provided by the Judiciary Act of 1789, for an order—a writ of mandamus—that would compel Madison to deliver the commission. Marshall, as chief justice, declared that Article III, section 2 of the Constitution allowed the Supreme Court to issue a writ of mandamus only under its appellate jurisdiction. Hence the provision of the Judiciary Act authorizing the writ of mandamus in an original proceeding, on which Marbury had relied, was invalid. The Constitution, said Marshall, is the fundamental law of the land; in cases of conflict between it and a statute, "an Act of the Legislature repugnant to the Constitution is void." Moreover, "It is emphati cally the province and duty of the judicial department to say what the law is."

Judicial review is exercised not only by the Supreme Court but also by the lower federal courts and the state courts. Actions of the executive branches of government as well as those of Congress and the state legislatures are subject to judicial review.

Martin v. Hunter's Lessee (1816)

The Virginia Supreme Court alleged that the appellate jurisdiction of the United States Supreme Court did not extend to decisions of state courts and that a provision of the Judiciary Act of 1789 so extending it was unconstitutional. Virginia argued that like all the other states it was bound by the supremacy clause (Article VI, section 2) and, furthermore, that its judges were as competent as those sitting on the U.S. Supreme Court to determine whether a conflict existed between state and federal law. Marshall and his colleagues disagreed, holding that the Constitution "was ordained and established, not by the States in their sovereign capacities, but emphatically, as the preamble of the Constitution declares, by 'the people of the United States'"; that the Constitution "is crowded with provisions which restrain or annul the sovereignty of the States in some of the highest branches of their prerogatives" (see Article I, section 10); that exercise of federal judicial power over the judgments of state courts is not more dangerous than over state legislatures and executives; and that, in order to avoid differences among state courts in the interpretation of the Constitution and federal laws and treaties, it is necessary that there should be a reviewing authority to control and harmonize the "jarring and discordant judgments" that might be handed down by "judges of equal learning and integrity" in the different states.

This decision thus provides the basis for a uniform interpretation of federal law. Without it, the supreme court of each state would determine for itself the meaning of the Constitution, acts of Congress, and U.S. treaties. What constitutes due process of law, interstate commerce, the meaning of the First Amendment, and so on, would vary from state to state.

United States v. Nixon (1974)

In a unanimous decision by the eight justices participating, the Court held that President Nixon must deliver to a U.S. district judge certain tapes of White House conversations subpoenaed for use in the criminal trials of former Nixon aides. Rejecting Nixon's contention, based on the doctrine of separation of powers, that he, as head of a coordinate branch of government, was not obliged to surrender the tapes, the Court reiterated the declaration in *Marbury v. Madison* (see above) that "it is emphatically the province and duty of the judicial department to say what the law is." The Court further stated that conversations between the president, his advisers, and others had no undifferentiated general immunity from judicial process; that the district judge, after listening to the tapes in private, could determine which portions, if any, contained sensitive military, diplomatic, or national security information, which need not be released. The importance of preserving confidentiality in White House conversations "must be balanced against the demonstrated need for evidence in a pending criminal trial."

FEDERAL SUPREMACY

United States v. Peters (1809)

A state legislature may not, by declaring that the decision of a lower federal court violated the Eleventh Amendment, impede the execution of the laws of the United States.

Ableman v. Booth (1859)

A Wisconsin court could not effect the release of a prisoner who was in the custody of a U.S. marshal for having violated federal law by helping a fugitive slave to escape. When a person is legally in federal custody for a federal offense and this fact has been communicated to state authorities, the state may not interfere.

Pennsylvania v. Nelson (1956)

This decision reversed a conviction under a state sedition law on the grounds that (1) Congress, in passing the Smith Act and other internal security legislation, intended to occupy the field of antisedition legislation to an extent that left no room for sup plementary state legislation; (2) the federal interest in internal security is dominant and pervasive; and (3) a state program might impermissibly conflict with federal objectives.

SEPARATION OF POWERS

Youngstown Sheet & Tube Co. v. Sawyer (1952)

The Court refused to uphold President Truman's seizure of steel mills in order to avert a strike that, he said, might hamper the Korean War effort by sharply reducing the supply of munitions. By a 6-to-3 vote and with seven separate opinions, the Court held that although Congress had considered granting the president power to seize strike-bound plants, it voted against doing so when it passed the Taft-Hartley Act. Nor could the Court find such authority in the clauses of Article II of the Constitution, which vest the president with executive power, make him commander in chief, and impose on him the duty to enforce federal law.

Train v. New York City (1975)

The president, as chief executive, has no power to countermand congressional authorization of funds for controlling and abating water pollution. Instead, the president must expend the full amounts authorized by Congress.

Nixon v. Administrator of General Services (1977)

See under *The Presidency*.

Immigration and Naturalization Service v. Chadha (1983)

Legislation authorizing one house or committee of Congress to "veto" or annul action of the executive branch or an administrative agency, which action was authorized by duly enacted legislation, violates the procedures of Article I, section 7 of the Constitution. This article requires that both houses of Congress pass a bill and present it to the president before it may take effect.

Bowsher v. Synar (1986)

The Court held unconstitutional a key provision of the Gramm-Rudman Deficit Reduction Act of 1985. The disallowed provision triggered automatic, across-the-board spending cuts aimed at eliminating the federal budget deficit by 1991. By vesting the comptroller general with the executive power of estimating the size of the deficit and mandating annually the spending reductions necessary to meet the deficit reduction target, Congress violated

the doctrine of separatio... al is
an agent of Congress wh... not
exercise executive powe... ty's
decision, observing tha... lent
officers in the entire fed...

JURISDICTION

Chisholm v. Georgia (1793)

Supreme Court jurisdiction over controversies "between a State and citizens of another State" included the power to hear and decide a case brought by Chisholm, a citizen of South Carolina, against the state of Georgia to obtain compensation for property taken during the Revolutionary War. This decision alarmed the states that had outstanding debts and led directly to the adoption of the Eleventh Amendment.

Martin v. Hunter's Lessee (1816)

See under *Judicial Review*.

Cohens v. Virginia (1821)

Though state courts may exercise final authority in cases that fall entirely within their jurisdiction, they are subject to the appellate jurisdiction of federal courts if their judgments involve the construction of federal laws or treaties or the Constitution. The Court also held that a federal court's review of a state court judgment against a defendant does not constitute a suit against a state (prohibited by the Eleventh Amendment) because the state itself initiated the lawsuit.

Ex parte McCardle (1869)

Congress may make exceptions to the Court's appellate jurisdiction even after hearings on a case have been concluded. McCardle had been tried for sedition by a military commission in Mississippi under authority provided by an act of Congress. He appealed to the Supreme Court. Some members of Congress feared that the Court would follow its precedent in *Ex parte Milligan* (see under *The President as Commander in Chief*) and void the act. Congress thereupon repealed the legislation giving the Supreme Court jurisdiction to hear McCardle's case on appeal. Said Chief Justice Chase: "Without jurisdiction the court cannot proceed at all in any cause. Jurisdiction is power to declare the law, and when it ceases to exist, the only function remaining to the court is that of announcing the fact and dismissing the cause."

Nashville, Chattanooga, and St. Louis R. Co. v. Wallace (1933)

The Court accepted jurisdiction to hear an appeal from a state court's "declaratory judgment," which was then a recent innovation. The Court said that the Constitution does not "crystallize into changeless form" the procedures that governed the access of litigants to the federal courts as they existed in 1789 and, "so long as the case retains the essentials of an adversary proceeding, involving a real, not a hypothetical controversy, which is finally determined by the judgment below," it is a "controversy" as this word is used in conferring jurisdiction on the federal courts in Article III.

Pennhurst State School & Hospital v. Halderman (1984)

Federal courts lack jurisdiction under the Eleventh Amendment to hear a suit against state and local officials because conditions in a state mental hospital violate state law.

DIVERSITY OF CITIZENSHIP

Swift v. Tyson (1842)

In adjudicating cases (as authorized by Article III, section 2) between residents of different states that contain no federal question, federal courts must apply relevant state statutes but need not follow state court decisions based on the common law. Where no state statute exists, federal courts are free to develop their own common law. Overruled by *Erie Railroad Co. v. Tompkins* (see below).

Erie Railroad Co. v. Tompkins (1938)

Tompkins, a resident of Pennsylvania, was injured while walking along the right-of-way of the Erie Railroad, a New York corporation. Under the common law of Pennsylvania, where the accident oc curred, Tompkins was a trespasser and not entitled to damages. The lower federal court, however, applied its own rule and held the railroad negligent and liable for damages. The Supreme Court overruled *Swift v. Tyson* (see above) for several reasons: the decision allowed plaintiffs to select the court where the law was most favorable to them; state and federal courts located in the same state might decide the same case differently; and in matters not governed by the Constitution or acts of Congress, "the law to be applied in any case is the law of the State. And whether the law of the State shall be declared by the legislature in a statute or by its highest court in a decision is not a matter of federal concern. There is no federal general common law."

JUDICIAL ORGANIZATION

Ex parte Bakelite Corporation (1929)

The Court differentiated the constitutional courts created under Article III—the federal district courts and the circuit courts of appeal—from the so-called legislative courts that have specialized jurisdiction limiting them to adjudicate claims of persons suing the United States for damages, to settle disputes over customs duties and patents, and to administer justice in U.S. territories created by Congress under Articles I and IV of the Constitution. In creating legislative courts, Congress is not bound by the limitations of Article III concerning the tenure and compensation of federal judges.

Glidden Co. v. Zdanok (1962)

After an act of Congress had provided that the Court of Claims and the Court of Customs and Patent Appeals should become constitutional courts under Article III, the Supreme Court ruled that judges of these specialized courts may not be assigned to sit on district or circuit courts, the regular constitutional courts, because they lack life tenure.

Northern Pipeline Construction Co. v. Marathon Pipe Line Co. (1982)

The federal bankruptcy courts may not constitutionally exercise all the power Congress provided them. Judges who exercise Article III jurisdiction, as bankruptcy judges did under the act of Congress, must also be provided the salary and tenure protections of Article III, which bankruptcy judges do not have.

COMITY AND THE ABSTENTION DOCTRINE

Railroad Commission v. Pullman Co. (1941)

The Court formulated the "abstention doctrine" to minimize conflict between state and federal courts. Applications of this doctrine have produced a system of "comity" by which the federal courts substantially avoid intruding themselves into ongoing state judicial proceedings. Comity accomplishes this by requiring litigants to exhaust their state's remedies, administrative as well as judicial, before gaining access to the federal courts. The policy gives the state courts the first opportunity to determine the constitutionality of their own laws. If the state court acts compatibly with the supremacy clause of Article VI, section 2 and gives force and effect to the federal law, there may be no need for federal court intervention.

Younger v. Harris (1971)

The defendant sought to avoid prosecution for violation of a state law that he contended was unconstitutional. The Court said that a federal court may enjoin a state criminal prosecution only where there is "great and immediate" danger "of irreparable loss" of federal rights. No such danger existed here.

Michigan v. Long (1983)

The Court used this case, an otherwise run-of-the-mill vehicular search-and-seizure suit, to overrule its traditional presumption regarding the "reviewability" of state court decisions. In cases where federal questions are bound up with issues of state law—which is true of most state criminal and civil rights litigation—the Supreme Court had declined review as long as the state court decision rested "on an adequate and independent state ground." In other words, if the state court would be able to adhere to its original decision notwithstanding a Supreme Court ruling on the federal aspects of the case, the Supreme Court would refuse to hear the matter. Now, if it is unclear whether the state court based its decision on state or on federal law, the Supreme Court will presume that it rests on federal law and, as such, consider the case reviewable. The effect of this holding, authored by Justice O'Connor, vastly broadens the Supreme Court's authority to review state court decisions. If it is adhered to and utilized regularly, the autonomy of the state courts will be undermined and seriously compromised.

Although the Supreme Court is ultimately responsible for interpreting the Constitution's other provisions, its use of judicial review, separation of powers, and national supremacy may be viewed as the foundation from which its policy-making capacity flows. The Court, however, does not have unbounded discretion with regard to these matters. It resolves disputes and makes policy only if a case falls within the jurisdiction of the federal courts and if its review comports with the rules it has formulated to review the decisions of state courts.

10

The Powers of Congress

*T*his chapter contains the major Supreme Court decisions that concern the structure, composition, and powers of Congress.

LEGISLATIVE MEMBERSHIP AND PREROGATIVES

Bond v. Floyd (1966)

The lower house of the Georgia legislature violated Julian Bond's First Amendment right to freedom of speech when it refused to accept him as a member because of his utterances in opposition to the Vietnam War.

Powell v. McCormack (1969)

The House of Representatives may not add to the constitutional qualifications of age, residence, and citizenship or exclude by a majority vote a duly elected member who possesses them. Adam Clayton Powell had been denied his seat because of charges that in previous sessions of Congress he had submitted false expense accounts and had misused committee funds. The residents of a congressional district are entitled to representation, the Court ruled, and this right can constitutionally be overridden only by a two-thirds vote of the House to expel.

Gravel v. United States (1972)

The speech or debate clause of Article I, section 6 allows the legislative aide of a member of Congress to share the member's immunity from being "questioned in any other place" than in the legislative chamber or committee. But when arrangements are made for private publication of government documents (here, the Pentagon Papers), the aide must tell a grand jury what he knows about how allegedly stolen documents came into the possession of a member of Congress.

Doe v. McMillan (1973)

The speech or debate clause absolutely immunizes the members and staff of a congressional committee who prepare and disseminate a derogatory report. However, a member of Congress may not with impunity repeat libelous statements from a report in circumstances that are "not an essential part of the legislative process."

Hutchinson v. Proxmire (1979)

The speech or debate clause does not apply to congressional newsletters or press releases. The "informing function" that the clause protects concerns the means that representatives and senators use to inform one another, not to communications to a member's constituents.

LEGISLATIVE APPORTIONMENT AND DISTRICTING

Colegrove v. Green (1946)

A suit to compel reapportionment of congressional districts presents a political question—one that courts are not competent to decide. Though the rural-dominated Illinois legislature had not changed the boundaries of the state's congressional districts since 1901, and though great population discrepancies existed, the Court declined to intervene because the justices deemed the Court ought not to become involved in partisan political disputes; it could not itself redistrict the state, and the Constitution in Article I, section 4 vests authority for dealing with such problems in Congress itself. Overruled by *Wesberry v. Sanders* (see below).

Baker v. Carr (1962)

The Court invalidated a Tennessee legislative apportionment that had remained unaltered for over sixty years despite losses of population in many counties and large increases in others. Rejecting the rule of *Colegrove v. Green* (see above), the Court held that the equitable apportionment of voters among legislative districts is a question that courts are competent to decide and, when the apportionment is inequitable, courts may provide relief.

Wesberry v. Sanders (1964)

The Court overruled *Colegrove v. Green* (see above) and invalidated the unequal apportionment of Georgia's congressional districts on the ground that since every voter is equal to every other voter, the districts from which members of Congress are chosen must be as nearly equal in population as practicable.

Reynolds v. Sims (1964)	The Court extended the principle of "one person, one vote" to apply to the apportionment of seats in both houses of a state's legislature.
Kirkpatrick v. Preisler (1969)	In dividing a state into congressional districts, the state legislature must make all districts equal in population or justify the variance.
Hadley v. Junior College District (1970)	Each district from which government officials are chosen must contain a population as nearly equal as practicable to every other district. This one-person, one-vote principle applies to all elected officials—local as well as state—who perform "public functions" and not only to those holding legislative office.
Mahan v. Howell (1973)	Greater variation in population (in this case, 16.4 percent) between the largest and smallest state legislative districts is more permissible than variation in congressional districts.
Salyer Land Co. v. Tulare Water District (1973)	The Court upheld weighted voting of elected officials in special-purpose governmental bodies that "disproportionately affect" a subset of the total population. Here a local water storage district chose its directors on the basis of one vote for every $100 worth of real estate an individual owned.

IMPLIED POWERS

M'Culloch v. Maryland (1819)	The Court's decision provides the classic exposition of the doctrine of implied powers, which allows for a loose, or broad, construction of the powers delegated to the federal government. The case arose from the refusal of the cashier of the Baltimore branch of the Bank of the United States to pay a tax levied by Maryland on notes issued by the bank. Chief Justice Marshall declared for the Court that the last clause of Article I, section 8 gives Congress the means to carry out its expressly granted powers, and that the bank was "necessary and proper" to taxing, borrowing, and conveying funds for the support of armies. "Let the end be legitimate, let it be within the scope of the Constitution, and all means which are appropriate, which are plainly adapted to that end, which are not prohibited, but consist with the letter and spirit of the Constitution, are constitutional."

Moreover, Maryland could not tax the bank because such a use of the state's taxing power threatens the supremacy of the federal government in matters committed to its jurisdiction. "The States have no power, by taxation or otherwise, to retard, impede, burden, or in any manner control, the operation of the constitutional laws enacted by Congress to carry into execution the powers vested in the general government."

LEGISLATIVE INVESTIGATIONS

Kilbourn v. Thompson (1881)	Congress has no authority to inquire into matters about which it has no power to legislate.

Watkins v. United States (1957)

The Court reversed the conviction of a labor leader who, when called before the House Committee on Un-American Activities, freely answered questions concerning his own involvement with the Communist party but refused to name other persons who long ago had severed their party connections. When Congress creates a committee it must spell out the committee's jurisdiction so that witnesses and reviewing authorities can determine whether questions asked are pertinent. "Investigations conducted solely for the personal aggrandizement of the investigators, or to 'punish' those investigated are indefensible," the Court stated. "The Bill of Rights is applicable to all investigations."

Barenblatt v. United States (1959)

By a 5-to-4 vote, the Court held that a college teacher's academic freedom under the First Amendment properly pertained to the classroom but did not protect him from the consequences of refusing to answer pertinent questions about his knowledge of Communist influence and his association with Communists on American college campuses when such questions were asked under the undoubted power of Congress to inquire into alleged Communist infiltration into the field of education.

WAR POWERS (See also THE PRESIDENT AS COMMANDER IN CHIEF)

Selective Draft Law Cases (1918)

The Court supported the compulsory features of the Selective Service Act of 1917, which required young men to register for military service. The power of Congress to raise and support armies is separate and distinct from its power to call the states' militia into federal service. The constitutional power to raise armies includes the power to compel military service. Such service is a citizen's obligation to his government and is sanctioned by numerous precedents. Subsequent cases emphasized and extended this decision.

Block v. Hirsh (1921)
The Court sustained state and federal emergency rent laws enacted at the close of World War I. The legislation, which fixed rents and temporarily extended leases, was held to be consistent with due process on the theory that the wartime emergency had clothed the relationship between landlord and tenant with a preponderant public interest and had made that relationship temporarily subject to the same sort of regulatory power that government may exert over the rates and services of public utilities.

Ashwander v. Tennessee Valley Authority (1936)
The case concerned a contract for the sale to a private company of surplus electric power generated at a government dam. The Court upheld the peacetime maintenance of the dam and the hydroelectric installations constructed in World War I, under both the power to improve navigation and the power to provide for the future supply of munitions. It upheld the acquisition by the Tennessee Valley Authority of transmission lines for the distribution and sale of its electric power on the principle that if the government owns property, Congress, acting in the public interest, may determine the manner and conditions of its disposition.

Woods v. Miller (1948)
The Court sustained the Housing and Rent Control Act of 1947. Congress, even after the cessation of hostilities, may remedy conditions resulting from wartime mobilization of men and matériel, under its war powers and the "necessary and proper" clause of Article I, section 8.

THE POWER TO TAX AND SPEND

Pollock v. Farmers' Loan and Trust Co. (1895)
The Court declared unconstitutional an act of Congress imposing an income tax without apportionment among the states (see Article I, section 9) on the ground that a tax on land is a direct tax and a tax on the income derived from land is indistinguishable from a tax on the land itself. In 1895 the Court applied the same principle to the income from stocks and bonds. Ratification of the Sixteenth Amendment canceled both decisions.

McCray v. United States (1904)

The Court refused to inquire into the motives of Congress when it imposed a tax of ten cents per pound on oleomargarine artificially colored to imitate butter and only one-fourth cent per pound on uncolored margarine. Opponents claimed that the tax was meant to achieve regulatory and not fiscal ends and that it destroyed property rights without due process. The majority, however, said that the act "on its face" is a revenue measure.

Bailey v. Drexel Furniture Co. (1922)

The Court declared unconstitutional an act of Congress imposing a 10 percent tax on the net profits of any business that knowingly employed children under certain specified ages. The Court ruled that the word "knowingly" applied to criminal law, not to taxation, and that the tax was not a bona fide revenue measure but rather a police regulation. As such, it ran afoul of the Tenth Amendment by invading matters reserved to the states. Effectively overruled by *Mulford v. Smith* (see below).

United States v. Butler (1936)

The Court invalidated the first Agricultural Adjustment Act because coercive federal regulation of farm production and prices infringes on powers reserved to the states. The Court ruled that processing taxes are an integral part of an unconstitutional scheme of regulation and that the revenue derived from the taxes, which was used to subsidize farmers, could not be sustained under the general welfare provision of the first clause of Article I, section 8.

Social Security Cases. [Helvering v. Davis (1937) and Steward Machine Co. v. Davis (1937)]

The Court upheld the constitutionality of federal taxes on employers and employees in certain businesses to finance the joint federal-state system of unemployment compensation, special assistance to wage earners and others, and the federal old-age insurance program of the Social Security Act of 1935. The five- member majority decreed that Congress had properly regarded social insecurity as a national problem that could be attacked nationally; that the cooperative federal-state features of the social security system do not violate the Tenth Amendment or coerce the states into abandoning their governmental responsibilities. The proceeds from the taxes were to be spent to promote the general welfare.

Mulford v. Smith (1939)

The Court effectively overruled *United States v. Butler* and *Bailey v. Drexel Furniture Co.* (see above) and sustained the second Agricultural Adjustment Act. Congress might constitutionally regulate the flow of an agricultural commodity to the interstate market in order to foster, protect, and conserve commerce or "to prevent the flow of commerce from working harm to the people of the nation."

THE SCOPE OF THE COMMERCE POWER

Gibbons v. Ogden (1824)

In a classic opinion, Chief Justice Marshall defined Congress's power to regulate foreign and interstate commerce to embrace every species of commercial intercourse, including navigation between the United States and foreign nations, as well as every commercial transaction that does not wholly occur within the boundaries of a single state. The power does not stop at a state's boundary but extends to activity within a state that affects other states.

After the Civil War until the mid-1930s, the Court tended to adhere to definitions of interstate commerce markedly more restrictive than Marshall's. Not until the eve of World War II did the Court allow Congress to use the commerce power as a regulatory tool, as the decisions summarized under *Federal Regulation of Business* and *Federal Regulation of Labor* illustrate.

Wickard v. Filburn (1942)

An Ohio farmer who planted twenty-three acres of wheat for his own consumption, exceeding the quota set by the secretary of agriculture, exerted "a substantial economic effect on interstate commerce." He thereby made himself liable for penalties imposed by the Agricultural Adjustment Act of 1938. This decision well illustrates the economic reach of the constitutional commerce power.

Katzenbach v. McClung (1964)

The 1964 Civil Rights Act outlaws race discrimination in places of public accommodation that affect interstate commerce. Without dissent, the justices agreed that the statute applied to a family-owned restaurant not patronized by interstate travelers, merely because $70,000 worth of food consumed on the premises had previously moved in interstate commerce.

FEDERAL REGULATION OF BUSINESS

United States v. E. C. Knight Co. (1895)

The Sherman Antitrust Act did not apply to a combination of four Pennsylvania companies that had a virtual monopoly on sugar refining, because (1) manufacture precedes commerce and is not a part of it, (2) interstate commerce does not commence until goods begin their final movement from one state to another, and (3) the manufacturing monopoly in this case had no "direct" effect on interstate commerce. Effectively overruled by *National Labor Relations Board v. Jones and Laughlin Steel Corp.* (see below).

Northern Securities Co. v. United States (1904)

This case resulted in the first successful prosecution under the Sherman Act. The Court ordered the dissolution of a holding company that controlled the Great Northern and the Northern Pacific Railroads on the grounds that it lessened competition and restrained interstate commerce.

Swift & Co. v. United States (1905)

The Court affirmed the power of Congress to punish conspiracies in restraint of trade among buyers and sellers in the Chicago stockyards. The Court stated that in the habitual course of commerce, livestock originating in one state paused at the Chicago stockyards only long enough to find a buyer before being shipped to another state. Therefore, they had remained within the "current," or stream, of commerce.

Standard Oil Co. v. United States (1911)

The Court ordered the dissolution of the Standard Oil Company of New Jersey, not because of its huge size, but because it had used its economic power through pricing and other manipulative policies to restrain trade unreasonably.

Schechter Poultry Co. v. United States (1935)

A unanimous Court declared the National Industrial Recovery Act unconstitutional because it delegated legislative powers to the president and attempted, under the guise of the commerce power in Article I, section 8, to regulate aspects of a business—the slaughtering and sale of locally grown poultry—that fall within the jurisdiction of the states.

National Labor Relations Board v. Jones and Laughlin Steel Corp. (1937)

The Court abandoned the doctrine outlined in *United States v. E. C. Knight Co.* (see above) that manufacturing is not commerce. It upheld provisions of the Wagner Act forbidding unfair labor practices that affect interstate commerce. (The case concerned clerical employees who had been dismissed for union-organizing activities.) Although the defendant steel company was not directly engaged in transportation, the successful conduct of its far-flung business depended on the free flow of interstate commerce to furnish it with raw materials and to market its products in other states and in foreign countries; hence the prohibition of unfair labor practices properly protects and promotes interstate commerce.

FEDERAL REGULATION OF LABOR

Adair v. United States (1905)

The Court invalidated a federal statute outlawing in interstate commerce those contracts under which a worker agreed not to join a union (yellow-dog contract). The Court declared the law a violation of the due process clause of the Fifth Amendment because it abridged freedom of contract. Employer and employee "have equality of right, and any legislation that disturbs that equality is an arbitrary interference with the liberty of contract." Subsequently overruled.

Loewe v. Lawlor **(1908)**

The famous Danbury Hatters' case. A nationwide boycott by a labor union of hats manufactured by nonunion shops was ruled to restrain trade under the Sherman Antitrust Act. The Clayton Act of 1914 nullified this decision by exempting labor unions from the operation of the Sherman Act.

Wilson v. New **(1917)**

The Court upheld the constitutionality of the Adamson Act, which provided for an eight-hour day and appropriate wage standards for interstate railroad workers.

Hammer v. Dagenhart **(1918)**

By a 5-to-4 vote the Court declared unconstitutional a federal law prohibiting the interstate shipment of goods made in factories employing children. The law, said the majority, is not a bona fide regulation of commerce but an effort to control the conditions of employment and manufacture within the states. Goods produced by child labor are not deleterious in themselves and are indistinguishable from those made by adults. Overruled by *United States v. Darby* (see below).

Adkins v. Children's Hospital **(1923)**

The Court declared the minimum wage law of the District of Columbia unconstitutional. The law violates the rights of the parties freely to contract with one another. It establishes standards of enforcement that are "too vague and fatally uncertain," requires employers to pay a minimum wage whether or not the employee was worth that much, and is "so clearly the product of a naked, arbitrary exercise of power that it cannot be allowed to stand under the Constitution," the Court stated. Overruled fourteen years later by *West Coast Hotel Co. v. Parrish*. See under *State Labor Regulation*.

United States v. Darby **(1941)**

The Court sustained provisions of the Fair Labor Standards Act of 1938 that fixed maximum hours and minimum wages for most employees and barred from interstate commerce the shipment of goods manufactured in violation of its provisions. According to the Court, "While manufacturing is not of itself interstate commerce, the shipment of manufactured goods interstate is such commerce." Overruled and repudiated the reasoning of *Hammer v. Dagenhart* (see above).

THE STATUS AND REGULATION OF INDIANS

The Cherokee Cases [Cherokee Nation v. Georgia (1831) and Worcester v. Georgia (1832)]

The Court held that Indian tribes are neither foreign nor subject nations, but rather "domestic dependent nations" whose "relation to the United States resembles that of a ward to his guardian." The powers vested in an Indian tribe are the inherent powers of a limited sovereign that have never been extinguished. The federal government, but not the states, may deal with the Indians through its treaty-making power and the Indian commerce clause in Article I, section 9 of the Constitution.

United States v. Winans (1905)

Treaties between Indian tribes and the United States are not grants of rights to Indians. They are grants of rights from them. The tribe reserves to itself all rights not granted to the United States.

Williams v. Lee (1959)

The Court allowed the states a measure of authority in Indian affairs "in cases where essential tribal relations were not involved and where the rights of Indians would not be jeopardized"; for example, suits by Indians in state courts against non-Indians and state court jurisdiction over non-Indians who commit crimes against each other on a reservation.

White Mountain Apache Tribe v. Bracker (1980)

Where a state asserts authority over the conduct of non-Indians on a reservation, federal courts must make a particularized inquiry into the nature of the state, federal, and tribal interests at stake. This inquiry must determine whether, in the specific context, the exercise of state authority would violate federal law. The supremacy clause (Article VI) makes state law inapplicable when it conflicts with federal law or where federal regulation comprehensively occupies the field. Here Arizona's efforts to tax a logging company hired by a tribe to fell trees on its reservation conflicted with pervasive federal policies and regulations.

This chapter has specified the major decisions that pertain to the powers that Congress may constitutionally exercise. It also includes those that concern membership in Congress and the constitutional bases on which officials exercising legislative power must be selected.

11

The Presidency

Unlike the first article of the Constitution which concerns the composition of Congress, along with its powers and procedures, Article II, which deals with the presidency, contains a less detailed listing of what presidents may do. Most importantly, as the initial words of Article II say, presidents exercise "The executive power." This includes, but is not necessarily limited to, removing officials from office, conducting foreign affairs, entering into treaties and executive agreements, commanding the armed forces, and pardoning persons convicted of federal crime.

PRESIDENTIAL PREROGATIVES

Kendall v. United States (1838)

An officer, in this case the postmaster general, may not refuse to perform a duty imposed on him by an act of Congress, even though the president has ordered him not to perform it. Congress may assign to any executive officer any duty it may think proper that is not repugnant to rights protected by the Constitution. The majority opinion stated: "To contend that the obligation imposed on the President to see the laws faithfully executed implies a power to forbid their execution is a novel construction of the Constitution and is entirely inadmissible."

Mississippi v. Johnson (1867)

In a decision arising from the attempt of Mississippi to obtain an injunction to prevent the president from enforcing one of the Reconstruction acts on the ground that the law was unconstitutional, the Court held that the president's responsibility to enforce the laws is not a mere ministerial duty, in which nothing is left to his discretion, but is rather an executive and political duty. Therefore, an injunction may not be issued against the president to restrain him from enforcing a law.

In re Neagle (1890)

The attorney general assigned a U.S. deputy marshal (Neagle) as a bodyguard for Justice Field, whose life had been threatened. While Field was on circuit duty in California, the marshal killed an assailant who was threatening the justice. A California court indicted Neagle for murder. Under federal law he could be released by writ of habeas corpus from state authority only if he had been acting under a law of the United States. No act of Congress authorized the attorney general to assign a bodyguard to a justice. However, the Court held that the writ could issue on the basis of an executive order, because the president's duty to execute the law includes the implied power to protect government officials while on duty.

In re Debs (1895)

The Court upheld a federal injunction against striking Pullman Company employees who had halted rail transportation in the Chicago area and sustained President Cleveland in sending in troops when the injunction was disobeyed, though the Illinois governor protested the president's action. The Court asserted "that the strong arm of the national Government may be put forth to brush away all obstructions to the freedom of interstate commerce or the transportation of the mails."

Nixon v. Administrator of General Services (1977)

The Court rejected former President Nixon's claim to his presidential papers after Congress had provided that the General Services Administration should determine which papers were public and which should be returned to him as private. Nixon based his claim on separation of powers, presidential privilege, and his right to privacy. By a 7-to-2 vote, the Court held that the test for violation of separation of powers is whether one branch unduly disrupts another. It held that nothing contained in the act of Congress was unduly disruptive; that the act's screening process was "a very limited intrusion" for which adequate justification had been shown; and that Nixon's privacy was only slightly infringed, whereas the justification for the screening process was substantial.

Butz v. Economou (1978)

Although federal officials may not be sued for mistakes of judgment, they are personally liable for acting in a way that they know, or should know, violates a person's constitutional rights. The Court majority, however, excluded government attorneys from this qualified immunity. They, along with judges and other officials whose duties involve adjudication, are absolutely immune from suit for injuries resulting from their official actions.

The Court also ruled in a 1987 decision (*United States v. Stanley*) that military personnel may not sue the government or their superior officers for service-connected injuries, even though the injury concerns a gross and deliberate violation of a constitutional right. Citing a 1950 precedent, *Feres v. United States*, the five-justice majority said that absolute immunity is necessary to preserve military discipline and to prevent the federal courts from second-guessing military actions. In Stanley's case, the action involved administering LSD to unknowing soldiers as part of a secret experiment to see how they reacted to mind-altering hallucinogenic drugs.

Nixon v. Fitzgerald (1982)

The Court ruled that no president may be sued for damages for any official action he takes while in office.

THE REMOVAL POWER

Myers v. United States (1926)

The Court declared unconstitutional the Tenure of Office Act of 1876, which required the consent of the Senate for the removal of certain classes of postmasters. The Court held that the president may remove at pleasure any officer appointed by himself and the Senate under the executive powers vested in him by Article II. He is responsible for the execution of the laws, and he can execute the laws only through subordinates. He must have the power, therefore, to remove subordinates in whom he lacks confidence. Limited by *Humphrey's Executor v. United States* (see below).

Humphrey's Executor (Rathbun) v. United States (1935)

The Court limited the scope of *Myers v. United States* (see above) by denying the president power to remove quasilegislative and quasijudicial officers when Congress made other provisions for their removal. As a result, Congress acted constitutionally when, in creating the Federal Trade Commission, it specified that the president could remove a commissioner only for inefficiency, neglect of duty, or malfeasance in office. The duties of such officers are not purely executive and, consequently, they are not exclusively subject to presidential control. The majority opinion stated: "It is quite evident that one who holds his office only during the pleasure of another cannot be depended upon to maintain an attitude of independence against the latter's will."

Wiener v. United States (1958)

Even though Congress had not limited the president's power to remove members of the War Claims Commission, their functions are intrinsically judicial; hence the president may not remove them at will, but only for cause.

FOREIGN AFFAIRS

Foster v.
Neilson (1829)

The Court refused to review the merits of a dispute over land grants in territory east of the Mississippi River claimed by both Spain and the United States. The Spanish grant had been made in 1804. The United States later claimed the territory as part of the Louisiana Purchase and occupied it by force. The Court said that decisions of the president and Congress bind the judiciary in all matters affecting the rights of the United States in foreign affairs.

United States v.
Curtiss-Wright
Corp.(1936)

The Court upheld an arms embargo imposed by the president under authority given to him by joint resolution of Congress. According to the Court, "The president is the sole organ of the Federal government in the field of international relations—a power which does not require as a basis for its exercise an act of Congress, but which . . . like every other governmental power, must be exercised in subordination to the applicable provisions of the Constitution."

TREATIES AND EXECUTIVE AGREEMENTS

Head Money
Cases (1884)

The Court sustained an act of Congress that levied a tax on steamship companies amounting to a small sum per capita on every immigrant brought to the United States, even though some of these immigrants came from countries with which the United States had treaties guaranteeing their free admission. The Court held treaties and statutes to be of equal weight. Hence if a self- executory treaty (one that requires no statute for its enforcement) and an act of Congress conflict, the one more recently enacted prevails.

Missouri v.
Holland (1920)

The Court sustained a federal statute to enforce a treaty with Great Britain for the mutual protection of migratory birds flying between the United States and British possessions in North America. Migratory birds involve "a national interest of very nearly the first magnitude," the Court said, which only "national action in concert with that of another power" can protect. The birds are "only transitorily within the State" and have "no permanent habitat therein." Lower federal courts had invalidated a federal statute for the protection of migratory birds, which antedated the treaty, as a usurpation of the reserved powers of the states and an encroachment on their property rights.

United States v. Belmont *(1937)*

The Court upheld an executive agreement that President Franklin Roosevelt, without consulting the Senate, entered into when he established diplomatic relations with the Soviet Union in 1933. The Court ruled that recognition, the establishment of diplomatic relations, and the agreement assigning American assets of a former Russian corporation to the U.S.S.R. were all part of a single transaction within the power of the president to make and that he spoke as the "sole organ" of the government in the transaction. To the objection that the Soviet Union had acquired the assets by confiscation, in violation of New York law, the Court replied that by recognizing the Soviet Union the United States accepted all actions of the U.S.S.R. pertaining to its own citizens and that the executive agreement overrode conflicting state laws.

Reid v. Covert *(1957)*

An international agreement whereby American servicemen and their dependents who committed crimes on British soil were to be tried by American courts did not authorize the United States to use a military tribunal to try the wife of a soldier. She was not a member of "the land and naval forces," for whose regulation Congress may provide in Article I, section 8; rather, she was a civilian, under the Fifth and Sixth amendments, answerable to indictment only by a grand jury, and entitled to trial by jury. The Court ruled that "no agreement with a foreign nation can confer power on the Congress, or on any other branch of Government, which is free from the restraints of the Constitution."

THE PRESIDENT AS COMMANDER IN CHIEF

The Prize Cases *(1863)*

In deciding four cases concerning vessels captured while running a naval blockade that President Lincoln had imposed by proclamation on southern ports shortly after the Civil War began, the Court sustained the president's action, saying: "If a war be made by invasion of a foreign nation, the President is not only authorized but bound to resist force, by force. He . . . is bound to accept the challenge without waiting for any special legislative authority. And whether the hostile party be a foreign invader, or States organized in rebellion, it is none the less a war." Congress later enacted legislation ratifying the president's proclamation.

Ex parte Milligan (1866)

A civilian was convicted of fomenting insurrection and other treasonable activities by a military commission sitting at Indianapolis in 1864. He applied to a U.S. circuit court for a writ of habeas corpus. On appeal, Milligan was held to have been unlawfully convicted because President Lincoln had acted unconstitutionally in establishing military commissions in places where the civil courts were open and their processes unobstructed. Such action was permissible only in an actual theater of war where civil courts were not functioning.

Ex parte Quirin (1942)

Seven Germans who landed secretly on American shores during World War II for the purpose of committing sabotage were tried and sentenced by a military commission after their capture. The Court determined that the military commission had been properly constituted; that though the saboteurs were captured and tried in a district where courts were open (see *Ex parte Milligan*, above), they were nonetheless subject to military jurisdiction as "unlawful belligerents" under the laws of war. A Sixth Amendment right to jury trial did not apply since that guarantee pertains to civil and not to military courts.

Korematsu v. United States (1944)

Korematsu, a native-born citizen of Japanese ancestry, was one of 112,000 Japanese Americans, 70,000 of whom were U.S. citizens, who were summarily removed from their homes in designated West Coast areas and shipped to inland "relocation centers" in accordance with a 1942 executive order. The Court sustained Korematsu's removal because "the properly constituted military authorities" feared an invasion of the West Coast and decided that military necessity required the removal of all persons of Japanese origin from the area. The decision—still valid law—seemed to constitutionalize guilt by association. Justice Jackson pointed out in dissent: Korematsu "has been convicted . . . of being present in the state whereof he is a citizen, near the place where he was born, and where all his life he has lived . . . merely because [he] is the son of parents as to whom he had no choice, and belongs to a race from which there is no way to resign."

Forty years later, a federal district court vacated Korematsu's conviction because government attorneys had failed to reveal to the Supreme Court key evidence that contradicted the military's claim that the Japanese Americans posed a threat to national security.

Toth v. Quarles (1955)

The Court held unconstitutional an act of Congress requiring discharged servicemen to be tried by courts martial for crimes allegedly committed during active duty. The Court said that such a requirement would deprive veterans of the safeguards enjoyed by other civilians under Article III of the Constitution and would encroach on the jurisdiction of the regular courts.

THE POWER TO PARDON

Ex parte Garland (1867)

The Court declared unconstitutional, as a bill of attainder, an act of Congress that required lawyers practicing in federal courts to take an oath that they had never voluntarily borne arms against the United States or given aid to its enemies. Garland, though pardoned by President Johnson for serving in both houses of the Confederate Congress, could not take the oath. The Court held that under Article II, section 2, a full pardon "releases the punishment and blots out of existence the guilt so that in the eye of the law the offender is as innocent as if he had never committed the offense." The pardoning power extends to every offense against the law and may be exercised before legal proceedings commence, while they are pending, or after conviction and judgment.

Ex parte Grossman (1925)

The Court ruled that the president may pardon and remit a sentence imposed by a federal court for criminal contempt on the ground that numerous precedents for such pardons exist in England and the United States. They are especially useful, the Court stated, when sentences are imposed "without the restraining influence of a jury and without many of the guarantees which the Bill of Rights offers to protect the individual against unjust conviction."

Schick v. Reed (1974)

The president may commute a death sentence to life imprisonment and constitutionally attach thereto a condition of no parole.

This Chapter has focused on the important Supreme Court decisions that have affected the powers of the president. Although fewer cases appear in this chapter than in Chapter 10, which concerns Congress, one should not conclude that the executive branch encounters the Supreme Court less often than the national legislature. The opposite is actually the case. The vast majority of executive action is performed by administrative agencies and bureaucrats. Although their activity may implement congressional action, litigation tends to focus on what the agency itself has or has not done rather than on the underlying congressional statute.

12

The States

This chapter focuses on the states and their place in the national scheme of things. Just as the federal government has obligations to the states, so also do the individual states have duties to one another.

In creating a federal system of government, the Framers did not sharply separate the powers of the states from those delegated to the national government. Although many provisions in the Constitution bar the states from engaging in certain activities (see Article I, section 10, for examples), the states and Washington have overlapping authority in certain significant areas. This overlap has produced conflict, which in turn has caused the Court to render a substantial number of landmark decisions as the cases in the sections on state labor regulation and state regulation of interstate commerce demonstrate.

THE PLACE OF THE STATES IN THE NATION

Texas v. White (1869)

No state may constitutionally secede from the Union. After the Civil War the governor of Texas sued to recover possession of United States bonds, acquired in 1850, that the secessionist legislature had sold to purchase supplies for the Confederate army. The Court held that Texas could recover the bonds. When entering the Union, a state becomes party to an indissoluble relationship. Hence, ordinances of secession and all other acts intended to give effect to it are absolutely void. "The Constitution, in all its provisions, looks to an indestructible Union composed of indestructible States."

Stearns v. Minnesota (1900)

Congressional restrictions on Minnesota's taxation of public lands at the time it became a state could be enforced because the provision did not impair Minnesota's sovereignty or legal equality with the other states.

Coyle v. Smith (1911)

The Court upheld the right of Oklahoma to change the location of its capital, contrary to a condition imposed by Congress when Oklahoma became a state. The location of its capital is a matter of state policy for state authorities to determine. And when admitted to the Union, Oklahoma became legally equal to every other state.

FEDERAL GUARANTEES TO THE STATES

Luther v. Borden (1849)

This case arose in the aftermath of the Dorr Rebellion in 1841, during which two rival governments existed in Rhode Island. One was regularly elected by residents who met a long-standing property qualification for voting. The other (Dorr's) was based on an informal election under universal manhood suffrage. At the request of the older government, President Tyler ordered militia into the state, and Dorr's government collapsed. In construing Article IV, section 4 of the Constitution, the Court declined to say which government was "republican" in form or whether or not on this occasion the president had been justified in suppressing "domestic violence." The Court held instead that these are "political questions" to be resolved as they arise by Congress and/or the president.

Pacific States Telephone and Telegraph Co. v. Oregon (1912)

Reiterated the holding of *Luther v. Borden* (see above) that the clause in Article IV, section 4 guaranteeing a republican form of government is nonjusticiable; i.e., its enforcement depends upon action by the legislative and/or executive branches rather than on decisions of the federal courts. The company had requested the Court to invalidate a state tax enacted by popular initiative, contending that the initiative had made the government unrepresentative and therefore unrepublican.

THE FULL FAITH AND CREDIT CLAUSE

International Shoe Co. v. Washington (1945)

The Court formulated the "minimum contacts" test that prevents a state court from taking action against a nonresident defendant unless said defendant has had sufficient contacts with the state wherein the court is located so that the lawsuit "does not offend traditional notions of fair play and substantial justice," wrote Chief Justice Stone. Although International Shoe, a Delaware corporation, had no office in Washington and entered into no contracts for the purchase or sale of shoes in the state, it did employ a dozen residents of Washington to solicit orders in the state for its shoes. The salesmen sent the orders to the company's out-of-state office for acceptance or rejection. If accepted, the shoes were shipped directly to the customer from the company's out-of-state office. These contacts were sufficient to subject International Shoe to the tax power of Washington.

As a result of this and subsequent decisions, the full faith and credit clause has the following scope and meaning: state court judgments in civil, not criminal, cases have as much force and effect in courts of other states as they do in the rendering state—provided that the court making the decision had jurisdiction, in a minimum contacts sense, over the litigants and the original state court's decision was a final judgment.

Most Supreme Court litigation involving full faith and credit traditionally involved divorce actions where the husband and wife resided in different states. Today most cases concern commercial transactions, insurance, and workers' compensation. Divorce litigation has faded because the states regularly recognize out-of-state decrees. This is not true, however, of child custody and support, and alimony decrees. In this area, courts commonly refuse to automatically enforce action taken by courts in another state. The Court explained why in *Thompson v. Thompson* (1988):

> . . . custody orders held a peculiar status under the full faith and credit doctrine which requires each State to give effect to the judicial procedures of other States. . . . The anomaly traces to the fact that custody orders characteristically are subject to modification as required by the best interests of the child. As a consequence, some courts doubted whether custody orders were sufficiently "final" to trigger full faith and credit requirements. . . . Because courts entering custody orders generally retain the power to modify them, courts in other States were no less entitled to change the terms of custody according to their own views of the child's best interest.

PRIVILEGES AND IMMUNITIES

Baldwin v. Montana Fish and Game Commission (1978)

The Court reaffirmed a long line of precedents that limit the scope of "privileges and immunities of citizens in the several States" to those "fundamental rights" that bear "upon the vitality of the Nation as a single entity," according to the Court. Most assuredly, said the majority, "elk hunting by nonresidents in Montana is not one of them." Hence, states may charge nonresidents more for hunting and fishing license fees than they charge their residents.

Hicklin v. Orbeck (1978)

In order to reduce unemployment, Alaska required all gas and oil companies doing business within the state to hire only residents. The Court unanimously agreed that Alaska had failed to show that nonresidents caused Alaska's high unemployment rate.

Supreme Court of New Hampshire v. Piper (1985)

No "substantial" reason, ruled the Court, supported New Hampshire's requirement that an attorney live in the state in order to practice law in its courts.

INTERSTATE EXTRADITION

Kentucky v. Dennison (1861)

Although Article IV speaks mandatorily, the Court refused Kentucky's demand that the governor of Ohio deliver up a fugitive from Kentucky justice. Said Chief Justice Taney:

> Given "the relations which the United States and the several States bear to each other . . . the words 'it shall be the duty' were not . . . compulsory, but [only] declaratory of . . . moral duty." Hence, governors can use their discretion whether or not to honor extradition requests. Over ruled by *Puerto Rico v. Branstad* (see below).

Puerto Rico v. Branstad (1987)

The Court unanimously overruled *Kentucky v. Dennison* (see above) as "the product of another time." The Court thereby gave force and effect to the plain words of the Constitution. Furthermore, because extradition is a duty directly imposed on the states by the Constitution itself, the reference in the Tenth Amendment to the reserved powers of the states has no applicability.

CONTRACT CLAUSE

Fletcher v. Peck (1810)

For the first time the Court declared a state law unconstitutional. In 1796 the Georgia legislature attempted to repeal a huge grant of land corruptly made by the previous session of the legislature, the members of which had been bribed by speculators. The Court voided the rescission. It considered the land grant to be a contract and, although legislative acts might be repealed, rights vested under prior acts could not be impaired.

Dartmouth College v. Woodward (1819)

The New Hampshire legislature could not constitutionally alter the charter of Dartmouth College without its consent. Corporate charters fall within the confines of the contract clause. The decision substantially immunized business and commercial interests from unilateral governmental action abrogating the terms and conditions of contracts and agreements freely made.

Charles River Bridge v. Warren Bridge (1837)

The Court sustained Massachusetts's charter to a competing company to build a bridge not far from an existing private toll bridge. The Court substantially modified the Dartmouth College decision by holding that the public interest and common law rules of construction require that the provisions of public grants, charters, and franchises given to private corporations be strictly construed. The only powers bestowed are those specifically provided. They afford their holders no implied protection against legislative action that may lessen the charter's value.

Home Building and Loan Association v. Blaisdell (1934)

The Court upheld a state statute extending a mortgagor's right to redeem foreclosed property for two years beyond the time stipulated in the mortgage. The contract clause is not breached because the state may subject existing contracts to regulation in the public interest. Just as a state may come to the relief of its citizens in cases of natural disaster, so also may it act in an economic crisis to safeguard the economic structure on which the good of all depends.

STATE LABOR REGULATION

Holden v. Hardy (1898)

The Court upheld a Utah law limiting underground miners to an eight-hour day. The majority saw no reason to doubt the legislature's judgment that working long hours at such an occupation is detrimental to health. In response to the argument that the law violates a worker's right to contract his labor, the Court replied that "the state still retains an interest in his welfare, however reckless he may be."

Lochner v. New York (1905)

By a 5-to-4 vote, the Court invalidated a state law limiting bakers to a ten-hour day and a sixty-hour week. Baking is not an unhealthy occupation; therefore the state may not regulate it. The statute unreasonably interfered with freedom of contract, which the due process clause of the Fourteenth Amendment protects. Modified by *Muller v. Oregon* (see below) and subsequently overruled.

Muller v. Oregon (1908)

The Court modified *Lochner v. New York* (see above) by upholding an Oregon statute forbidding the employment of women in certain industries for more than ten hours per day, apparently on the ground that women require legislative protection because they are less able than men to endure sustained labor.

West Coast Hotel Co. v. Parrish (1937)

The Court reversed earlier decisions, such as *Adkins v. Children's Hospital* (see under *Federal Regulation of Labor*) by upholding, 5 to 4, minimum wage legislation for women. The majority rejected arguments that such legislation violates the due process clause of the Fourteenth Amendment, stating that "the liberty safeguarded is liberty in a social organization which requires the protection of law against the evils which menace the health, safety, morals and welfare of the people."

This decision signaled the end of the Court's use of the due process clause as a means of preventing the state legislatures from passing regulations incompatible with the principles of laissez-faire economics. Hereafter, states were free to regulate prices and working conditions, establish minimum wages and maximum hours of work, and ban child labor without fear that they would run afoul of federal judges. This decision thus did for state economic regulation what *National Labor Relations Board v. Jones and Laughlin Steel Corp*, decided two weeks later, did for federal economic regulation. (See under *Federal Regulation of Business*.)

STATE REGULATION OF INTERSTATE COMMERCE

Cooley v. Board of Wardens (1851)

The Court formulated the doctrine that Congress's commerce power is not exclusive and that where a uniform national rule is not required, the states may apply their own regulations to foreign and interstate commerce. (Here the issue concerned the piloting of ships in the port of Philadelphia.) Such regulations remain valid until such time as Congress supersedes them.

Shreveport Rate Case (Houston E. & W. Texas R. Co. v. United States [1914])

The Texas Railway Commission fixed unreasonably low rates between distributing centers in Texas and points near the state's borders, thereby putting at a disadvantage shippers in other states, whose rates were fixed by the Interstate Commerce Commission. The Court ordered the Texas commission to end the discrimination.

South Carolina Highway Dept. v. Barnwell Bros. (1938)

In the absence of congressional regulation, a state may impose limits on the weight and width of motor vehicles traveling from state to state over its highways. The states and their local subdivisions have built the highways and are responsible for their safe use, and the regulation in question does not discriminate against interstate commerce.

Southern Pacific Co. v. Arizona (1945)

The Court invalidated a law that prohibited railroad train lengths of more than fourteen passenger cars or seventy freight cars. The burden on interstate commerce outweighs the law's problematical advantages as a safety measure inasmuch as longer trains operate safely in states other than Arizona.

Huron Portland Cement Co. v. Detroit (1960)

A municipality may apply its smoke abatement ordinance to ships operating in interstate commerce, though the ships' boilers and equipment have been federally inspected and licensed. The regulation is valid because it looks to the health of the local community and imposes no discriminatory burden on interstate commerce. Federal legislation, by contrast, concerns maritime safety and does not preempt the field to the exclusion of local police regulations.

Kassel v. Consolidated Freightways (1981)

Although reluctant to invalidate state regulations concerning highway safety, the Court ruled that Iowa unconstitutionally burdened interstate commerce by banning double tractor-trailer trucks from its roads. The six justices in the majority could not agree on an opinion, but four of them did observe that Iowa's "real concern was not safety but an effort to limit the use of its highways by deflecting some through traffic" to neighboring states.

THE TENTH AMENDMENT AS A LIMITATION ON FEDERAL REGULATION

Maryland v. Wirtz (1968)	Federal wage and hour legislation applies to public school and hospital employees. In exercising its powers, stated the Court, the federal government "may override countervailing state interests," regardless of whether they are " 'governmental' or 'proprietary' in character."
National League of Cities v. Usery (1976)	The Court declared unconstitutional congressional extension of minimum wage laws to the employees of states and their subdivisions. The Tenth Amendment prevents Congress from using the commerce power to interfere with any state activity the performance of which may be characterized as an "attribute of sovereignty," according to the majority opinion. Besides increasing costs, such laws burden the states and interfere with their right to manage their own affairs. Overruled by *Garcia v. San Antonio Metropolitan Transit Authority* (see below).
United Transportation Union v. Long Island Rail Road Co. (1982)	The Tenth Amendment does not prohibit application of the Railway Labor Act to a state-owned railroad engaged in interstate commerce. The operation of a railroad is not an activity in which states typically engage. Hence, the Court ruled, the federal law does not regulate the "states as states"; neither does it address a matter that is indisputably an attribute of state sovereignty.
Garcia v. San Antonio Metropolitan Transit Authority (1985)	Justice Blackmun, who provided the key vote in *National League of Cities v. Usery* (see above), switched to the other side and wrote the Court's opinion overruling Usery. Application of federal wage and hour provisions to employees of a city-owned transportation system "contravened no affirmative limit on Congress's power under the commerce clause," stated the majority opinion. One may assume that the Court has come full circle and now reoccupies the position it took in *Maryland v. Wirtz* (see above).

THE FOURTEENTH AMENDMENT AS A LIMITATION ON STATE ECONOMIC REGULATION

Munn v. Illinois (1877)   The Court sustained state regulation of grain elevators, declaring that the "public has a direct and positive interest" in private businesses "clothed with a public interest." Property put to such uses is subject to public control. As a consequence, the rates and services of public utilities could be regulated, notwithstanding judicial support for the principles of laissez-faire economics.

Euclid v. Ambler Realty Co. (1926)   The Court upheld a comprehensive zoning ordinance restricting and regulating the location of businesses, industries, and various types of dwellings. Despite the losses sustained by many property owners in the zoned areas, the Court held zoning to be a reasonable exercise of the state's police power—the power to regulate on behalf of public health, safety, welfare, morals, and/or convenience—and as such does not violate due process.

Tyson v. Banton (1927)   The Court invalidated a New York State law limiting the resale price of theater tickets, on the ground that ticket brokerage is not a business affected with a public interest. Hence, its regulation is not a legitimate exercise of the state's police power. Effectively overruled by *Gold v. DiCarlo* (1965).

Nebbia v. New York (1934)   The Court upheld governmental fixing of minimum and maximum prices of milk. The majority thus expanded the scope of regulation under the police power beyond the limited category of public utilities and virtually abandoned the concept that only "businesses affected with a public interest" could be regulated.

West Coast Hotel Co. v. Parrish (1937)   See under *State Labor Regulation*

This chapter has outlined various aspects of the federal system of government that the Constitution established. Although the resolution of conflicts between the United States and the individual states is currently and historically the most salient, the Supreme Court has also addressed such relatively mundane matters as the extradition of fugitives from one state to another and the scope of the full faith and credit clause.

13

First Amendment Freedoms

This and the succeeding chapter focus on the Bill of Rights. The cases that concern these guarantees are in two groups. The decisions in this chapter pertain to the First Amendment, which guarantees individuals the freedom to communicate with one another. Those in the succeeding chapter largely, but not completely, concern the rights of persons accused of crime.

The reader should note that the vast majority of cases in both chapters are of relatively recent vintage. Almost none of them antedates the 1920s. Prior to that time the federal government enacted few laws that concerned the liberties protected from abridgment by the Bill of Rights. The state and local governments, by contrast, did enact such laws. But persons so deprived had no redress in the federal courts. The reason why is detailed in the two cases that are summarized immediately below.

THE APPLICABILITY OF THE BILL OF RIGHTS TO THE STATES

Barron v. Baltimore (1833)

Barron claimed that Baltimore's refusal to compensate him for a wharf rendered unusable by a city street-grading project violated the Fifth Amendment. The Court held the Bill of Rights applicable only to actions of the federal government, not to those of the states and their subdivisions. Chief Justice Marshall reasoned that the Constitution grants powers to government and that therefore the Bill of Rights could limit only the powers that had been granted. Furthermore, the Bill of Rights was added to the Constitution because the public feared oppression by the federal government, not by the states. Effectively overruled by the Supreme Court's interpretation of the scope of the due process clause of the Fourteenth Amendment.

Gitlow v. New York (1925)

The Court upheld a state law that made it a crime to advocate the duty, necessity, or propriety of overthrowing government by force or violence: ". . . the legislative body itself has previously determined the danger of substantive evil arising from utterances of a specified character," stated the majority of the Court. In the middle of the opinion, almost as an aside, appears the statement: "For present purposes we may and do assume that freedom of speech and of the press—which are protected by the First Amendment from abridgment by Congress—are among the fundamental personal rights and 'liberties' protected by the due process clause of the Fourteenth Amendment from impairment by the states." The Court offered no logical or historical justification for abandoning the rule of *Barron v. Baltimore* (see above). From this incidental beginning, almost all the provisions of the first eight amendments have by degrees been incorporated into the due process clause of the Fourteenth Amendment. Accordingly, the language that prohibits the states from depriving "any person of life, liberty, or property, without due process of law" reads as though it also includes the language of the first eight amendments.

FREEDOM OF SPEECH

Schenck v. United States (1919)

The Court sustained the conviction of a Socialist party official who had violated the Espionage Act of 1917 by urging young men who had been called for military service to assert their constitutional rights by opposing the draft. Justice Holmes, who wrote the opinion, suggested limitations for government encroachment on the First Amendment's guarantee of free speech: "The question in every case is whether the words used are used in such circumstances and are of such a nature as to create a clear and present danger that they will bring about the substantive evils that Congress has a right to prevent. . . . When a nation is at war many things that might be said in time of peace are such a hindrance to its effort that their utterance will not be endured."

Whitney v. California (1927)

The Court affirmed the conviction, under the California Criminal Syndicalism Act of 1919, of Anita Whitney, an organizer and executive committee member of the Communist Labor party, which advocated sabotage, violence, and terror as means of effecting economic and political change.

Though Whitney testified that she did not believe in violence, the Court held that united and joint action by such a group involves greater danger to the public peace and security than the isolated utterances of individuals. Overruled by *Brandenburg v. Ohio* (see below).

Chaplinsky v. New Hampshire (1942) — Freedom of speech does not include use of lewd, obscene, profane or libelous expressions, or words such as "damned racketeer" or "God-damned Fascist." By their very utterance, such phrases inflict injury or tend to incite an immediate breach of the peace. "Fighting words" are "no essential part of any exposition of ideas" and are of such slight social value that the First Amendment does not protect them.

American Communications Association v. Douds (1950) — The Court upheld a provision of the Taft-Hartley Labor Management Relations Act of 1947 that denied the facilities of the National Labor Relations Board to unions whose officials refused to take non- Communist loyalty oaths. The majority ruled that Congress did not violate the First Amendment when it used its commerce power to prevent political strikes fomented by agitators who had infiltrated labor unions.

Dennis v. United States (1951) — The Court affirmed the conviction of eleven leaders of the American Communist party under the Smith Act's prohibition of willfully advocating and teaching the overthrow of the government of the United States by force and violence. Citing Circuit Judge Learned Hand's interpretation of Justice Holmes's clear and present danger rule: "Whether the gravity of the 'evil,' discounted by its improbability, justifies such invasion of free speech as is necessary to avoid the danger," the Court decided that the danger here justified restraining freedom of speech. The government cannot wait "until the putsch is about to be executed, the plans have been laid and the signal is awaited."

Adler v. Board of Education (1952) — The Court sustained a New York law that prohibited from holding any position in the public schools any person who advocated the overthrow of the government by force or violence. The statute authorized the Board of Regents to establish a list of organizations that advocated such action. Membership in an organization on that list constituted evidence to disqualify a person from public school employment. "School authorities have the right and duty to screen the officials, teachers, and employees as to their fitness in order to maintain the integrity of the schools," the Court stated. Overruled by *Keyishian v. Board of Regents* (see below).

Burstyn v. Wilson (1952) — A state may not deny a license to show a motion picture on the ground that it is "sacrilegious." Motion pictures are "a significant medium for the communication of ideas" and thus are protected by the First Amendment.

Yates v. United States (1957)   Mere advocacy of a revolutionary philosophy, such as that of Karl Marx, is not enough to convict a Communist party member under the Smith Act. In order to convict, the prosecution must prove the accused guilty of advocating forcible overthrow of the government and of inciting others to take specific action toward this end.

Barenblatt v. United States (1959)   See under *Legislative Investigations*.

Scales v. United States (1961)   The First Amendment does not protect the speech or the association of an active member of a group, ostensibly a political party, if the group advocates forcible overthrow of the government. Neither does the due process clause of the Fifth Amendment protect an individual who was an active and knowing member of an organization that was conspiring to overthrow the government by force, even though the threat was not immediate.

Communist Party v. Subversive Activities Control Board (1961)   The case arose out of an effort to compel the American Communist party to register under the terms of the Internal Security Act of 1950. The Court accepted the congressional conclusion that Communism is a movement dominated by the Soviet Union, a nation that is dangerous to the United States and its institutions. Hence, a requirement that the Communist party register with the Justice Department, list its members, and file financial statements does not violate freedom of expression or association. The Court, however, did not consider what, if anything, could be done to the Party if it refused to register.

Keyishian v. Board of Regents (1967)   The Court overruled *Adler v. Board of Education* (see above) and voided New York's loyalty oath for teachers. A state may protect its educational system against subversion, but not by vague and uncertain methods that do not inform teachers of the sanctions involved in a complicated scheme of control that "casts a pall of orthodoxy over the classroom," according to the Court. The Court further stated that Communist party membership may not disqualify a public school teacher unless specific intent to further the unlawful aims of the Party is shown.

Brandenburg v. Ohio (1969)   The Court overruled *Whitney v. California* (see above) and held that the First Amendment does not permit a state to forbid advocacy of force or lawlessness as a means to effect change "except where such advocacy is directed to inciting or producing imminent lawless action and is likely to incite or produce such action."

SYMBOLIC SPEECH

Stromberg v. California (1931)

The Court invalidated California's "anti-red flag" law in a case involving the display of a red flag at a children's camp. The peaceful display of a red flag as a "sign, symbol or emblem of opposition to organized government" is protected by the First Amendment. In Chief Justice Hughes's words: "The maintenance of the opportunity for free political discussion to the end that government may be responsive to the will of the people and that changes may be obtained by lawful means is a fundamental principle of our constitutional system."

Thornhill v. Alabama (1940)

The Court declared unconstitutional a state law against "loitering or picketing," which, as interpreted by the state courts, prohibited a single picket from carrying a placard on the street in front of a factory. The Court, through Justice Murphy, held that peaceful picketing communicates the nature and causes of a labor dispute and thereby informs the public about a matter of public concern.

United States v. O'Brien (1968)

The Court affirmed the conviction of a young man who, in order to influence others to adopt his antiwar beliefs, violated federal law by burning his draft card. An incidental limitation on First Amendment freedoms is justified if it falls within the constitutional powers of government, it furthers an important or substantial governmental interest, the governmental interest is unrelated to the suppression of expression, and the incidental restriction on communication is no greater than necessary to further that interest.

Tinker v. Des Moines School District (1969)

The Court voided a regulation banning the wearing of black arm bands to protest the Vietnam War. The Court majority found no relation between the regulation and student discipline. Students do not shed their freedom of expression "at the schoolhouse gate." Nor may they be "confined to the expression of those sentiments that are officially approved."

Cohen v. California (1971)

A person may not be convicted of disturbing the peace because he wears a jacket in a courtroom emblazoned with the phrase "Fuck the Draft." A state may not "forbid particular words without also running a substantial risk of suppressing ideas. . . ."

Texas v. Johnson (1989)

The Court affirmed the decision of the Texas Supreme Court that declared unconstitutional the state's flag burning law. With two of President Reagan's three nominees (Scalia and Kennedy) among the five-member majority, the Court ruled that Texas's law criminalized a content-based restriction on expressive conduct. It did not attempt to protect the physical integrity of the flag in all circumstances, but only against impairments that gave offense to onlookers who disapproved of flag burning as a form of political protest. Said Justice Brennan for the majority: "If there is a bedrock principle underlying the First Amendment, it is that the Government may not prohibit the expression of an idea simply because society finds the idea itself offensive or disagreeable."

One year later, the same five justices declared unconstitutional a federal flag-desecration law that Congress enacted in reaction to the Court's decision in the Texas case (*United States v. Eichman, 1990*).

FREEDOM OF ASSEMBLY AND ASSOCIATION

DeJonge v. Oregon (1937)

The Court made the First Amendment right to freedom of assembly binding on the states. The Court reversed a state court's conviction of a speaker at a meeting called by the Communist party to protest police efforts to break up a strike. The right of peaceable assembly is essential in order "to maintain the opportunity for free political discussion to the end that Government may be responsive to the will of the people, and that changes, if desired, may be obtained by peaceful means."

Hague v. C.I.O. (1939)

The Court voided a Jersey City ordinance that required a permit from the director of public safety to conduct a public meeting. The Court held that people have a right to publicly assemble to communicate their views and to discuss public questions in an orderly and peaceful manner.

NAACP v. Alabama (1958)

The Court rejected Alabama's demand for the membership lists of the NAACP. The Court unanimously ruled that "inviolability of privacy in group association may in many circumstances be indispensable to preservation of freedom of association, particularly where a group espouses dissident beliefs."

Shelton v. Tucker (1960)

The Court ruled unconstitutional an Arkansas statute requiring public school teachers to list all organizations to which they belonged or contributed. The law, said the five-member majority, was overly broad. It "goes far beyond" what a "legitimate inquiry into the fitness and competency" of teachers warrants.

Edwards v. South Carolina (1963)

The state infringed petitioners' constitutionally protected rights of free speech, free assembly, and freedom to solicit redress of grievances when it broke up an orderly demonstration by two hundred students on the grounds of the state capitol and arrested their leaders.

Cox v. Louisiana (1965)
The Court reversed a state court's conviction of a civil rights demonstrator for blocking a street. Since Louisiana had permitted labor unions and other organizations to block streets, it could not use a double standard for civil rights. The Court, however, warned that it would not sanction "demonstrations, however peaceful or commendable their motives, which conflict with properly drawn statutes and ordinances designed to promote law and order, protect the community against disorder, regulate traffic, safeguard legitimate interests in private and public property, or protect the administration of justice and other essential governmental functions."

Communist Party of Indiana v. Whitcomb (1974)
The Court unanimously voided a state law barring from the ballot the candidates of any party whose officers had not taken an oath that the party did not advocate the overthrow of government by force or violence. The majority held that the law violated a First Amendment right to advance common ideas and cast an effective ballot. Four justices (the Nixon appointees) filed a concurring opinion arguing that inasmuch as the major parties' candidates had been listed on the ballot without their taking a loyalty oath, discrimination against the Communist party violated the equal protection clause of the Fourteenth Amendment.

Rutan v. Illinois Republican Party (1990)
Partisan political considerations may be not be used to hire, promote, or transfer those government employees for whom party affiliation is an inappropriate job requirement. Earlier decisions had restricted the jobs for which politics was an appropriate consideration. In a dissenting opinion signed by three others, Justice Scalia observed that federal judges are overwhelmingly appointed on the basis of party affiliation. "Thus, the . . . principle that the Court . . . announces will be enforced by a corps of judges (the members of this Court included) who . . . owe their office to its violation."

FREEDOM OF THE PRESS

Near v. Minnesota (1931)
The Court declared unconstitutional a state law directed at a weekly newspaper in Minneapolis that scurrilously attacked the integrity of law enforcement officials. The law prohibited the publication of scandalous, malicious, defamatory or obscene matter and provided for enforcement by

injunction against persons doing so. The Court held that the law prevented future publication and thus placed publishers under "an effective censorship," whereas freedom of the press means "principally, although not exclusively, immunity from previous restraint or censorship."

Grosjean v. American Press Co. (1936)

The Court invalidated a Louisiana statute that imposed a heavy and discriminatory tax on the advertising revenue of newspapers in the larger cities of the state, most of which had opposed the Huey Long machine. The Court held that this action was "a deliberate and calculated device in the guise of a tax to limit the circulation of information to which the public is entitled."

New York Times v. Sullivan (1964)

Libel laws cannot be used to "cast a pall of fear and timidity" over the press. Alabama courts had awarded heavy damages to Birmingham law enforcement officials who had sued the *New York Times* for inaccuracies in a paid political advertisement. The justices unanimously reversed this decision, holding that "debate on public issues should be uninhibited, robust and wide open"; that injury to an official's reputation "affords no warrant for suppressing speech that would otherwise be free"; and that a public official may not recover damages for libel unless he proves "actual malice," that is, that the statement was made "with knowledge that it was false or with reckless disregard of whether it was false or not."

Branzburg v. Hayes (1972)

The majority rejected arguments that preserving the confidentiality of news sources is essential to the operation of a free press and held, 5 to 4, that a reporter must testify, and reveal the contents of his notebooks, to a grand jury. "We cannot seriously entertain the notion that the First Amendment protects a newsman's agreement to conceal the criminal conduct of his source, or evidence thereof, on the theory that it is better to write about crime than to do something about it." Ergo: freedom of the press is not to be equated with immunity for the press.

Miami Herald Publishing Co. v. Tornillo (1974)

The Court declared unconstitutional a Florida statute that gave a political candidate the right to reply to newspaper criticism of his character or official record. State-mandated publication intrudes on the right of editors to decide what their publications should contain.

Time, Inc. v. Firestone (1976)

The Court sustained a libel judgment against *Time* magazine for publishing a sixty-seven-word report alleging that a socialite's husband was granted a divorce "on grounds of extreme cruelty and adultery" when, in fact, the decree specified no basis. Although the trial judge had observed that the proceedings "produced enough testimony of extramarital adventures on both sides to make Dr. Freud's hair curl," the Supreme Court ruled that Mrs. Firestone was a "private person," not a "public figure"; hence, the actual malice test of *New York Times v. Sullivan* (see above) does not apply. Instead, state courts may impose a standard of liability less protective of the media than where the plaintiff is a public official or a public figure.

FREEDOM OF THE PRESS VERSUS THE RIGHT TO A FAIR TRIAL

Nebraska Press Association v. Stuart (1976)

The justices unanimously struck down a state court order restraining the media from publishing pretrial confessions made by a person accused of a ghastly mass murder. Chief Justice Burger declared that although circumstances may sometimes warrant the prohibition of certain communications, barriers to prior restraint remain high. In a concurring opinion, Justices Brennan, Stewart, and Marshall wrote that the Constitution bars prior restraint as a means of ensuring a fair trial of an accused person.

Zurcher v. The Stanford Daily (1978)

The Court sustained a search warrant of the offices of a student newspaper issued because the newspaper possessed photographs revealing the identity of demonstrators who had assaulted police officers. The Court held that the critical element in a reasonable search "is not that the property owner is suspected of a crime, but that there is reason . . . to believe that the 'things' to be searched for . . . are located on the property to which entrance is sought."

Richmond Newspapers, Inc., v. Virginia (1980)

The order of a trial judge closing a murder trial to the press and the public at the accused's request violated their First Amendment right to attend criminal trials. Absent an overriding interest, such trials must be open.

Globe Newspaper Co. v. Superior Court (1982)

The Court declared unconstitutional a state law requiring the exclusion of press and public during the testimony of victims at criminal trials for sex offenses against minors. Though the protection of minors from further trauma or embarrassment is a compelling governmental interest, the First Amendment requires that the public's exclusion from criminal trials be established on a case-by-case, rather than a mandatory, basis.

OBSCENITY

Roth v. United States (1957)

The Court affirmed a conviction for mailing obscene materials. The majority held obscenity to be beyond the pale of constitutional protection and defined it as follows: "Whether to the average person, applying contemporary community standards, the dominant theme of the material taken as a whole appeals to prurient interest."

Jacobellis v. Ohio (1964)

The justices held a French film, *The Lovers*, not to be obscene because the contemporary community standards in the Roth definition of obscenity (see above) constitute a single national standard. "It is, after all, a national Constitution we are expounding." Overruled by *Miller v. California* (see below).

Memoirs v. Massachusetts (1966)

The Court reversed a ruling that the book *Fanny Hill* was obscene because it was prurient and offensive, even though it had "some minimal literary value." To be obscene, a publication must: (1) have an overall appeal to prurient interest, (2) be patently offensive, and (3) be "utterly without redeeming social importance."

Miller v. California (1973)

By a 5-to-4 vote, the majority redefined obscenity: "A work may be subject to state legislation when that work, taken as a whole, appeals to the prurient interest in sex, portrays in a patently offensive way sexual conduct specifically defined in the applicable state law, and, taken as a whole, does not have serious literary, artistic, political, or scientific value." Nor did a jury need to apply national community standards. Overruling Jacobellis (see above), it could now use local ones.

Jenkins v. Georgia (1974)

To be obscene, material must be hard-core pornography. Hence, a theater manager could not be convicted for showing a film (in this case, *Carnal Knowledge*) not X-rated, that received critical acclaim, and whose female lead was nominated for an Academy Award.

Osborne v. Ohio (1990)

Though persons have a constitutional right to view obscenity in private, this right does not extend to the possession and viewing of child pornography.

COMMERCIAL SPEECH

Bigelow v. Virginia (1975)

Paid commercial advertisements are not without First Amendment protection. A state may not constitutionally sanction a newspaper editor for publishing an out-of-state abortion clinic ad.

Virginia State Pharmacy Board v. Virginia Citizens Consumer Council (1976)

Individual consumers and society in general have a strong interest in the free flow of commercial information. Maintenance of professional standards does not justify a state's banning advertisements containing the price of prescription drugs.

Bates v. State Bar of Arizona (1977)

The Court invalidated a state disciplinary rule prohibiting lawyers from advertising. Such a restriction "serves to inhibit the free flow of commercial information and keep the public in ignorance," according to the Court. Routine legal services lend themselves to advertising and the legal profession is not demeaned thereby. But false, deceptive, or misleading legal advertising can be regulated.

Bolger v. Youngs Drug Products Corp. (1983)

The justices unanimously declared unconstitutional a federal statute that prohibited the mailing of unsolicited advertisements for contraceptives. In the opinion of the Court, Justice Marshall said, "The level of discourse reaching a mailbox simply cannot be limited to that which would be suitable for a sandbox."

FREE EXERCISE OF RELIGION

Pierce v. Society of Sisters (1925)

The Court invalidated an Oregon law that required parents to send their children to public schools until they had completed the eighth grade, thus preventing their attendance at accredited parochial and other private schools. The law unreasonably interfered with the liberty of parents to direct the upbringing and education of their children and deprived the parochial schools of their property and business without due process of law.

Cantwell v. Connecticut (1940)	The First Amendment's guarantee of religious freedom, including an absolute freedom of belief and a qualified freedom of action, applies to the states. In reversing the convictions of three Jehovah's Witnesses, the Court declared that a government may not license religious solicitors or proselytizers because no official may constitutionally determine what is or what is not "religious."
Flag Salute Cases [Minersville School District v. Gobitis (1940) and West Virginia State Board of Education v. Barnette (1943)]	These cases concerned the power of the state to exclude children from the public schools because they refused, on religious grounds, to salute the American flag during school exercises. In the first case, the Court upheld the flag salute as a means of inculcating loyalty, holding that the requirement does not interfere with religious freedom. The second case, three years later, overruled the earlier decision. Any official effort to prescribe orthodoxy in politics or religion or to force persons to profess adherence to such orthodoxy violates the First Amendment.
Wisconsin v. Yoder (1972)	The justices unanimously voided the conviction of Amish parents who, on religious grounds, refused to send their children to high school.
Wooley v. Maynard (1977)	The Court declared unconstitutional a New Hampshire law that required most automobile license plates to display the state motto "Live Free or Die." Jehovah's Witnesses attacked the law as repugnant to their moral, religious, and political beliefs. The Court ruled that an individual may not be required to participate in the dissemination of an ideological message by displaying it on his or her private property.
Thomas v. Review Board of the Indiana Employment Security Division (1981)	To deny unemployment compensation benefits to a Jehovah's Witness who voluntarily quit his job because a transfer would have required him to produce armaments, contrary to his religious beliefs, violates his free exercise of religion.
Oregon Department of Human Resources v. Smith (1990)	Individuals may be punished for using illegal drugs as part of a religious ceremony. Members of an American Indian church need not be exempted from a law that prohibits the use of peyote. For the first time, the Court ruled that a state need not show a compelling governmental interest in order to justify an across-the-board criminal prohibition of conduct, even if the prohibition burdens a religious ritual. This standard could allow government to ban Moslem circumcision, the slaughter of animals to make meat kosher, and the use of wine at Mass.

ESTABLISHMENT OF RELIGION

Everson v. Board of Education (1947)

Busing children to parochial schools so that parents can "get their children, regardless of their religion, safely and expeditiously to and from accredited schools" does not breach the wall of separation between church and state.

McCollum v. Board of Education (1948)

School authorities of Champaign, Illinois, infringed the establishment of religion clause when they allowed representatives of Catholic, Jewish, and Protestant faiths to give religious instruction on school property during school hours, even though the school authorities did not pay for the religious instruction. School officials, however, enforced the attendance of those children whose parents enrolled them in the program. Tax-supported schools, said the Court, may not disseminate religious doctrines, and the compulsory-education law may not promote sectarian causes.

Zorach v. Clauson (1952)

The Court upheld New York City's released-time religious education program that allowed students, at their parents' written request, to receive religious instruction during school hours on premises other than public school property. The Court construed the establishment clause less rigorously than in McCollum v. Board of Education (see above), holding that it does not mandate absolute separation of church and state because, said the majority, "we are a religious people whose institutions presuppose a Supreme Being."

Engel v. Vitale (1962)

The Court invalidated a twenty-two-word prayer composed by the State Board of Regents, New York's ultimate educational authority. The Court said of the prayer—which was to be recited at the start of each school day—"that it is no part of the business of government to compose official prayers for any group . . . to recite as part of a religious program carried on by government."

School District of Abington Township v. Schempp (1963)

The Court held that recitation of the Lord's Prayer or Bible reading during school exercises violates the First Amendment no less than reciting a composed school prayer. The Constitution requires a "wholesome neutrality" between church and state "that neither advances nor inhibits religion." This, however, does not prevent nonsectarian study of the Bible or religion in the public schools.

Walz v. Tax Commission of the City of New York (1970)

The Court upheld tax exemptions for properties used exclusively for religious purposes. These exemptions do not establish, support, or sponsor religion; they rather treat religious organizations the same as any other charitable, nonprofit entity. Moreover, restricting the fiscal relation between church and state tends to complement and reinforce the desired separation between them.

Lemon v. Kurtzman (1971)

Salary supplements to parochial school teachers and reimbursement of costs to teach secular subjects in private schools are unconstitutional. For such parochial programs to pass constitutional muster, three criteria must be met: (1) they must serve "a secular legislative purpose"; (2) they must have a "principal or primary effect . . ., that neither advances nor inhibits religion"; and (3) they "must not foster 'an excessive government entanglement with religion.' "

Chief Justice Burger, speaking for the Court, found numerous reasons why the programs could not be sustained: the religious purpose of the church-related elementary and secondary schools; the enhanced opportunities for religious indoctrination of children of impressionable age; the necessity for state surveillance of teachers to ensure observance of restrictions on course content; the necessity for state supervision, as well, of parochial school expenditures to determine which were secular and which were not; "the potential divisiveness" of "political division along religious lines," which would be "a threat to the normal political process"; and the "self- perpetuating and self- expanding propensities" of these innovative programs, given parochial schools' desperate need for money.

Tilton v. Richardson (1971)

The Court upheld federal aid to church-related and other private colleges to construct academic buildings. College students are "less impressionable and less susceptible to religious indoctrination" than younger students; furthermore, a one-time, single-purpose construction grant causes few entanglements between church and state. The Court, however, did invalidate a provision that would have allowed religious use of the buildings after twenty years.

Mueller v. Allen (1983)

By a 5-to-4 vote, the Court upheld tax deductions for public and private school tuition, fees, books, and transportation. No impermissible promotion of religion occurs because deductions may be taken by all parents regardless of whether their children attend public, parochial, or nonsectarian private schools.

Lynch v. Donnelly (1984)

Inclusion of a nativity scene in a city Christmas display has a secular legislative purpose that does not impermissibly advance religion or excessively entangle the city with religion; namely, to celebrate a public holiday and the origins of that holiday.

Wallace v. Jaffree (1985)

A moment of legislatively mandated silence in public schools "for meditation or voluntary prayer" runs afoul of the establishment clause. The record clearly indicated that the law's sole purpose is to return voluntary prayer to the public schools.

Grand Rapids School District v. Ball (1985)

By a 5-to-4 vote, the Court voided a shared-time program in which classes in parochial schools were financed with tax dollars and taught by public school teachers. The program promoted religion in three ways: "The state-paid instructors, influenced by the pervasively sectarian nature of the religious schools in which they work, may subtly or overtly indoctrinate the students in particular religious tenets at public expense. The symbolic union of church and state inherent in the provision of secular, state-provided instruction in the religious school buildings threatens to convey a message of state support for religion to students and to the general public. Finally, the programs in effect subsidize the religious functions of the parochial schools by taking over a substantial portion of their responsibility for teaching secular subjects."

Edwards v. Aguillard (1987)

Louisiana law requiring public schools that teach evolution to teach "creation science" as well advances religion and thereby violates the establishment clause. The law's primary purpose, said the Court, "was to restructure the science curriculum to conform with a particular religious viewpoint."

*T*his chapter has concentrated on the freedoms provided by the First Amendment, with emphasis on controversies of current import.

14

The Bill of Rights

*T*he cases in this chapter proceed through the remainder of the Bill of Rights, commencing with the Second Amendment. No Third Amendment cases appear because no Supreme Court decisions have been based on it. The little litigated Ninth Amendment is considered in the first section of chapter 15, The Right to Privacy. The Tenth Amendment is the subject of the final section in chapter 12 which deals with the states.

Consequently, this chapter primarily concerns the rights of persons accused of crime, as these rights are enumerated in the Fourth through the Eighth amendments. Because the Fifth Amendment bars government from the civil act of taking persons' property without just compensation and has also been construed to provide for the substantive civil right to travel, sections dealing with each of these rights are included in this chapter.

RIGHT TO KEEP AND BEAR ARMS

United States v. Miller (1939)

Because a sawed-off shotgun is not the type of weapon a "well-regulated" militia uses, the Second Amendment does not apply to such guns, and Miller's conviction for violating federal law was affirmed by the Court.

In decisions dating from the nineteenth century, the Supreme Court has consistently ruled that the Second Amendment does not bind the states. Hence, state and local governments are constitutionally free to enact gun control laws if they so desire.

UNREASONABLE SEARCHES AND SEIZURES

Mapp v. Ohio (1961)

The exclusionary rule, which precludes the admission of evidence that the police unconstitutionally obtain, applies to state criminal prosecutions. In this case, allegedly obscene material, seized without a search warrant, that could not have been admitted in a federal prosecution, also had to be excluded from a state prosecution.

Terry v. Ohio (1968)

The Court upheld a "stop and frisk" law. When experienced police officers observe unusual conduct that leads them to believe that a crime is about to be committed, they may "frisk" or gently pat down the outer clothing of the suspicious person. If weapons or other contraband is found, it is admissible as evidence.

United States v. Matlock (1974)

The Court ruled admissible evidence seized in a warrantless search of a room occupied by a suspected bank robber and the woman with whom he lived. When the suspect was arrested in front of the house, he was not asked to consent to a search; his companion, however, admitted police officers to his room. The majority held that permission for a warrantless search may be obtained from "a third party who possessed common authority or other sufficient relationship to the premises."

Zurcher v. The Stanford Daily (1978)

See under *Freedom of the Press versus the Right to a Fair Trial.*

Mincey v. Arizona (1978)

The Court reversed a state supreme court's decision that had approved a murder-scene exception to the Fourth Amendment's search warrant requirement and the admissibility of the accused's subsequent confession. No emergency existed threatening the destruction or loss of evidence. A warrant could have been obtained quickly and easily. Mincey's statements while hospitalized in a barely conscious condition, isolated from his attorney and family, could not be considered voluntary.

United States v. Ross (1982)

The justices overruled their 1981 decision limiting the scope of the automobile's exception to the requirement for a search war rant. If police have probable cause to search a car, the search may extend to every part of the vehicle, including all packages and containers that may conceal the object of the search.

Illinois v. Gates (1983)

The Court overruled two Warren Court decisions for determining whether an informant's tip establishes probable cause for issuance of a search warrant. Six justices held that a "totality of the circumstances" approach is all that the Fourth Amendment requires.

United States v. Leon (1984)	The justices established a "good faith" exception to the exclusionary rule. Evidence secured under a defective search warrant (in this case, one issued without probable cause) may be used to prosecute the accused, provided the searchers did not know the warrant was defective.
Michigan v. Sitz (1990)	The Court upheld the constitutionality of sobriety checkpoints. Drivers passing a certain point are stopped and, while the driver remains in the car, briefly examined for signs of intoxication. The Court said that though the checkpoints are a "seizure," they nevertheless are "reasonable."

WIRETAPPING

Olmstead v. United States (1928)	Federal agents did not violate the prohibition against unreasonable searches and seizures when, without actually entering a person's premises, they obtained evidence by tapping his telephone. (Six years later the Federal Communications Act prohibited anyone not authorized by the sender from wiretapping or publishing the substance of any intercepted communication.) Overruled by *Katz v. United States* (see below).
Katz v. United States (1967)	The Court overruled *Olmstead v. United States* (see above) and brought electronic surveillance within the purview of the Fourth Amendment. In Katz a listening device was hidden in the top of a glass-enclosed public telephone booth often used by a suspected bookmaker. The police listened in only when the suspect used the booth. The Court held that a conversation is a "thing" that may be seized. Hence, the police invaded the suspect's privacy. All participating justices except Black agreed with Stewart's statement that "the Fourth Amendment protects people, not places. What a person knowingly exposes to the public, even in his own house or office, is not a subject of Fourth Amendment protection. . . . But what he seeks to preserve as private, even in an area accessible to the public, may be constitutionally protected."
United States v. United States District Court (1972)	The justices declared unconstitutional a long-standing government practice of tapping, without prior judicial approval, the telephones of individuals who have no significant connection with a foreign government but who are suspected of domestic subversion. The Court held: "Fourth Amendment freedoms cannot properly be guaranteed if domestic surveillance may be

conducted solely within the discretion of the executive branch. . . . Nor must the fear of unauthorized official eavesdropping deter vigorous citizen dissent and discussion of Government action in private conversation."

United States v. Kahn (1974)

The Court, interpreting a recently enacted federal law, held that a district judge who finds probable cause that a home telephone is being used by the owner and "others as yet unknown" to conduct illegal gambling may properly issue an order to tap the telephone, and evidence so obtained may be used against them.

SELF-INCRIMINATION

Twining v. New Jersey (1908)

The states may constitutionally compel individuals to testify against themselves. Overruled by *Malloy v. Hogan* (see below).

Chambers v. Florida (1940)

The police denied due process of law to four blacks when they obtained "sunrise confessions" after five days of interrogation in the absence of family, friends, or counsel "under circumstances calculated to break the strongest nerves and the stoutest resistance," stated the Court.

Adamson v. California (1947)

A statute permitting judicial comment on the failure of a defendant to take the stand does not violate the self-incrimi nation clause. Overruled by *Malloy v. Hogan* (see below).

Ullman v. United States (1956)

The Court upheld the constitutionality of legislation granting immunity from criminal prosecution to persons whose testimony in national security matters congressional committees demanded. A witness can be compelled to testify under such immunity even though loss of a job, denial of a passport, or public opprobrium may result. Protection against compulsory self-incrimination applies only to prosecution for crime.

Slochower v. Board of Higher Education (1956)

The Court invalidated the discharge of a tenured professor in a municipal college who invoked the Fifth Amendment in a congressional investigation of Communist activity. Invocation of the self-incrimination clause provides only procedural protection; it does not imply guilt or professional incompetence.

Mallory v. United States (1957)

The justices unanimously invalidated a confession because it had been obtained from a defendant who was detained by arresting officers for an unduly long time (about eighteen hours) before he was brought before a magistrate, in violation of the Federal Rules of Criminal Procedure.

Malloy v. Hogan (1964)   The Court reversed a witness's contempt citation for refusing to answer questions on the ground that his answers might incriminate him. The decision overruled *Twining v. New Jersey* and *Adamson v. California* (see above) and made the self-incrimination clause binding on the states. The Court held it would be "incongruous to have different standards determine the validity of a claim of privilege" depending on "whether the claim was asserted in a state or a federal court."

Albertson v. Subversive Activities Control Board (1965)   The Court voided provisions of the Internal Security Act requiring individual Communists to register, because admission of Communist affiliation would expose the registrant to criminal prosecution. The decision rendered inoperative provisions of other laws requiring the registration of the Communist party and Communist-front organizations.

Zicarelli v. New Jersey State Commission of Investigation (1972)   This decision upheld a sentence for contempt of court against a witness who refused to testify when state laws provided that neither the testimony given nor leads therefrom could be used in any subsequent prosecution. The prohibition against compulsory self-incrimination had not been breached because the witness remained in the same position whether testifying or silent, according to the Court. Immunized individuals may be prosecuted only on evidence "derived from a legitimate source wholly independent of the compelled testimony."

MIRANDA WARNINGS

Miranda v. Arizona (1966)   The Court extended the protection of the self-incrimination clause by requiring the police to clearly inform persons in custody prior to questioning them that they have the right to remain silent; that anything they do say may be used against them; that they have the right to consult an attorney; and that if they cannot afford an attorney, one will be provided them. Any questions answered by a person in custody who has not been given these warnings is not admissible as evidence against that person.

Harris v. New York (1971)   Statements made by a suspect who had not been read the Miranda warnings, though inadmissible as direct evidence, may be used to impeach his courtroom testimony. The Miranda ruling, said the majority, "cannot be perverted into a license to use perjury"; the advantage of exposing false testimony outweighs the "speculative possibility that impermissible police conduct will be encouraged."

Doyle v. Ohio (1976)

After receiving the Miranda warnings, defendants chose to remain silent. At trial, defendants claimed narcotics agents framed them. To impeach their testimony, the prosecutor cross-examined them about their failure to offer this alibi at the time of their arrest. The Court ruled that it is fundamentally unfair to allow an arrestee's silence to be used to impeach a courtroom explanation, given Miranda's assurance that silence carries no penalty.

Rhode Island v. Innis (1980)

An offhand remark by a police officer does not constitute interrogation, even though the remark leads the suspect to incriminate himself. The Court stated that interrogation occurs only when "a person in custody is subjected to either express questioning or its functional equivalent"; that is, "any words or actions on the part of the police that the police should know are reasonably likely to elicit an incriminating response from the suspect."

DOUBLE JEOPARDY

Palko v. Connecticut (1937)

The Court sustained the right of a state to appeal a criminal case verdict. Palko, after having been convicted of second-degree murder, was retried, convicted of first-degree murder, and sentenced to death. Because double jeopardy is not "implicit in a scheme of ordered liberty," no constitutional violation occurred. In this case, all that the state sought was "a trial free from the corrosion of substantial legal error." Overruled by *Benton v. Maryland* (see below).

Louisiana ex rel. Francis v. Resweber (1947)

A convicted murderer who had escaped death because of mechanical failure of the electric chair sought to prevent a second attempt at execution on the grounds of double jeopardy and cruel and unusual punishment. The Court held, 5 to 4, that the state's second effort to execute him does not violate the Constitution.

Bartkus v. Illinois (1959)

The Court, 5 to 4, reiterated its position that the due process clause of the Fourteenth Amendment does not apply all the provisions of the Bill of Rights to the states. In this case, conviction for an offense (robbery of a federally insured loan association) in a state court, after the defendant had been acquitted of the same offense in a federal court, did not violate due process or raise any valid question of double jeopardy.

Benton v. Maryland (1969)   This decision overruled *Palko v. Connecticut* (see above) and made binding on the states the Fifth Amendment's guarantee against double jeopardy. In a trial for burglary and larceny, the defendant was convicted of burglary but acquitted of larceny. On retrial (held because of errors in the burglary conviction), he was convicted of both larceny and burglary. The Court held that the larceny conviction subjected the defendant to jeopardy a second time.

Waller v. Florida (1970)   An individual may not be prosecuted in a Florida state court for the same offense he was convicted of in a Florida municipal court. State and local courts are part of the same governmental entity, unlike state and federal courts. Compare *Bartkus v. Illinois* (see above).

Ashe v. Swenson (1970)   A person acquitted of robbing one member of a group may not be retried on the same evidence for robbing a second member of the same group.

Crist v. Bretz (1978)   The federal rule that jeopardy attaches when the jury is impaneled and sworn applies to the states as well.

TAKING OF PROPERTY BY GOVERNMENT

Berman v. Parker (1954)   Congress did not violate the Fifth Amendment by authorizing the taking of private property to redevelop and make more attractive "blighted territory" in the District of Columbia. Once a public purpose for the taking is established, private enterprise may constitutionally be "one of the means chosen" to complete the project.

Penn Central Transportation Co. v. New York City (1978)   "Diminution in property value, standing alone," cannot "establish a 'taking'." The Court instead focused "on the character of the action and on the nature and extent of the interference." Here a landmark preservation law prohibiting the construction of an office tower above Grand Central Terminal does not take Penn Central's property.

Pruneyard Shopping Center v. Robins (1980)   California's constitutional provision permitting individuals to distribute literature and solicit petition signatures in a privately owned shopping center does not take property.

Hawaii Housing Authority v. Midkiff (1984)

A land reform act authorizing a state to take residential property from lessors and transfer it to lessees on payment of just compensation does not violate the Fifth Amendment's public use clause. A government properly exercises its power of eminent domain to lessen the concentration of land ownership in a few hands. Transferring the land so taken to private beneficiaries does not invalidate the taking. Government does not have to use the taken property itself to legitimate the taking.

THE RIGHT TO TRAVEL

Kent v. Dulles (1958)

The secretary of state, in issuing passports under "such rules as the President shall designate," is limited to restrictions specifically authorized by Congress or established by usage. "The right to travel is part of the 'liberty' of which the citizen cannot be deprived without the due process of law of the Fifth Amendment."

Aptheker v. Secretary of State (1964)

The Court declared unconstitutional those provisions of the Internal Security Act of 1950 that denied passports to persons belonging to organizations required by the act to register with the attorney general. The Court refused to uphold the restrictions because they are too broad: they do not consider whether a person's membership in such an organization is knowing or unknowing or whether his or her participation is active or inactive, and they do not consider the purpose for which one desires to travel.

Zemel v. Rusk (1965)

Congress constitutionally granted the executive branch the authority to refuse to issue passports to American citizens traveling to Cuba. Such travel "might involve the Nation in dangerous international incidents."

TRIAL BY JURY

Strauder v. West Virginia (1880)

This decision declared unconstitutional a statute requiring jury lists to be made up entirely of white male citizens. The statute violated the rights of blacks under the equal protection clause of the Fourteenth Amendment and deprived them of due process of law.

Hurtado v. California (1884)

A state need not indict persons with a grand jury. "Information" certifying "probable guilt" suffices.

Maxwell v. Dow (1900)

A state may use eight-person juries, instead of the twelve required in federal courts.

Patton v. United States (1930)

The Court sustained a verdict reached by eleven jurors in a federal court. The twelfth had become ill after the trial had begun, and the defense and prosecution agreed to proceed without him. Inasmuch as a defendant in a federal court may waive a jury trial altogether, he or she may also consent to trial by eleven jurors. Absent such a waiver, federal courts must use twelve-member juries; a federal judge must superintend the trial; and the jury's verdict must be unanimous.

Norris v. Alabama (Second Scottsboro Case) (1935)

The justices reversed the conviction of a black youth for rape because of a "long-continued, unvarying and wholesale exclusion of Negroes from jury service" in the county in which the trial occurred. Going behind the record in the case, the Court found that no black had ever been called for jury duty in the court and concluded that no black names had ever been placed on the lists of potential jurors, though many were qualified for jury service and some had served on federal court juries.

Duncan v. Louisiana (1968)

The Court reversed a conviction in a nonjury trial for an offense for which the maximum sentence was two years in prison, even though Duncan received only sixty days. The Court ruled that the right to trial by jury prevails in state criminal cases that, if tried in federal court, would require a jury.

United States v. Jackson (1968)

The majority voided a provision of the Federal Kidnapping Act that authorized a jury to impose a death sentence if the kidnapper had harmed his or her victim. The Court said that the provision required a defendant to risk his or her life in order to obtain a jury trial.

Witherspoon v. Illinois (1968)

The justices prohibited a death sentence when the jury that imposed or recommended it excluded prospective jurors who had expressed conscientious or religious scruples against capital punishment.

Taylor v. Louisiana (1975)

The Court reversed a rape conviction because state law, for all practical purposes, excluded women from the pool from which jurors were chosen. The defendant was thus deprived of the right to be tried by an impartial jury drawn from a fair cross section of the community. Sex could no longer be a valid basis for determining eligibility for jury service. Overruled *Hoyt v. Florida (1961)*, which had sustained exemption of women from jury duty on the ground that "woman is still regarded as the center of home and family life."

Ballew v. Georgia (1978) — Conviction by a jury of less than six members deprives the accused of the right to trial by jury.

Burch v. Louisiana (1979) — A state may not constitutionally convict a person of a nonpetty offense by a nonunanimous vote of a six-member jury.

Batson v. Kentucky (1986) — See under *Race Discrimination*.

Lockhart v. McCree (1986) — This case resolved a question that had been explicitly left open in *Witherspoon v. Illinois* (see above): whether persons opposed to capital punishment can be excluded from juries that determine the guilt as well as the sentence of persons accused of a capital offense. The states may exclude such persons because the practice, said the majority, does not create a biased jury nor one that fails to represent a fair cross section of the community. These excluded jurors are not a distinctive group, and a state has the right to impanel a single jury that can impartially decide all the issues in a case.

RIGHT TO CONFRONT AND CROSS-EXAMINE WITNESSES

Pointer v. Texas (1965) — The Sixth Amendment's guarantee that an accused has the right to confront witnesses against him or her is binding on the states. Hence, the prosecution may not introduce a transcript of a witness's testimony at a pretrial hearing where the defendant was without an attorney and had no opportunity to cross-examine the witness.

Davis v. Alaska (1974) — The credibility of a prosecution witness is impeachable by cross-examination even though the impeachment conflicts with a state's interest in preserving the confidentiality of juvenile delinquency proceedings. The witness here was a sixteen-year-old on probation for robbery whose testimony was crucial to the prosecution's case.

Ohio v. Roberts (1980) — Use of testimony given at a pretrial hearing when the witness could not be located to appear at trial does not violate the confrontation clause.

Maryland v. Craig (1990)

Victims of child abuse may testify without actually appearing in the courtroom and personally confronting those they accuse. The majority held that, while important, confrontation was not an "indispensable element" of the Sixth Amendment. Speaking for four dissenters, Justice Scalia focused on the literal words of the provision and sarcastically observed that the majority gave the accused "virtually everything the confrontation clause guarantees (everything, that is, except confrontation)."

RIGHT TO COUNSEL

Powell v. Alabama (First Scottsboro Case) (1932)

The Court reversed the conviction of a black youth for rape, on the ground that the trial judge had not effectively provided counsel for his defense. No attorney was appointed until the morning of the trial, which left no time to prepare a defense. "The right to be heard would be, in many cases, of little avail if it did not comprehend the right to be heard by counsel. . . . The failure of the trial court to make an effective appointment of counsel was a denial of due process."

Johnson v. Zerbst (1938)

The justices reversed the conviction for forgery of a young marine who had informed the federal district judge that, though he had no attorney, he was ready to stand trial. Ignorant of the law, he failed to assert important rights while representing himself. An accused person may waive the right to counsel, but the waiver must be clearly and intelligently made. The trial judge has the "serious and weighty responsibility . . . of determining whether there is an intelligent and competent waiver by the accused."

Gideon v. Wainwright (1963)

The right to counsel applies to state criminal prosecutions. Indigents accused of a felony have the right to be represented by appointed counsel.

Escobedo v. Illinois (1964)

The police denied a murder suspect's repeated requests to consult his attorney. On the assumption that the same standard ought to apply in the station house as in the courtroom (since what one says in the former place may be used in the latter, and statements resulting from lengthy inquisitions may jeopardize a person as much as courtroom admissions—arguably, even more. What happens in court occurs in full public view, unlike police interrogation), the majority held that "when the process shifts from investigatory to inquisitory—when its focus is on the accused and its purpose is to elicit a confession—our adversary system begins to operate, and, under the circumstances here, the accused must be permitted to consult with his lawyers." (Compare *Miranda v. Arizona* under *Miranda Warnings*.)

Argersinger v. Hamlin (1972)

The Court extended the right to counsel to all cases in which a judge or magistrate wishes to preserve the option of imposing a jail sentence. No person may be sentenced to jail "without a knowing and intelligent waiver of his right" to counsel, stated the Court. If indigent, an accused must be provided with a lawyer's services.

Nix v. Whiteside (1986)

An attorney's refusal to cooperate with the accused in presenting perjured testimony at trial does not deprive the defendant of effective representation by counsel. "Whatever the scope of a constitutional right to testify, it . . . does not extend to testifying falsely."

RIGHT TO BAIL

United States v. Salerno (1987)

Pretrial detention without bail of persons deemed a threat to public safety does not violate the excessive bail provision of the Eighth Amendment. The majority observed that the amendment "says nothing about whether bail shall be available at all."

CRUEL AND UNUSUAL PUNISHMENT

Trop v. Dulles (1958)

The Court declared unconstitutional a provision of the Nationality Act of 1940 that automatically revoked the citizenship of members of the armed forces who were convicted of wartime desertion.

Furman v. Georgia (1972)

The justices held 5 to 4 that the death penalty was so infrequently and randomly imposed that it no longer credibly deterred crime. Hence, it constituted cruel and unusual punishment. Each justice delivered a separate opinion. Those in the majority said: The death penalty has in fact been imposed on a capriciously selected handful (Stewart). It is uniquely degrading and is tolerated only because of its disuse (Brennan). The threat of execution is too attenuated to service criminal justice (White). The death penalty falls disproportionately on the poor and minorities (Marshall). Capital punishment has no application to society at large, but only to some selected outcasts (Douglas). The minority justices disagreed about the value of the death penalty but all said that if it were abolished, abolition should result from popular action, not judicial decree.

Gregg v. Georgia (1976)

This decision involved one of a group of cases in which the Court ruled the death penalty permissible if it is not imposed capriciously or arbitrarily, if the sentencing authority follows strict guidelines, and if it is not made mandatory for any particular crime.

Ingraham v. Wright (1977)

Disciplinary paddling of public school children is not cruel and unusual punishment, said a majority of five justices.

Coker v. Georgia (1977)

The death penalty may not be meted out for the nonfatal rape of an adult woman, according to seven of the nine justices.

Ford v. Wainwright (1986)

In its final death penalty decision, the Burger Court ruled 5 to 4 that the Constitution bars the execution of murderers who become insane while on death row. If such persons regain their sanity, however, they may be executed.

McCleskey v. Kemp (1987)

Statistical evidence demonstrating that the death penalty was imposed more frequently on killers of whites than blacks violates neither the Eighth nor the Fourteenth Amendments.

Penry v. Lynaugh (1989)

The death sentence for mentally retarded persons is not unconstitutional per se. Such persons, however, are entitled to instructions that jurors may treat evidence of mental retardation as mitigating the effect of the murder.

Stanford v. Kentucky (1989)

Persons as young as sixteen may be sentenced to death.

This concludes the inventory of landmark decisions construing the provisions of the Bill of Rights. Like the various issues involving the First Amendment, those concerning the rights of persons accused of crime have undergone substantial modification in recent years. Nothing in the composition of the current Court or the makeup of its docket suggests that the justices will lessen their consideration of them in future years.

15

The Right to Privacy

*T*his chapter summarizes the leading cases that deal with modern aspects of what is loosely and nontechnically called the right to privacy. With but a single exception, all the cases were decided within approximately the past twenty-five years. They concern sexual activity, marital and family rights, abortion, and the right to die.

PRIVACY

*Griswold v.
Connecticut
(1965)*

The justices established a right to privacy independent of freedom of association, the Fourth Amendment, and the self-incrimination clause. At issue, according to Justice Stewart, was "an uncommonly silly law" that made the sale or use of contraceptives a criminal offense. The Court voided the law and, citing a long list of precedents, said that "specific guarantees in the Bill of Rights have penumbras, formed by emanations from those guarantees that help give them life and substance." In other words, the provisions in the Bill of Rights have a broader scope than their language suggests. These penumbras "create zones of privacy." Douglas, speaking for the majority, rhetorically inquired: "Would we allow the police to search the sacred precincts of marital bedrooms for telltale signs of the use of contraceptives? The very idea is repulsive to the notions of privacy surrounding the marriage relationship." He concluded:

> We deal with a right of privacy older than the Bill of Rights, older than our political parties, older than our school system. Marriage is a coming together for better or for worse, hopefully enduring, and intimate to the degree of being sacred. It is an association that

promotes a way of life, not causes; a harmony in living, not political faiths; a bilateral loyalty, not commercial or social projects. Yet it is an association for as noble a purpose as any involved in our prior decisions.

Eisenstadt v. Baird **(1972)**   The Court refused to accept Massachusetts's argument against use of contraceptives by unmarried persons: "to protect purity, to preserve chastity . . . and thus to engender in the State and nation a virile and virtuous race of men and women." The Court considered it "plainly unreasonable to assume that Massachusetts has prescribed pregnancy and the birth of an unwanted child as punishment for fornication." Chief Justice Burger dissented, believing it proper that only physicians dispense contraceptives.

Moose Lodge v. Irvis **(1972)**   A provision in the Civil Rights Act of 1964 exempting from its coverage "a private club or other establishment not in fact open to the public" is constitutionally permissible. The right to privacy may take precedence over a racially open society.

Whalen v. Roe **(1977)**   The Court sustained a state law that required the computerized listing of the names and addresses of every person obtaining a prescription for a dangerous drug, such as opium or amphetamines, against a charge that it invaded "zones of privacy." The law, said the majority, contains "careful safeguards against indiscriminate disclosure" and evidences "a proper concern with, and protection of, the individual's interest in privacy."

Bowers v. Hardwick **(1986)**   The due process clause confers no right on consenting adult homosexuals to engage in oral or anal intercourse. In its opinion, the five-justice majority rejected the view "that any kind of private sexual conduct between consenting adults is constitutionally insulated from state proscription." Choices fundamental to heterosexual life —marriage, procreation, child rearing, and family relationships—were sharply distinguished from homosexual acts. The majority also emphasized the "ancient roots" of laws outlawing homosexual conduct and noted that "24 States and the District of Columbia continue to provide criminal penalties for sodomy performed in private and between consenting adults."

FAMILY RIGHTS

Meyer v. Nebraska **(1923)**   The Court voided a statute that both prohibited teaching foreign languages in elementary schools and forbade teaching any subject in a language other than English. The law unreasonably infringed on the liberty to teach and the liberty of parents to secure instruction for their children, both of which the due process clause of the Fourteenth Amendment protects.

Loving v. Virginia (1967)

The Court unanimously and emphatically voided laws prohibiting interracial marriage as a deprivation of liberty as well as a denial of equal protection.

Mathews v. Lucas (1976)

Provisions of the Social Security Act requiring illegitimate children to show dependency on their deceased father in order to qualify for survivor's benefits do not unconstitutionally discriminate against them. Although the act makes it more difficult for illegitimate than for legitimate children to qualify, the classification reasonably relates to a permissible governmental purpose: to determine the likelihood of dependency only where documentary evidence—a legitimated birth, support order, or paternity decree—exists.

Lassiter v. Department of Social Services (1981)

This decision upheld a state's refusal to appoint an attorney to represent an indigent mother, who had been convicted of second-degree murder, in claiming custody of her child. By a 5-to-4 vote, the Court ruled that the state's invasion of Lassiter's rights was "not so serious or unreasonable as to compel us to hold that appointment of counsel to indigent parents is constitutionally mandated." A state, however, is free to do so if it wishes.

Santosky v. Kramer (1982)

Due process requires "clear and convincing evidence" that parents are unfit before a state can permanently remove children from the custody of abusive or neglectful parents. The traditional standard, "preponderance of the evidence," insufficiently protects parents' fundamental rights in the care, custody, and management of their children.

Palmore v. Sidoti (1984)

A parent may not lose custody of a child because of remarriage to a person of a different race. Speaking for a unanimous Court, Chief Justice Burger said that "the reality of private biases and the possible injury they might inflict" are impermissible considerations "for removal of an infant child from . . . its natural mother." Although "the Constitution cannot control such prejudices . . . neither can it tolerate them."

ABORTION

Roe v. Wade (1973)

The Court voided state laws that made abortions criminal offenses (except when performed to preserve the woman's life or health). Such laws violate the due process clause of the Fourteenth Amendment, which protects the right to privacy. This includes a qualified right to terminate a pregnancy. The state, however, does have a legitimate interest in protecting the pregnant woman's health and the potentiality of human life, both of which interests grow and reach a "compelling point" at different stages of pregnancy. For the first three months, abortion procedures must be left to the judgment of the woman and her physician. For the second trimester, the state may regulate abortion procedures in order to protect the woman's life or health. During the final three months, the state may regulate abortions, or even forbid them, except to preserve the life or health of the woman.

Planned Parenthood of Central Missouri v. Danforth (1976)

This decision voided a state law requiring parental consent for an unmarried woman under eighteen and spousal consent for a married woman to obtain an abortion. The majority said that what the state cannot do itself, it cannot delegate to another and, although a husband may be deeply concerned about his wife's pregnancy, she bears the child and is the more directly and immediately affected.

Beal v. Doe (1977)

One of three decisions that respectively hold that state refusal to use Medicaid funds for nontherapeutic abortions violates neither federal law nor the Constitution, and that public hospitals may constitutionally adopt a flat no-abortion policy. One result: a pregnant woman has a constitutional right to an abortion only if she can pay for it and can find a hospital or clinic willing to perform the operation. Other results: taxpayers are not compelled to pay for other people's abortions and hospitals can set their own medical policy.

Akron v. Akron Center for Reproductive Health (1983)

The Court reaffirmed a woman's right to an abortion and barred a variety of curbs that increased their cost; for example, that all second trimester abortions be performed in a hospital and that twenty-four hours elapse between consent and performance of an abortion. Such requirements are invalid unless justified "by a compelling state interest."

Thornburgh v. American College of Obstetricians (1986)

This was the Burger Court's final abortion decision. It voided the requirements that physicians (1) provide patients with detailed information about the risks of an abortion and alternatives to abortion, (2) compile records of abortions and make them available to the public, (3) use the method more likely to promote a live birth, and (4) have a second physician in attendance when an abortion is performed. "The states are not free," said the five--member majority, "under the guise of protecting maternal health or potential life, to intimidate women into continuing pregnancies."

*Webster v.
Reproductive
Health Services
(1989)*

The Court reaffirmed the states' rights to regulate abortion within the broad confines of the guidelines laid down in *Roe v. Wade* (see above). Justice O'Connor, whose vote was crucial to the Court's decision, indicated that the concept of viability should replace Roe's trimester scheme and that state regulations were constitutional so long as they do "not impose an undue burden on a woman's abortion decision."

*Hodgson v.
Minnesota
(1990)*

Unemancipated minors (dependent females under the age of eighteen) may be required to notify their parents before obtaining an abortion as long as the state's law allows a pregnant teenager the option of a judicial hearing in lieu of parental notification.

RIGHT TO DIE

*Cruzan v.
Director,
Missouri
Department of
Health (1990)*

Persons who make their wishes clearly known have a constitutional right to terminate life-sustaining care. The Court, with only Justice Scalia dissenting, said that "the principle that a competent person has a constitutionally protected liberty inter est in refusing unwanted medical treatment [though not previously articulated] may be inferred from our prior decisions."Here, however, the majority ruled that the comatose, brain-dead Cruzan had not made her wishes known with the clarity that Missouri's law required.

On remand, the Missouri attorney general withdrew his opposition to Cruzan's death. With the approval of her family and her court- appointed legal guardian, a local court permitted her feeding tube to be disconnected in December 1990, six months after the Supreme Court's decision.

Although the cases in this chapter are relatively few in number, they by no means span the spectrum of constitutionally protected privacy rights. The respective prohibitions in the Fourth and Fifth amendments on unreasonable searches and seizures and self- incrimination, plus the First Amendment's guarantee of freedom of association, also pertain to privacy.

The small number of Supreme Court decisions in the areas of privacy that this chapter has considered will certainly swell in future years. Controversies about sexual orientation, marriage and family matters, abortion, and the right to life and death are not likely to disappear. Neither does it seem that the decisions that the justices have rendered to date are necessarily set in concrete. Much additional policy-making may be expected at all governmental levels.

16

Discrimination

*T*he cases included in this chapter concern the equal protection clause.
Although the Framers of the amendment meant it to apply to the newly freed
slaves, the Supreme Court has broadly extended its scope to encompass all
bases of discrimination, e.g., sex, age, disability, handicap, alienage, income,
geography, literacy, education.

The Court, however, does not treat all bases for categorizing and classi-
ifying people as equally suspect. Invidious racial discrimination, for example,
is much more offensive than a classification that categorizes people on the
basis of their income.

The clause does not require people to be treated equally. The constitutional language is negatively phrased: "deny to any person." Consequently,
government is only barred from arbitrarily or unreasonably treating people
differently. In other words, reasonable governmental discrimination does not
violate the Constitution. Whether governmental action is reasonable or not
depends on why it has classified or categorized people, and the basis for that
classification.

Because of the virulent character of race discrimination in the United
States, most of the landmark decisions summarized below pertain to it.

RACE DISCRIMINATION

*Civil Rights
Cases (1883)*   The Court voided the Civil Rights Act of 1875, which forbade proprietors
of public conveyances, hotels, restaurants, and places of amusement to refuse
admission to a person because of race, color, or previous condition of
servitude. The Court held that the Fourteenth Amendment prohibited only

governmental discrimination, not that in which individuals and private organizations engage.

Yick Wo v. Hopkins (1886)   The Court invalidated a San Francisco laundry-licensing ordinance on the ground that it arbitrarily classified persons so as to discriminate against Chinese laundrymen.

Plessy v. Ferguson (1896)   The Court upheld a Louisiana law that required railroads to provide "separate but equal" accommodations for white and black passengers. The Court said that a law that recognizes a difference in color "has no tendency to destroy the legal equality of the two races." The Fourteenth Amendment was not intended to enforce "social, as distinguished from political, equality or a commingling of the races upon terms unsatisfactory to either." If the enforced segregation "stamps the colored race with the badge of inferiority," it is solely because "the colored race chooses to put that construction upon it." The elder Justice Harlan's dissent strongly presaged the Court's opinion in *Brown v. Board of Education* (see *Equal Protection in Education*), which overruled Plessy.

Buchanan v. Warley (1917)   The Court voided a city ordinance that sought to establish residential segregation by prohibiting a member of one race from occupying premises in districts where a majority of the dwellings were occupied by members of another race. The decision was circumvented by resort to restrictive covenants—contracts that prohibited a home buyer from selling the house to a member of specified racial or ethnic groups. These were later denied enforcement in *Shelley v. Kraemer* (see below).

Morgan v. Virginia (1946)   The justices invalidated a law requiring race separation on motor carriers on the ground that the law interfered with interstate commerce by disturbing the comfort of interstate passengers and limiting their freedom to select seats. The Court ruled that interstate buses require a "single, uniform rule to promote and protect national travel."

Shelley v. Kraemer (1948)   The Court denied judicial enforcement to restrictive racial covenants (long-term agreements between private parties limiting the right to own, lease or occupy housing to members of only one race), holding that though such private voluntary agreements do not violate the equal protection clause of the Fourteenth Amendment, their enforcement by state courts does.

Washington v. Davis (1976)   The justices held that a racially neutral employment qualification cannot be considered discriminatory simply because a greater proportion of blacks fails to qualify than persons of other races or ethnic groups. A purpose or intention to discriminate, not merely a discriminatory effect, must be shown for a violation of the equal protection clause to occur.

Batson v. Kentucky (1986)   By a 7-to-2 vote, the Burger Court, usually conservative on racial issues, overruled *Swain v. Alabama*, a conservative decision of the Warren Court, usually liberal on racial issues. A defendant may establish a prima facie case of purposeful discrimination—violating the equal protection clause—when a prosecutor uses peremptory challenges to exclude blacks from a jury. (Such challenges permit an attorney to exclude a specified number of prospective jurors without any reason being given.)

St. Francis College v. Al-Khazraji (1987)   White ethnic and nationality groups, as well as those of nonwhite ancestry, are covered by federal civil rights legislation that prohibits housing, job, and other contract-based discrimination.

EQUAL PROTECTION IN EDUCATION

Missouri ex rel. Gaines v. Canada (1938)   The Court introduced a modification of the "separate but equal" doctrine regarding educational opportunities for blacks. It sustained a black man's right to a professional education equal to that of whites by requiring that he be admitted to the all-white law school of a state university at least until a black law school was established. The Court explicitly rejected Missouri's offer to finance the student's legal education at an out-of-state institution as less than equal treatment.

McLaurin v. Oklahoma State Regents (1950)   A black man, admitted as a graduate student to the University of Oklahoma, was required by state law to occupy segregated seating in classrooms, the library, and the cafeteria. This policy denied him equal protection, ruled the Court, because it impaired "his ability to study, to engage in discussions and exchange views with other students, and, in general, to learn his profession."

Sweatt v. Painter (1950)   The Court ordered a black man admitted to the University of Texas Law School, from which he had been excluded because of his race, even though Texas had recently established a black law school. The justices observed that the separate facilities were not equal in faculty, course offerings, library, alumni achievements, or reputation.

Brown v. Board of Education (1954, 1955)   The Court overruled *Plessy v. Ferguson* (see under *Race Discrimination*). The justices unanimously declared separate educational facilities to be "inherently unequal." They requested further argument concerning the means to achieve desegregation. In 1955 they ordered local authorities to "make a prompt and reasonable start" and instructed the federal district courts to "proceed with all deliberate speed" to end segregation in public schools.

Bolling v. Sharpe (1954)

This was a companion case to *Brown v. Board of Education* (see above) that ordered desegregation of the public schools in the District of Columbia. There being no equal protection clause limiting the federal government, the justices based their decision on the due process clause of the Fifth Amendment.

Green v. County School Board (1969)

The justices disallowed as "intolerable" a school board plan to give parents "freedom of choice" to send their children either to a formerly all-white school or to a formerly all-black school, because the plan shifted responsibility for complying with *Brown v. Board of Education* (see above) from the school board to the parents. Declaring that the "time for mere deliberate speed has run out," the Court said that "the burden on a school board today is to come forward with a plan that promises realistically to work and that promises realistically to work now."

Swann v. Charlotte-Mecklenburg County Board of Education (1971)

This case addressed the means available for dismantling racially separate schools "in states having a long history of maintaining two sets of schools in a single school system . . . to carry out a governmental policy to separate pupils in schools solely on the basis of race." Given that the objective remains the elimination of "all vestiges of state-imposed segregation" and that in pursuance thereof "a district court has broad power to fashion a remedy that will assure a unitary system," could courts order busing and the use of racial ratios to achieve this goal? The justices' unanimous response: Yes, indeed.

Noting that "bus transportation has been an integral part of the public education system for years, and was perhaps the single most important factor in the transition from the one-room schoolhouse to the consolidated school," the Court found "no basis for holding that the local school authorities may not be required to employ bus transportation as one tool of school desegregation. Desegregation plans cannot be limited to the walk-in school."

Racial quotas are also permissible. The Court was not saying that "any particular degree of racial balance or mixing" is required "as a matter of substantive constitutional right." But the presence of all-black schools creates a presumption of discrimination, and the use of racial ratios as "a starting point" in shaping a remedy therefore falls within courts' "discretionary powers." However, "the constitutional command to desegregate does not mean that every school in every community must always reflect the racial composition of the school system as a whole." This is a significant limitation: ratios and quotas are acceptable, but each and every school need not be balanced precisely. Indeed, the Court went further: "The existence of some small number of one-race, or virtually one-race, schools within a district is not in and of itself the mark of a system which still practices segregation by law." But if a district contemplates continuance of predominantly one-race schools, it bears "the burden of showing that such school assignments are genuinely nondiscriminatory."

Milliken v. Bradley (1974)

Cross-district busing between Detroit and fifty-three suburban school districts, said a five-member majority, may not be ordered to remedy purposeful segregation in one district unless it can be shown that the other districts had also acted unconstitutionally. The evidence showed that only Detroit had purposefully segregated its schools. A metropolitan remedy that encompassed both city and suburban school districts would also disrupt local control of school operations ("no single tradition in public education is more deeply rooted" than this) and would pose large-scale financial and administrative problems, to say nothing of the problems posed by the busing operation itself. In supporting the federal district court's metropolitan remedy, the dissenters emphasized that the state, not the local districts, is responsible for education and asserted that a Detroit-only remedy could not effectively desegregate Detroit's schools inasmuch as they were already overwhelmingly black.

Missouri v. Jenkins (1990)

Federal courts have no authority to directly levy property taxes to fund court-ordered school desegregation. Federal courts do, however, have authority to order discriminating school districts to levy such taxes.

AFFIRMATIVE ACTION

Regents of the University of California v. Bakke (1978)

A thirty-three-year-old white student who had a medical aptitude test score slightly below that required for regular admission applied to the newly established medical school of the University of California at Davis. The school had reserved 16 of 100 positions for blacks, Mexican Americans, and other minorities. Persons occupying these positions had less distinguished academic records than Bakke, who was denied admission.

Six of the nine justices wrote opinions, with no single opinion garnering majority support. Four of the justices—Burger, Stewart, Rehnquist, and Stevens—considered the Davis quota system a violation of Title VI of the 1964 Civil Rights Act, which stipulates that "no person in the United States shall, on the ground of race, color, or national origin, be excluded from participation in, be denied benefits of, or be subjected to discrimination under any program or activity receiving Federal financial assistance." Citing the rule that the resolution of a constitutional issue should be avoided if a case can be fairly decided on a statutory ground, these four justices interpreted Title VI to mean that it should be color blind in its application and concluded that the "ban on exclusion is crystal clear: Race cannot be the basis of excluding anyone from participation in a federally funded program."

At the other extreme were Justices Brennan, Marshall, White, and Blackmun, who decided that the Davis program violated neither the Constitution nor Title VI. According to their view, preferential treatment is a permissible means "of remedying past societal discrimination," and Title VI was enacted "to induce voluntary compliance with the requirement of non-discriminatory treatment." This being so, "It is inconceivable that Congress intended to encourage voluntary efforts to eliminate the evil of racial discrimination while at the same time forbidding the voluntary use of race-conscious remedies."

The opinion of Justice Powell, whose vote was decisive, refused to prohibit admissions officers "from any consideration of the race of any applicant." But because rights are personal, because "racial and ethnic distinctions of any sort are inherently suspect and thus call for the most exacting judicial scrutiny," and because the medical school had not been found guilty of discrimination, its quota system was unconstitutional.

Fullilove v. Klutznick *(1980)*

The enforcement clause of the Fourteenth Amendment, ruled the Court, permits Congress to require that 10 percent of federal funds for local public works projects be used to procure supplies or services from minority owned businesses.

Firefighters Local Union v. Stotts *(1984)*

Title VII of the 1964 Civil Rights Act, which outlaws race or sex discrimination, also explicitly protects bona fide seniority systems that do not purposefully discriminate against minorities. Hence, an injunction prohibiting a "last-hired, first- fired" layoff to save the jobs of blacks cannot stand.

Wygant v. Jackson Board of Education *(1986)*

The Court declared unconstitutional a plan to lay off teachers that gave preference to racial minorities. However, public employers may establish affirmative action programs that serve an "important" or "compelling" governmental interest, according to the Court. One such interest is "remedying past or present racial discrimination." Furthermore, employers may begin affirmative action plans without a prior judicial finding of discrimination, and such plans need not be "victim specific." Instead, they may penalize individual whites who have not themselves discriminated. But such plans must be "narrowly tailored" to remedy past or present discrimination. Therefore, racial preferences in hiring or promotion are more acceptable than layoffs. "Though hiring goals may burden some innocent individuals," said the prevailing opinion, "they simply do not impose the same kind of injury that layoffs impose."

Note, however, that the Court in this and in other cases distinguishes "goals" from "quotas." Only the latter are presumptively unconstitutional.

Firefighters v. Cleveland (1986)

Inasmuch as "Congress intended voluntary compliance to be the preferred means of achieving the objectives" of the employment discrimination provisions of the Civil Rights Act of 1964, a court may enter a consent decree in which employers, over the objections of white employees, agree to take preferential, affirmative action to promote or hire minorities, even though the decree benefits persons who were not actual victims of the city's race discrimination. Because of the voluntary character of consent decrees, judges may approve broader relief than in cases where the employer objects.

Johnson v. Transportation Agency (1987)

See under *Sex Discrimination*.

Richmond v. Croson Company (1989)

The Court ruled that the city's 30 percent set-aside for minority contractors violated the equal protection clause for three reasons: (1) the city failed to show discrimination in the local construction industry, (2) the program was not narrowly tailored to serve the alleged compelling interest; i.e., remedying past discrimination, because it included Eskimos and Asians, along with blacks, among the benefitted groups, and (3) the set-aside was a "quota" rather than a "goal." The Court was also troubled by the fact that blacks comprised half the city's population and controlled a majority of the seats on the city council. Thus, the set-aside program could be viewed as one that benefitted the majority rather than racial minorities.

Metro Broadcasting Co. v. FCC (1990)

The justices reaffirmed the decision in *Fullilove v. Klutznick* (see above) and thereby made it clear that the federal government has more leeway than state and local governments to establish affirmative action programs. Such congressionally authorized programs need not remedy "past societal discrimination" but may be directed toward future objectives, such as promoting racial and ethnic diversity. These programs, moreover, do not have to be "closely connected to a compelling governmental interest"; they need only be "substantially related to important governmental interests."

EMPLOYMENT DISCRIMINATION

St. Francis College v. Al-Khazraji (1987)

See under *Race Discrimination.*

Ward's Cove Packing Co. v. Atonio (1989)

By a 5-to-4 vote, the Court overruled a unanimously decided Burger Court case, *Griggs v. Duke Power Co.*, and construed federal civil rights laws to make it much more difficult for workers to prove race and sex discrimination. Most notably, workers must prove that no business justification exists for the company's hiring practices.

Martin v. Wilks (1989)

White and male workers may challenge consent decrees that settle race and sex discrimination cases. Here, white firefighters challenged an eight-year-old court-approved settlement intended to increase the number of blacks hired and promoted.

Patterson v. McLean Credit Union (1989)

The 1866 Civil Rights Act, a major federal antidiscrimination statute, prohibits racial discrimination only in the formation of private contracts. It does not apply to racial discrimination or harassment on the job.

Supporters of civil rights are making a major effort to get Congress to overturn the three preceding decisions by legislation that would prohibit discrimination in all aspects of contractual relationships. The proposed legislation would reassert the pre–*Ward's Cove* standards for proving discrimination and setting the burden of proof. It would also provide notice to nonparties and an opportunity for them to be heard prior to—but not after—a proposed court settlement of a job discrimination case.

SEX DISCRIMINATION

Hoyt v. Florida (1961)

This was the Warren Court's only sex discrimination case. A woman convicted of murdering her husband with a baseball bat argued that her all-male jury deprived her of the right to an impartial jury. Not so, said a unanimous Court:

> Despite the enlightened emancipation of women from the restrictions and protections of bygone years, and their entry into many parts of community life formerly considered to be reserved to men, woman is still regarded as the center of home and family life. We cannot say that it is constitutionally impermissible for a State, acting in pursuit of the general welfare, to conclude that a woman should be relieved from the civic duty of jury service unless she herself determines that such service is consistent with her own special responsibilities.

Overruled by *Taylor v. Louisiana.*

Cleveland Board of Education v. LaFleur (1974)

This decision held that mandatory pregnancy leaves for school teachers violated due process of law. To assume that no teacher can perform her duties once she becomes four or five months pregnant and that she continues to be incapable until her child is at least three months old is "arbitrary" and bears "no rational relationship to the valid state interest of preserving continuity of instruction." So long as teachers are required to give "substantial advance notice" of their condition, "dates later in pregnancy" serve the state interest just as well, "while imposing a far lesser burden" on the exercise of the constitutionally protected "freedom of personal choice in matters of marriage and family life," especially since "the ability of any particular pregnant woman to continue at work past any fixed time in her pregnancy is very much an individual matter."

Craig v. Boren (1976)

Oklahoma prohibited the sale of "nonintoxicating" 3.2-percent beer to males under twenty-one and to females under eighteen. Over the dissents of Burger and Rehnquist, the majority ruled that sex classifications withstand constitutional challenge only if they serve "important governmental objectives" and are "substantially related to achievement of those objectives." The Court ruled the law unconstitutional because the "relationship between gender and traffic safety" is "far too tenuous" to satisfy this standard.

Califano v. Goldfarb (1977)

The Court declared a sex-based distinction in the distribution of social security benefits unconstitutional because it discriminated against widowers of female wage earners. Widows of male workers received survivor's benefits, but widowers did only if over half of their support came from their wives. It was discriminatory that widowers had to prove they were dependent, while widows were assumed to be so.

Rostker v. Goldberg (1979)

The majority upheld the constitutionality of the all-male draft and the exclusion of women from combat positions in the armed forces.

Mississippi University for Women v. Hogan (1982)

A state university may not constitutionally limit enrollment in its nursing program to women. Said Justice O'Connor's majority opinion, the school's policy is based on "the stereotyped view of nursing as an exclusively woman's job." The four dissenters maintained that the issue is the right of a state to honor wom en's "traditionally popular and respected choice" to attend a single-sex college.

Arizona Governing Committee v. Norris (1983)

The justices construed Title VII of the 1964 Civil Rights Act to forbid a state to establish a retirement plan that paid lower benefits to women than to men because of their longer life expectancy. Here, a state employee sued because after retirement she would receive $34 less than a man who had put aside the same amount of money.

Hishon v. King & Spalding (1984)

In forbidding sex discrimination, Title VII of the Civil Rights Act of 1964 prohibits business partnerships—in this case a law firm—from discriminating against women employees (here by denying partnership to a female attorney).

Johnson v. Transportation Agency (1987)

In the Court's first affirmative action decision involving women, the justices endorsed their preferential treatment in the work place, holding that sex—like race—could legally and constitutionally be a factor in hiring and promotion even though the employer had no history of previous discrimination.

ALIENS

Truax v. Raich (1915)

An Arizona statute requiring private employers to hire 80 percent of their work force from among American citizens unconstitutionally infringes on aliens' "right to work for a living in the common occupations of the community," ruled the Court.

Graham v. Richardson (1971)

Because aliens are "a discrete and politically powerless minority," the Court held that state laws that discriminate against them are "inherently suspect and subject to close judicial scrutiny." Consequently, states may not condition eligibility for welfare benefits on U.S. citizenship.

Ambach v. Norwick (1979)

States may require governmental employees "who participate directly in the formulation, execution, or review of broad public policy" or who "perform functions that go to the heart of representative government" to be citizens, the Court stated. Thus, a city may exclude aliens from its police force. In this case, aliens may be made ineligible for certification as public schoolteachers. "Public education, like the police function, 'fulfills a most fundamental obligation of government to its constituency.' "

Plyler v. Doe
(1982)

Texas law withholding funds from local school districts for the education of the children of illegal aliens violates the equal protection clause. Dividing 5 to 4, Justice Brennan's majority opinion asserted that though public education is not a fundamental right, denial of access thereto must serve a "substantial" state interest when it "imposes a lifetime hardship on a discrete class of children not accountable for their disabling status." Texas failed to show such an interest.

JUVENILE JUSTICE

Kent v. United
States (1966)

Without granting a hearing, a juvenile court judge waived jurisdiction over a sixteen-year-old boy accused of housebreaking, robbery, and rape, thus permitting him to be indicted and tried in the regular adult courts, where the maximum sentences for these crimes are much greater. Speaking though Justice Fortas, the Court ruled that a valid waiver requires a hearing on the matter, access by counsel to the social records and probation reports considered by the juvenile court, and a statement of the reasons for the waiver of jurisdiction. Absent these protections, "the child receives the worst of both worlds," getting neither "the protections accorded to adults nor the solicitous care and regenerative treatment postulated for children."

In re Gault
(1967)

A boy was committed to the state industrial school for having made an obscene telephone call, for which an adult would have received a $50 fine or been imprisoned for no more than two months. The majority declared that "the condition of being a boy does not justify a kangaroo court"; consequently, "neither the Fourteenth Amendment nor the Bill of Rights is for adults alone." The Court specifically required juvenile courts to give timely advance notice of charges; to guarantee the right to representation by counsel, either retained or appointed; to ensure confrontation and cross-examination of adverse witnesses; and to inform defendants of the privilege against self-incrimination and the right to remain silent.

Tinker v. Des Moines School District (1969)	See under *Symbolic Speech*.

In re Winship (1970)	In the first of its decisions concerning juveniles, the Burger Court prohibited juvenile courts from convicting minors unless the standard "beyond a reasonable doubt" is employed when the adolescent is charged with an offense that would be considered a crime if committed by an adult. This standard, said the majority, "is a prime instrument for reducing the risk of convictions resting on factual error," for ensuring that "the moral force of the criminal law not be diluted by a standard of proof which leaves people in doubt whether innocent men are being condemned." The same considerations "which demand extreme caution in factfinding to protect the innocent adult apply as well to the innocent child."

McKeiver v. Pennsylvania (1971)	The right to a jury trial in criminal prosecutions does not apply to juvenile delinquency proceedings. The Court stated: "If the jury trial were to be injected into the juvenile court system as a matter of right, it would bring with it . . . the traditional delay, the formality, and the clamor of the adversary system and, possibly, the public trial."

Goss v. Lopez (1975)	This case established public education as a property right of children. Accordingly, the Court ruled, students facing temporary suspension "must be given some kind of notice and afforded some kind of hearing." The notice can be oral or written. If the student denies the charges, "an explanation of the evidence the authorities have and an opportunity to present his side of the story" must be provided, and "as a general rule" the notice and hearing must precede "removal of the student from school."

Parham v. J.R. (1979)	Due process does not require a formal, adversarial-type hearing before a parent or guardian may commit a minor to a state mental institution. The law recognizes "that natural bonds of affection lead parents to act in the best interests of their children."

Santosky v. Kramer (1982)	See under *Family Rights*.

Schall v. Martin (1984)	A statute authorizing pretrial detention for up to seventeen days of juveniles who present a serious risk of committing an offense does not violate due process. The statute serves legitimate state interests and satisfies procedural safeguards.

DeShaney v. Winnebago County Department of Social Services (1989)

The Constitution does not obligate state and local governments to protect their residents against harm from private individuals. Here, social workers failed to protect a four-year-old boy from his father's brutality that left him permanently institutionalized with severe brain damage, even though they received periodic reports of abuse and at one point took custody of the child. Said Chief Justice Rehnquist: Though government may not arbitrarily deprive persons of life, liberty, or property, the due process clauses "confer no affirmative right to governmental aid, even where such aid may be necessary" to preserve life, liberty, or property. In sum:

> The most that can be said of the state functionaries in this case is that they stood by and did nothing when suspicious circumstances dictated a more active role for them. In defense . . . it must also be said that had they moved too soon to take custody of the son away from the father, they would likely have been met with charges of improperly intruding into the parent-child relationship, charges based on the same due process clause that forms the basis for the present charge of failing to provide adequate protection.

Maryland v. Craig (1990)

See under *Right to Confront and Cross-Examine Witnesses.*

HANDICAPPED PERSONS

Buck v. Bell (1927)

The Court upheld compulsory sterilization of "mental defectives" under a statute that applied only to inmates of state mental hospitals and provided for notice, hearing, and judicial approval before sterilization. Justice Holmes, speaking for the Court, minced no words: "It is better for all the world, if instead of waiting to execute degenerate offspring for crime, or to let them starve for their imbecility, society can prevent those who are manifestly unfit from continuing their kind. The principle that sustains compulsory vaccination is broad enough to cover cutting the Fallopian tubes. . . . Three generations of imbeciles are enough."

O'Connor v. Donaldson (1975)

The justices ruled unanimously that individuals cannot constitutionally be confined to mental institutions against their will and without treatment if they are dangerous to no one and capable of surviving in the outside world.

Youngberg v. Romeo (1982)	Again unanimously, the Court held that involuntarily committed retarded persons have substantive due process liberty interests that require a state to provide minimally adequate training to ensure their safety and their freedom from undue restraint.
Cleburne v. Cleburne Living Center (1985)	Although the Constitution does not provide the mentally retarded with special protection against governmental discrimination, a Texas city's denial of a zoning permit for a group home was so irrational as to be unconstitutional. The permit requirement "appears to us to rest on an irrational prejudice against the mentally retarded." The record reveals "no rational basis for believing that the [proposed] home would pose any special threat to the city's legitimate interests."

POVERTY LAW

Goldberg v. Kelly (1970)	If state or federal law "entitles" a welfare recipient to certain benefits, then, the Court ruled, the due process clause requires government to adhere to certain "procedural safe guards" before the recipient is deprived of them: timely and adequate notice detailing the reasons for termination, an opportunity to present evidence orally and to confront and cross-examine adverse witnesses at a hearing prior to the termination of benefits, the right to retain an attorney, an impartial decision maker to conduct the hearing, and a decision that must rest solely on legal rules and the evidence presented at the hearing.
Dandridge v. Williams (1970)	Reductions in welfare entitlements, as distinct from their termination, do not violate the Constitution if they are reasonably related to a legitimate governmental purpose or interest. Budgetary and fiscal constraints are such.
Fuentes v. Shevin (1972)	Contracts between debtors and creditors and between buyers and sellers must accord with the requirements of due process—specifically, giving notice and conducting a hearing—in order for a seller to repossess property for nonpayment of debt.
Mathews v. Eldridge (1976)	. The due process clause does not always require an adversarial type of hearing prior to the termination of governmentally provided "entitlements," as specified in *Goldberg v. Kelly* (see above). Three factors determine what process is constitutionally required: (1) the importance of the entitlement to the individual recipient, (2) the importance of the government's interest, and

(3) the "risk of an erroneous determination" because of deficiencies in the agency's fact- finding procedures. In this case, involving medical disability benefits, the decision turned on "routine, standard, and unbiased medical reports by physician specialists." Hence, an informal, nonadversarial hearing after termination suffices because the fact-finding procedures minimized the risk that indi viduals would improperly lose their benefits.

T his chapter, like the one concerning the right to privacy, contains many highly controversial matters. Not only those pertaining to race and affirmative action, but also those that relate to the rights of indigents, handicapped persons, the mentally ill, and juveniles. As with privacy, we may expect the Supreme Court to confront a steady stream of cases in future years that apply to these and related issues. In their broadest context these decisions will continue to specify the extent to which the United States values equality.

17

Citizenship and Voting

*N*o subject is addressed in more provisions of the Constitution than the right to vote. According to Article I, section 2 of the original document, individuals have a right to vote in federal elections if they are enfranchised by their state of residence to vote for the more populous house of the state legislature. In addition to other provisions in Articles I and II that address the time, place, and manner of electing members of Congress and the president and vice-president, the Twelfth, Fourteenth, Fifteenth, Seventeenth, Nineteenth, Twentieth, and Twenty-Second through the Twenty-Sixth amendments all concern voting and elections of one sort or another. Nonetheless, the United States has the lowest participation rate among the world's self-governing societies.

THIRTEENTH AMENDMENT: SERVITUDE

Pollock v. Williams (1944)

The Thirteenth Amendment prohibits all legislation that would compel a person to work in order to pay off a debt. A state may not "directly or indirectly command involuntary servitude even if it was voluntarily contracted for."

Jones v. Alfred H. Meyer Co. (1968)

The justices sustained an 1866 act of Congress that prohibited both public and private racial discrimination in the sale or rental of housing. The law had not previously been enforced, and similar civil rights legislation had been declared unconstitutional in 1883 (see the Civil Rights Cases under *Race Discrimination*). Justice Stewart said for the Court that the Thirteenth Amendment was intended to remove "the badges and incidents of slavery" from the United States. "When racial discrimination herds men into ghettos and makes their ability to buy property turn on the color of their skins, then it too is a relic of slavery. The Thirteenth Amendment includes the right to buy whatever a white man can buy, the right to live wherever a white man can live."

FOURTEENTH AMENDMENT: CITIZENSHIP

Scott v. Sandford (1857)   A slave had resided with his master for several years in the free state of Illinois and at Fort Snelling, which was in a territory that had been made free by the Missouri Compromise. On returning to Missouri, Scott sued for his freedom. The Court held that neither Scott nor any other black—slave or free—could be a U.S. citizen. As a result, Scott could not bring a lawsuit in a federal court under the diversity of citizenship clause of Article III of the Constitution. Furthermore, no constitutional provision protected blacks because "for more than a century before" the ratification of the Constitution, blacks had

> . . . been regarded as beings of an inferior order; and altogether unfit to associate with the white race, either in social or political relations; and so far inferior, that they had no rights which the white man was bound to respect; and that the negro might justly and lawfully be reduced to slavery for his own benefit. He was bought and sold, and treated as an ordinary article of merchandise and traffic, whenever a profit could be made by it. This opinion was at that time fixed and universal in the civilized portion of the white race.

The majority accordingly declared the Missouri Compromise unconstitutional. Congress may not prevent citizens from transporting their slaves into a territory because slave ownership is a property right with which Congress may not interfere.

United States v. Wong Kim Ark (1898)   A child born in the United States and subject to its jurisdiction is an American citizen, even if his parents are aliens ineligible for naturalization. However, children born in the United States, but not subject to its jurisdiction, are not citizens. These include children of foreign diplomats, children born on foreign ships in American territorial waters, and Indians born on reservations. Congress later (1924) made all Indians American citizens.

Perez v. Brownell (1958)   The Court upheld a provision of the Smith Act (1940) that a native-born American might forfeit citizenship by participating in an election in a foreign country. Under its power to legislate on foreign relations, Congress may prevent interference by Americans in the affairs of a foreign country. Overruled by *Afroyim v. Rusk* (see below).

Schneider v. Rusk (1964)

The justices voided a section of the Immigration and Nationality Act of 1952 that deprived of citizenship a naturalized person who lived three consecutive years in his native land. Justice Douglas, for the Court, said that depriving naturalized citizens of a right that native-born citizens may exercise makes them sec ond- class citizens.

Afroyim v. Rusk (1967)

The decision overruled *Perez v. Brownell* (see above) and held that Afroyim, who had voted in an Israeli election, did not thereby lose his American citizenship. The Fourteenth Amendment's definition of citizenship binds Congress and prevents "forcible destruction" or deprivation of citizenship without an individual's consent.

VOTING

Ex parte Siebold (1880)

The Court let stand a federal conviction of a state-appointed election commissioner for violating both state and federal laws by stuffing a ballot box. Under Article I, section 4, Congress has plenary and paramount jurisdiction over the election of members of Congress and may supervise such elections "so as to give every citizen his free right to vote without molestation or injury."

Guinn v. United States (1915)

The Court voided Oklahoma's "grandfather clause," which required a literacy test for all voters in state and national elections except those who, under any form of government, were entitled to vote on January 1, 1866, or who then resided in some foreign nation, or were the lineal descendants of such persons. Though the law did not mention race, color, or previous servitude, the selection of a date prior to the adoption of the Fifteenth Amendment made it obvious that the intention was to disenfranchise black residents "in direct and positive disregard" of that amendment.

Harper v. Virginia State Board of Elections (1966)

The Court put a final end to the poll tax. Following passage of the Twenty-Fourth Amendment, which banned the tax in federal, but not state, elections, only four southern states retained it. Said the Court: A state violates the equal protection clause "whenever it makes the affluence of the voter or the payment of any fee an electoral standard." The amount of the Virginia fee: $1.50.

South Carolina v. Katzenbach (1966)

With only a partial dissent by Justice Black, the Court upheld the constitutionality of the Voting Rights Act of 1965. As a result, southern blacks, for the first time in history, were able to vote with relative ease.

The Voting Rights Act bans discriminatory practices, such as literacy and "understanding" tests, in all fifty states and also prohibits states from using any voting test if, in the 1964 presidential election, fewer than 50 percent of their residents who were of age registered or voted. This provision applied to Alabama, Georgia, Louisiana, Mississippi, South Carolina, and Virginia, plus twenty-six counties in North Carolina, and a few counties in other states. Tests could be restored in these places only with the approval of the federal district court in the District of Columbia upon a showing that such tests had not produced racial discrimination in the preceding five years. Any new voting qualification has to receive the attorney general's approval. The act also authorizes the U.S. attorney general to appoint voting examiners to register applicants wanting to vote.

Oregon v. Mitchell (1970)

A majority of the justices upheld the constitutionality of a 1970 amendment to the Voting Rights Act of 1965 that lowers the minimum voting age to eighteen in federal elections, but declared the provision unconstitutional for state and local elections. After the decision, Congress submitted and the state legislatures ratified the Twenty-Sixth Amendment, which lowers the voting age to eighteen in all elections.

Dunn v. Blumstein (1972)

Tennessee's requirements for voting in state elections (a year's residence in the state and ninety days in the county) violated the equal protection of the law. "The State," said the Court, "must show a substantial and compelling reason" for such requirements because they impinge on the constitutionally protected right to travel from one state to another. And "any classification which serves to penalize the exercise of that right, unless shown to be necessary to promote a compelling state interest, is unconstitutional." No such interest had been shown. Durational requirements do not correlate with informed or intelligent voting. "Knowledge or competence has never been a criterion for participation in Tennessee's electoral process for long-time residents. Indeed, the State specifically provides" for absentee balloting by persons who "have only the slightest political interest, and from whose political debates they are likely to be cut off."

Rosario v. Rockefeller (1973)

Different concerns permit varying durations before voters may participate in primary elections. New York State required persons wishing to vote in a state primary to register eight to eleven months in advance. The law affected only new voters and those who wanted to change their registration from one party to another. This, said the majority, does not prohibit these voters from participating in primaries but only sets time limits for the legitimate purpose of preventing a political raid by members of one party who switch to another. "Indeed, under the New York law, a person may, if he wishes, vote in a different party primary each year." By no means are voters locked "into an unwanted pre-existing party affiliation from one primary to the next." The four dissenters charged that the law unduly restricted party enrollment. Concern with raiding could be as effectively discouraged by a thirty- to sixty-day deadline. "Partisan political activities do not constantly engage the attention of large numbers of Americans, especially as party labels and loyalties tend to be less persuasive than issues and the qualities of individual candidates. The crossover in registration from one party to another is most often impelled by motives quite unrelated to a desire to raid or distort a party primary."

Buckley v. Valeo *(1976)*

The justices invalidated portions of the Federal Election Campaign Acts that limit the amount of money a candidate or an independent group may spend in an election. Such laws, which ignore the high cost of media advertising in modern campaigning, excessively restrict "the number of issues discussed, the depth of their exploration, and the size of the audience reached." But the Court upheld limitations on contributions made directly to candidates and requirements reporting and disclosing money spent. Public financing of presidential elections was also sustained.

Mobile v. Bolden *(1980)*

The Constitution does not guarantee the election of black candidates but only prohibits purposefully discriminatory voting standards, practices or procedures. Mobile's at-large voting system is not such even though blacks, totaling more than 35 percent of the city's population, have never won election to the three-member city council.

Congress limited the applicability of the decision when, in 1982, it approved a twenty-five year extension of the Voting Rights Act. Voters no longer need to prove intentional discrimination to secure relief under the act, although they must still do so if their lawsuits allege violations of the Fourteenth and Fifteenth amendments. Minority voters may instead focus on the effect of the challenged system and show that the "totality of the circumstances" produces "an aggregate" of discriminatory results.

Although none of the provisions in the Constitution that concern voting directly bestow the right to vote on any person, the net effect of the Supreme Court's decisions has given all citizens eighteen and older a right to vote in both the state and federal general elections.

18

The Organization of the Federal Courts

This chapter outlines the organization of the various federal courts.

SUPREME COURT

It has jurisdiction over all cases arising in the lower federal courts, and over cases containing federal questions from the highest state court that has jurisdiction to hear the case.

COURTS OF APPEALS

They consist of eleven numbered districts into which the United States (except for the District of Columbia) is divided, plus a separate court of appeals for the District of Columbia.

These courts have final jurisdiction over cases arising in federal courts except those heard by the Supreme Court. In addition, the court of appeals for the District of Columbia has jurisdiction to review determinations of quasijudicial federal agencies and commissions as well as cases arising in the District that in a state would be decided by the highest state court.

DISTRICT COURTS

There currently are ninety-one of these courts, at least one of which is located in every state. Puerto Rico and the District of Columbia also have a district court.

As the major trial courts of the federal system, these courts have original jurisdiction over cases arising under U.S. law. The Puerto Rico district court also determines some matters arising under the Commonwealth's local law.

SPECIAL COURTS

These are (1) the Court of Military Appeals, (2) the Court of International Trade, which was formerly known of as the Customs Court, (3) the Tax Court, and (4) the Court of Appeals for the Federal Circuit.

The last of these courts was created in 1982 from the merger of the Court of Customs and Patent Appeals and the Court of Claims. It has jurisdiction over such matters as appeals in suits for damages against the United States and over appeals from the Court of International Trade. It also hears appeals from various federal agencies and commissions: the Patent and Trademark Office, the Merit System Protection Board, and the boards of contract appeals. It also has jurisdiction over patent appeals from the district courts.

Special district courts also exist in various territories possessed by the United States: Guam, the Virgin Islands, and the Northern Mariana Islands. These courts have jurisdiction over cases arising under the laws of the United States as well as local territorial laws.

A set of local courts also exists in Puerto Rico, which has jurisdiction over laws enacted by local legislative bodies.

*T*he number and composition of the foregoing courts, with the exception of the U.S. Supreme Court, are within the constitutional power of Congress to determine. So also is their jurisdiction. The Constitution only provides for the Supreme Court and a chief justice of the United States. Except for the original jurisdiction that the Constitution specifies for the Supreme Court, the justices also depend on Congress to provide them with their appellate jurisdiction.

Congress's power to create, modify, and abolish the federal courts, and the number of judges serving thereon, is the major check that Congress has over the judiciary.

19

Supreme Court Justices Since 1789

*W*hat follows is a list of the individuals who have served as justices of the Supreme Court. One person, Edwin M. Stanton, is excluded from the list. He was nominated by President Grant on December 20, 1869 and confirmed by the Senate on the same day. He died four days later without having taken his seat.

The Supreme Court originally consisted of a chief justice and five associate justices. Congress reduced the number of associate justices to four in 1801, increased it to six in 1807, to eight in 1837, to nine in 1863, and reduced it to six in 1866. In 1869 Congress raised the number of associate justices to eight where it has remained ever since. Justices serve for life unless they resign or retire or are impeached and convicted.

Justices who have no number preceding their name were originally appointed as an associate justice. **Boldface** indicates chief justices.

Name	State	Term
1. **John Jay**	New York	1789 –1795
2. John Rutledge	South Carolina	1789 –1791
3. William Cushing	Massachusetts	1789 –1810
4. James Wilson	Pennsylvania	1789 –1798
5. John Blair	Virginia	1789 –1796
6. James Iredell	North Carolina	1790 –1799
7. Thomas Johnson	Maryland	1791 –1793
8. William Paterson	New Jersey	1793 –1806

Name	State	Term
9. Samuel Chase	Maryland	1796–1811
10. **Oliver Ellsworth**	Connecticut	1796–1799
11. Bushrod Washington	Virginia	1798–1829
12. Alfred Moore	North Carolina	1799–1804
13. **John Marshall**	Virginia	1801–1835
14. William Johnson	South Carolina	1804–1834
15. Brockholst Livingston	New York	1806–1823
16. Thomas Todd	Kentucky	1807–1826
17. Joseph Story	Massachusetts	1811–1845
18. Gabriel Duval	Maryland	1812–1835
19. Smith Thompson	New York	1823–1843
20. Robert Trimble	Kentucky	1826–1828
21. John McLean	Ohio	1829–1861
22. Henry Baldwin	Pennsylvania	1830–1844
23. James M. Wayne	Georgia	1835–1867
24. **Roger B. Taney**	Maryland	1836–1864
25. Philip P. Barbour	Virginia	1836–1841
26. John Catron	Tennessee	1837–1865
27. John McKinley	Alabama	1837–1852
28. Peter V. Daniel	Virginia	1841–1860
29. Samuel Nelson	New York	1845–1872
30. Levi Woodbury	New Hampshire	1845–1851
31. Robert C. Grier	Pennsylvania	1846–1870
32. Benjamin R. Curtis	Massachusetts	1851–1857
33. John A. Campbell	Alabama	1853–1861
34. Nathan Clifford	Maine	1858–1881
35. Noah H. Swayne	Ohio	1862–1881
36. Samuel F. Miller	Iowa	1862–1890

Name	State	Term
37. David Davis	Illinois	1862 –1877
38. Stephen J. Field	California	1863 –1897
39. **Salmon P. Chase**	Ohio	1864 –1873
40. William Strong	Pennsylvania	1870 –1880
41. Joseph P. Bradley	New Jersey	1870 –1892
42. Ward Hunt	New York	1873 –1882
43. **Morrison R. Waite**	Ohio	1874 –1888
44. John M. Harlan	Kentucky	1877 –1911
45. William B. Woods	Georgia	1881 –1887
46. Stanley Matthews	Ohio	1881 –1889
47. Horace Gray	Massachusetts	1882 –1902
48. Samuel Blatchford	New York	1882 –1893
49. Lucius Q.C. Lamar	Mississippi	1888 –1893
50. **Melville W. Fuller**	Illinois	1888 –1910
51. David J. Brewer	Kansas	1890 –1910
52. Henry B. Brown	Michigan	1891 –1906
53. George Shiras, Jr.	Pennsylvania	1892 –1903
54. Howell E. Jackson	Tennessee	1893 –1895
55. Edward D. White	Louisiana	1894 –1910
56. Rufus W. Peckham	New York	1896 –1909
57. Joseph McKenna	California	1898 –1925
58. Oliver W. Holmes	Massachusetts	1902 –1932
59. William R. Day	Ohio	1903 –1922
60. William H. Moody	Massachusetts	1906 –1910
61. Horace H. Lurton	Tennessee	1910 –1914
62. Charles E. Hughes	New York	1910 –1916
Edward D. White	Louisiana	1910 –1921
63. Willis Van Devanter	Wyoming	1911 –1937

Name	State	Term
64. Joseph R. Lamar	Georgia	1911–1916
65. Mahlon Pitney	New Jersey	1912–1922
66. James C. McReynolds	Tennessee	1914–1941
67. Louis D. Brandeis	Massachusetts	1916–1939
68 John H. Clarke	Ohio	1916–1922
69. William H. Taft	Ohio	1921–1930
70. George Sutherland	Utah	1922–1938
71. Pierce Butler	Minnesota	1922–1939
72. Edward T. Sanford	Tennessee	1923–1930
73. Harlan F. Stone	New York	1925–1941
Charles E. Hughes	New York	1930–1941
74. Owen J. Roberts	Pennsylvania	1930–1945
75. Benjamin N. Cardozo	New York	1932–1938
76. Hugo L. Black	Alabama	1937–1971
77. Stanley F. Reed	Kentucky	1938–1957
78. Felix Frankfurter	Massachusetts	1939–1962
79. William O. Douglas	Connecticut	1939–1975
80. Frank Murphy	Michigan	1940–1949
Harlan F. Stone	New York	1941–1946
81. James F. Byrnes	South Carolina	1941–1942
82. Robert H. Jackson	New York	1941–1954
83. Wiley B. Rutledge	Iowa	1943–1949
84. Harold H. Burton	Ohio	1945–1958
85. **Fred M. Vinson**	Kentucky	1946–1953
86. Tom C. Clark	Texas	1949–1967
87. Sherman Minton	Indiana	1949–1956
88. **Earl Warren**	California	1953–1969
89. John M. Harlan	New York	1955–1971

Name	State	Term
90. William J. Brennan	New Jersey	1956 –1990
91. Charles E. Whittaker	Missouri	1957 –1962
92. Potter Stewart	Ohio	1958 –1981
93. Byron R. White	Colorado	1962 –
94. Arthur J. Goldberg	Illinois	1962 –1965
95. Abe Fortas	Tennessee	1965 –1969
96. Thurgood Marshall	New York	1967 –
97. **Warren E. Burger**	Minnesota	1969 –1986
98. Harry A. Blackmun	Minnesota	1970 –
99. Lewis F. Powell	Virginia	1971 –1987
100. William H. Rehnquist	Arizona	1971 –1986
101. John P. Stevens	Illinois	1975 –
102. Sandra Day O'Connor	Arizona	1981 –
William H. Rehnquist	Arizona	1986 –
103. Antonin Scalia	Illinois	1986 –
104. Anthony M. Kennedy	California	1988 –
105. David H. Souter	New Hampshire	1990 –

20

Unconfirmed and Declining Supreme Court Nominees

*T*he following list indentifies the individuals who failed to be confirmed after being nominated to the Supreme Court. The Senate rejected twelve nominees, took no action on five, and postponed consideration of three. The president withdrew his nominee on six occasions and another seven declined their nomination.

The list excludes the three individuals who were confirmed after the president nominated them a second time: William Paterson whose initial nomination was withdrawn in 1793, Roger Taney whose consideration the Senate postponed in 1835, and Stanley Matthews on whom the Senate took no action in 1881.

Name	Reason Not Seated	Date
1. Robert H. Harrison	Declined	9/26/1789
2. John Rutledge	Rejected, 10 to 14	12/15/1795
3. William Cushing	Declined	1/27/1796
4. John Jay	Declined	12/19/1800
5. Levi Lincoln	Declined	1/3/1811
6. Alexander Wolcott	Rejected, 9 to 24	2/13/1811
7. John Quincy Adams	Declined	2/22/1811
8. John J. Crittenden	Postponed	2/12/1829
9. William Smith	Declined	3/8/1837

Name	Reason Not Seated	Date
10. John C. Spencer	Rejected, 21 to 26	1/31/1844
11. Edward King	Postponed	6/15/1844
12. Reuben H. Walworth	Withdrawn	6/17/1844
13. Edward King	Withdrawn	2/7/1845
14. John M. Read	No Action	1845
15. George W. Woodward	Rejected, 20 to 29	1/22/1846
16. Edward A. Bradford	No Action	1852
17. George E. Badger	Postponed	2/11/1853
18. William C. Micou	No Action	1853
19. Jeremiah S. Black	Rejected, 25 to 26	2/21/1861
20. Henry Stanbery	No Action	1866
21. Ebenezer R. Hoar	Rejected, 24 to 33	2/3/1870
22. George H. Williams	Withdrawn	1/8/1874
23. Caleb Cushing	Withdrawn	1/13/1874
24. Roscoe Conkling	Declined	3/2/1882
25. William B. Hornblower	Rejected, 24 to 30	1/15/1894
26. Wheeler H. Peckham	Rejected, 32 to 41	2/16/1894
27. John J. Parker	Rejected, 39 to 41	5/7/1930
28. Abe Fortas	Withdrawn	10/4/1968
29. Homer Thornberry	No Action	1968
30. Clement Haynsworth, Jr.	Rejected, 45 to 55	11/21/1969
31. G. Harrold Carswell	Rejected, 45 to 51	4/8/1970
32. Robert H. Bork	Rejected, 42 to 58	10/23/1987
33. Douglas H. Ginsburg	Withdrawn	11/8/1987

Selected Readings

Abraham, Henry J. *The Judiciary: The Supreme Court in the Governmental Process,* (8th ed., 1991).

Baum, Lawrence. *The Supreme Court* (2d ed., 1985).

Beard, Charles A. *An Economic Interpretation of the Constitution of the United States* (rev. ed., 1935).

Cannon, Mark W., and David M. O'Brien. eds. *Views from the Bench* (1985).

Carp, Robert A., and Ronald Stidham. *The Federal Courts* (2d. ed., 1990).

Danelski, David J. *A Supreme Court Justice Is Appointed* (1964).

Ducat, Craig R., and Harold Chase. *Constitutional Interpretation* (4th ed., 1987).

Farrand, Max. *The Records of the Federal Convention of 1787* (3 vols., 1937).

Fine, Sidney. *Laissez Faire and the General-Welfare State* (1956).

Frank, Jerome. *Law and the Modern Mind* (1930).

Frank, John P. *Marble Palace: The Supreme Court in American Life* (1958).
    Justice Daniel Dissenting (1964).

Friedman, Lawrence M. *A History of American Law* (1973).

Garraty, John A. ed. *Quarrels That Have Shaped the Constitution* (rev. ed., 1987).

Gates, John B., and Charles A. Johnson, eds. *The American Courts* (1990).

Goldman, Sheldon, and Thomas P. Jahnige. *The Federal Courts As a Political System* (3d ed., 1985).

Hall, Kermit L. *The Magic Mirror: Law in American History* (1989).

Halpern, Stephen C., and Charles M. Lamb, eds. *Supreme Court Activism and Restraint* (1982).

Jensen, Merrill. *The Articles of Confederation* (1948).

Kamisar, Yale. *Police Interrogation and Confessions* (1980).

Kelly, Alfred H., and Winfred Harbison. *The American Constitution* (5th ed., 1976).

Kutler, Stanley I. *Judicial Power and Reconstruction Politics* (1968).

Lewis, Anthony. *Gideon's Trumpet* (1964).

McCloskey, Robert G. *The American Supreme Court* (1960).

Murphy, Bruce Allen. *The Brandeis/Frankfurter Connection* (1982).

Murphy, Walter F. *Elements of Judicial Strategy* (1964).

Neely, Richard. *How Courts Govern America* (1981).

O'Brien, David M. *Storm Center: The Supreme Court in American Politics* (2d ed., 1990).

Palmer, Jan. *The Vinson Court Era* (1990).

Pritchett, C. Herman. *The Roosevelt Court* (1948).
    Civil Liberties and the Vinson Court (1954).

Provine, D. Marie. *Case Selection in the United States Supreme Court* (1980).

Rodell, Fred. *Nine Men* (1955).

Schubert, Glendon A. *Quantitative Analysis of Judicial Behavior* (1959).

Schwartz, Bernard. *Super Chief: Earl Warren and His Supreme Court* (1983).

    The Unpublished Opinions of the Burger Court (1989).

Scigliano, Robert. *The Supreme Court and the Presidency* (1971).

Spaeth, Harold J. *An Introduction to Supreme Court Decision Making* (rev. ed., 1972).

    Supreme Court Policy Making (1979).

Spaeth, Harold J., and Saul Brenner. *Studies in U.S. Supreme Court Behavior* (1990).

Stern, Robert L., Eugene Gressman, and Stephen Shapiro. *Supreme Court Practice* (6th ed., 1986).

Tribe, Laurence H. *God Save This Honorable Court* (1985).

Warren, Charles. *The Supreme Court in United States History* (3 vols., 1922).

Wasby, Stephen L. *The Supreme Court in the Federal Judicial System* (3d ed., 1987).

Witt, Elder, ed. *The Supreme Court and Its Work* (1981).

Wolfe, Christopher. *Judicial Activism* (1991).

Woodward, Bob, and Scott Armstrong. *The Brethren* (1979).

Glossary

abstention doctrine

The main feature of comity (q.v.). As a general rule, the federal courts should not intrude themselves into or otherwise duplicate ongoing state court litigation.

appellant

A party who appeals the decision of a lower court to a higher court.

appellate jurisdiction

The authority that a court of appeals has to review cases decided by lower courts. Distinguished from original jurisdiction (q.v.).

appellee

A party against whom an appeal is taken.

attainder, bill of

A legislative act that declares a person guilty of a crime without trial or conviction.

Bill of Rights

The first ten amendments to the Constitution.

certiorari, writ of

A request from a losing litigant that the case be reviewed by a higher court. It is the most frequently used basis for requesting Supreme Court review.

collateral estoppel

A rule that bars the relitigation of issues between the same parties that were previously resolved.

comity

A set of rules established by the Supreme Court that minimizes conflict between the federal and state court systems.

common law

The legal rules, remedies, customs, practices, and principles that have no statutory or constitutional basis. Cf. equity, statute.

defendant

The party against whom legal action is taken; particularly, a person accused or convicted of crime.

diversity jurisdiction

That aspect of the jurisdiction of the federal courts that authorizes them to hear controversies between residents of different states.

due process of law

The procedures that government must employ to constitutionally deprive persons of life, liberty, or property. It also refers to the substantive limits on government's power to deprive persons of freedom of speech, press, religion, association, and the right to privacy.

equal protection

Prohibits government from classifying people on arbitrary or unreasonable bases.

equity

Judicial rules, remedies, practices, and principles that supplement those of the common law (q.v.).

ex post facto law   A law that (1) declares an action that was innocent when done a crime; or (2) retroactively increases the punishment for a crime; or (3) retroactively alters the rules for conviction in order to make conviction easier.

federal question   A case arising under the Constitution, act of Congress or treaty of the United States. Lawsuits involving such matters may be heard in federal court.

final judgment   A court decision that is sufficiently final to warrant review by a higher court.

habeas corpus, writ of   An order from a court ordering a sheriff or jailer to produce a prisoner so that the court may determine the legality of the prisoner's detention. It is also a means whereby persons convicted under state law may request a federal court to review their conviction.

injunction   A writ forbidding a specified person from performing some specified action.

judgment of the Court   An opinion of the Supreme Court that announces the Court's decision but with which less than a majority of the participating justices agree.

judicial activism   A rule that views judges as primarily responsible for the protection of constitutional rights. Cf. judicial restraint.

judicial restraint   A rule that courts should defer to the decisions of elected officials, bureaucrats, and, in the case of federal courts, to the decisions of state court judges. Cf. judicial activism.

litigant   A party to a lawsuit.

mandamus   A writ ordering a person or official to perform some specified action.

original jurisdiction   The authority that a court has to hear and decide a case from its inception. Distinguished from appellate jurisdiction (q.v.).

per curiam   An opinion of a court that is anonymously authored.

petitioner   A party who initiates legal action. Also known as a plaintiff or complainant.

plaintiff   A party who initiates legal action. Also known as a petitioner or complainant.

political question   An issue that a court declines to decide because it considers the matter more appropriate for resolution by legislative or executive officials.

prima facie   On first appearance.

res judicata   An adjudicated matter. A case or controversy that the court has previously resolved.

respondent   A party against whom a legal action is brought.

standing to sue   The qualifications that a person must possess in order to initiate a lawsuit.

stare decisis   Precedent: to adhere to what was previously decided.

statute   A law enacted by a lawmaking body. Cf. common law, equity.

strict construction   The rule that states (1) that constitutional provisions should be construed literally, and (2) that any ambiguity in the language of a criminal law should be resolved in the accused person's favor.

sub silentio   Without notice being taken.

Appendix A

VIRGINIA BILL OF RIGHTS[*]

**Adopted
June 12, 1776**

A declaration of rights made by the representatives of the good people of Virginia, assembled in full and free convention; which rights do pertain to them and their posterity, as the basis and foundation of government.

Section 1. That all men are by nature equally free and independent, and have certain inherent rights, of which, when they enter into a state of society, they cannot, by any compact, deprive or divest their posterity; namely, the enjoyment of life and liberty, with the means of acquiring and possessing property, and pursuing and obtaining happiness and safety.

Section 2. That all power is vested in, and consequently derived from, the people; that magistrates are their trustees and servants, and at all times amenable to them.

Section 3. That government is, or ought to be, instituted for the common benefit, protection, and security of the people, nation, or community; of all the various modes and forms of government, that is best which is capable of producing the greatest degree of happiness and safety, and is most effectually secured against the danger of maladministration; and that, when any government shall be found inadequate or contrary to these purposes, a majority of the community hath an indubitable, inalienable, and infeasible right to reform, alter, or abolish it, in such manner as shall be judged most conducive to the public weal.

Section 4. That no man, or set of men, are entitled to exclusive or separate emoluments or privileges from the community, but in consideration of public services; which, not being descendible, neither ought the offices of magistrate, legislator, or judge to be hereditary.

---

[*] B. P. Poore, ed., *The Federal and State Constitutions, Colonial Charters, and Other Organic Laws of the United States* (2d ed., Washington, D.C.: Government Printing Office, 1878), II, 1908 ff.

Section 5. That the legislative and executive powers of the State should be separate and distinct from the judiciary; and that the members of the two first may be restrained from oppression, by feeling and participating the burdens of the people, they should, at fixed periods, be reduced to a private station, return into that body from which they were originally taken, and the vacancies be supplied by frequent, certain, and regular elections, in which all, or any part of the former members, to be again eligible, or ineligible, as the laws shall direct.

Section 6. That elections of members to serve as representatives of the people in assembly, ought to be free; and that all men, having sufficient evidence of permanent common interest with, and attachment to, the community, have the right of suffrage, and cannot be taxed or deprived of their property for public uses, without their own consent, or that of their representatives so elected, nor bound by any law to which they have not, in like manner, assented, for the public good.

Section 7. That all power of suspending laws, or the execution of laws, by any authority, without consent of the representatives of the people, is injurious to their rights, and ought not to be exercised.

Section 8. That in all capital or criminal prosecutions a man hath a right to demand the cause and nature of his accusation, to be confronted with the accusers and witnesses, to call for evidence in his favor, and to a speedy trial by an impartial jury of twelve men of his vicinage, without whose unanimous consent he cannot be found guilty; nor can he be compelled to give evidence against himself; that no man be deprived of his liberty, except by the law of the land or the judgment of his peers.

Section 9. That excessive bail ought not to be required, nor excessive fines imposed, nor cruel and unusual punishment inflicted.

Section 10. That general warrants, whereby an officer or messenger may be commanded to search suspected places without evidence of a fact committed, or to seize any person or persons not named, or whose offence is not particularly described and supported by evidence, are grievous and oppressive, and ought not to be granted.

Section 11. That in controversies respecting property, and in suits between man and man, the ancient trial by jury is preferable to any other, and ought to be held sacred.

Section 12. That the freedom of the press is one of the great bulwarks of liberty, and can never be restrained but by despotic governments.

Section 13. That a well-regulated militia, composed of the body of the people, trained to arms, is the proper, natural, and safe defence of a free State; that standing armies, in time of peace, should be avoided, as dangerous to liberty; and that in all cases the military should be under strict subordination to, and governed by, the civil power.

Section 14. That the people have a right to uniform government; and, therefore, that no government separate from, or independent of the government of Virginia, ought to be erected or established within the limits thereof.

Section 15. That no free government, or the blessings of liberty, can be preserved to any people, but by a firm adherence to justice, moderation, temperance, frugality, and virtue, and by frequent recurrence to fundamental principles.

Section 16. That religion, or the duty which we owe to our Creator, and the manner of discharging it, can be directed only by reason and conviction, not by force or violence; and therefore all men are equally entitled to the free exercise of religion, according to the dictates of conscience; and that it is the mutual duty of all to practise Christian forbearance, love, and charity towards each other.

Appendix B

The Declaration of Independence

A DECLARATION
by the Representatives of the
United States of America
in General Congress Assembled
July 4, 1776

When, in the course of human events, it becomes necessary for one people to dissolve the political bands which have connected them with another, and to assume, among the powers of the earth, the separate and equal station to which the laws of nature and of nature's God entitle them, a decent respect to the opinions of mankind requires that they should declare the causes which impel them to the separation.

We hold these truths to be self-evident, that all men are created equal; that they are endowed by their Creator with certain inalienable rights; that among these, are life, liberty, and the pursuit of happiness. That, to secure these rights, governments are instituted among men, deriving their just powers from the consent of the governed; that, whenever any form of government becomes destructive of these ends, it is the right of the people to alter or to abolish it, and to institute a new government, laying its foundation on such principles, and organizing its powers in such form, as to them shall seem most likely to effect their safety and happiness. Prudence, indeed, will dictate that governments long established, should not be changed for light and transient causes; and, accordingly, all experience hath shown, that mankind are more disposed to suffer, while evils are sufferable, than to right themselves by abolishing the forms to which they are accustomed. But, when a long train of abuses and usurpations, pursuing invariably the same object, evinces a design to reduce them under absolute despotism, it is their right, it is their duty, to throw off such government and to provide new guards for their future security. Such has been the patient sufferance of these colonies, and such is now the necessity which constrains them to alter their former systems of government. The history of the present King of Great Britain is a history of repeated injuries and usurpations, all having, in direct object, the establishment of an absolute tyranny over these States. To prove this, let facts be submitted to a candid world:—

He has refused his assent to laws the most wholesome and necessary for the public good.

He has forbidden his governors to pass laws of immediate and pressing importance, unless suspended in their operation till his assent should be obtained; and, when so suspended, he has utterly neglected to attend to them.

He has refused to pass other laws for the accommodation of large districts of people, unless those people would relinquish the right of representation in the legislature: a right inestimable to them, and formidable to tyrants only.

He has called together legislative bodies at places unusual, uncomfortable, and distant from the depository of their public records, for the sole purpose of fatiguing them into compliance with his measures.

He has dissolved representative houses repeatedly for opposing, with manly firmness, his invasions on the rights of the people.

He has refused, for a long time after such dissolutions, to cause others to be elected; whereby the legislative powers, incapable of annihilation, have returned to the people at large for their exercise; the state remaining, in the meantime, exposed to all the danger of invasion from without, and convulsions within.

He has endeavored to prevent the population of these States; for that purpose, obstructing the laws for naturalization of foreigners, refusing to pass others to encourage their migration hither, and raising the conditions of new appropriations of lands.

He has obstructed the administration of justice, by refusing his assent to laws for establishing judiciary powers.

He has made judges dependent on his will alone, for the tenure of their offices, and the amount and payment of their salaries.

He has erected a multitude of new offices, and sent hither swarms of officers, to harass our people, and eat out their substance.

He has kept among us, in time of peace, standing armies, without the consent of our legislatures.

He has affected to render the military independent of, and superior to, the civil power.

He has combined, with others, to subject us to a jurisdiction foreign to our Constitution, and unacknowledged by our laws; giving his assent to their acts of pretended legislation:

For quartering large bodies of armed troops among us:

For protecting them by a mock trial, from punishment, for any murders which they should commit on the inhabitants of these States:

For cutting off our trade with all parts of the world:

For imposing taxes on us without our consent:

For depriving us, in many cases, of the benefit of trial by jury:

For transporting us beyond seas to be tried for pretended offenses:

For abolishing the free system of English laws in a neighboring province, establishing therein an arbitrary government, and enlarging its boundaries, so as to render it at once an example and fit instrument for introducing the same absolute rule into these colonies:

For taking away our charters, abolishing our most valuable laws, and altering, fundamentally, the powers of our governments:

For suspending our own legislatures, and declaring themselves invested with power to legislate for us in all cases whatsoever.

He has abdicated government here, by declaring us out of his protection, and waging war against us.

He has plundered our seas, ravaged our coasts, burnt our towns, and destroyed the lives of our people.

He is, at this time, transporting large armies of foreign mercenaries to complete the works of death, desolation, and tyranny, already begun, with circumstances of cruelty and perfidy scarcely paralleled in the most barbarous ages, and totally unworthy of the head of a civilized nation.

He has constrained our fellow citizens, taken captive on the high seas, to bear arms against their country, to become the executioners of their friends, and brethren, or to fall themselves by their hands.

He has excited domestic insurrections amongst us, and has endeavored to bring on the inhabitants of our frontiers, the merciless Indian savages, whose known rule of warfare is an undistinguished destruction of all ages, sexes, and conditions.

In every stage of these oppressions, we have petitioned for redress, in the most humble terms; our repeated petitions have been answered only by repeated injury. A prince, whose character is thus marked by every act which may define a tyrant, is unfit to be the ruler of a free people.

Nor have we been wanting in attention to our British brethren. We have warned them, from time to time, of attempts made by their legislature to extend an unwarrantable jurisdiction over us. We have reminded them of the circumstances of our emigration and settlement here. We have appealed to their native justice and magnanimity, and we have conjured them, by the ties of our common kindred, to disavow these usurpations, which would inevitably interrupt our connections and correspondence. They, too, have been deaf to the voice of justice and consanguinity. We must, therefore, acquiesce in the necessity which denounces our separation, and hold them, as we hold the rest of mankind, enemies in war, in peace, friends.

We, therefore, the representatives of the United States of America, in general Congress assembled, appealing to the Supreme Judge of the world for the rectitude of our intentions, do, in the name, and by the authority of the good people of these colonies, solemnly publish and declare, that these united colonies are, and of right ought to be, free and independent states: that they are absolved from all allegiance to the British Crown, and that all political connection between them and the state of Great Britain is, and ought to be, totally dissolved; and that, as free and independent states, they have full power to levy war, conclude peace, contract alliances, establish commerce, and to do all other acts and things which independent states may of right do. And, for the support of this declaration, with a firm reliance on the protection of Divine Providence, we mutually pledge to each other our lives, our fortunes, and our sacred honor.

Appendix C

Articles of Confederation

Proposed by Congress November 15, 1777
Ratified and effective March 1, 1781

To all to whom these Presents shall come, we the undersigned Delegates of the States affixed to our Names send greeting.

Whereas the Delegates of the United States of America, in Congress assembled, did, on the fifteenth day of November in the Year of our Lord One Thousand Seven Hundred and Seventy seven, and in the Second Year of the Independence of America, agree to certain articles of Confederation and perpetual Union between the States of Newhampshire, Massachusetts-bay, Rhodeisland and Providence Plantations, Connecticut, New York, New Jersey, Pennsylvania, Delaware, Maryland, Virginia, North-Carolina, South-Carolina, and Georgia in the words followings, viz. "Articles of Confederation and perpetual Union between the states of Newhampshire, Massachusetts-bay, Rhodeisland and Providence Plantations, Connecticut, New-York, New-Jersey, Pennsylvania, Delaware, Maryland, Virginia, North-Carolina, South-Carolina and Georgia."

Article I. The Stile of this Confederacy shall be "The United States of America."

Article II. Each state retains its sovereignty, freedom, and independence, and every Power, Jurisdiction and right, which is not by this confederation expressly delegated to the United States, in Congress assembled.

Article III. The said states hereby severally enter into a firm league of friendship with each other, for their common defence, the security of their Liberties, and their mutual and general welfare, binding themselves to assist each other, against all force offered to, or attacks made upon them, or any of them, on account of religion, sovereignty, trade, or any other pretence whatever.

Article IV. The better to secure and perpetuate mutual friendship and intercourse among the people of the different states in this union, the free inhabitants of each of these states, paupers, vagabonds and fugitives from justice excepted, shall be entitled to all privileges and immunities of free citizens in the several states; and the people of each state shall have free ingress and regress to and from any other state, and shall enjoy therein all the privileges of trade and commerce, subject to the same duties, impositions and restrictions as the inhabitants thereof respectively, provided that such restrictions shall not extend so far as to prevent the removal of property imported into any state, to any other state of which the Owner is an inhabitant; provided also that no imposition, duties or restrictions shall be laid by any state, on the property of the united states, or either of them.

If any Person guilty of, or charged with treason, felony, or other high misdemeanor in any state, shall flee from justice, and be found in any of the united states, he shall, upon demand of the Governor or executive power, of the state from which he fled, be delivered up and removed to the state having jurisdiction of his offence.

Full faith and credit shall be given in each of these states to the records, acts and judicial proceedings of the courts and magistrates of every other state.

Article V. For the more convenient management of the general interests of the united states, delegates shall be annually appointed in such manner as the legislature of each state shall direct, to meet in Congress on the first Monday in November, in every year, with a power reserved to each state, to recall its delegates, or any of them, at any time within the year, and to send others in their stead, for the remainder of the Year.

No state shall be represented in Congress by less than two, nor by more than seven Members; and no person shall be capable of being a delegate for more than three years in any term of six years; nor shall any person, being a delegate, be capable of holding any office under the united states, for which he, or another of his benefit receives any salary, fees or emolument of any kind.

Each state shall maintain its own delegates in a meeting of the states, and while they act as members of the committee of the states.

In determining questions in the united states in Congress assembled, each state shall have one vote.

Freedom of speech and debate in Congress shall not be impeached or questioned in any Court, or place out of Congress, and the members of congress shall be protected in their persons from arrests and imprisonments, during the time of their going to and from, and attendance on Congress, except for treason, felony, or breach of the peace.

Article VI. No state without the Consent of the united states in congress assembled, shall send any embassy to, or receive any embassy from, or enter into any conference, agreement, alliance or treaty with any King, prince or state; nor shall any person holding any office of profit or trust under the united states, or any of them, accept of any present, emolument, office or title of any kind what ever from any king, prince or foreign state; nor shall the united states in congress assembled, or any of them, grant any title of nobility.

No two or more states shall enter into any treaty, confederation or alliance whatever between them, without the consent of the united states in congress assembled, specifying accurately the purposes for which the same is to be entered into, and how long it shall continue.

No state shall lay any imposts or duties, which may interfere with any stipulations in treaties, entered into by the United States in Congress assembled, with any king, prince or state, in pursuance of any treaties already proposed by congress, to the courts of France and Spain.

No vessels of war shall be kept up in time of peace by any state, except such number only, as shall be deemed necessary by the united states in congress assembled, for the defence of such state, or its trade; nor shall any body of forces be kept up by any state, in time of peace, except such number only, as in the judgment of the united states, in congress assembled, shall be deemed requisite to garrison the forts necessary for the defence of such state; but every state shall always keep up a well regulated and disciplined militia, sufficiently armed and accoutred, and shall provide and constantly have ready for use, in public stores, a due number of field pieces and tents, and a proper quantity of arms, ammunition and camp equipage.

No state shall engage in any war without the consent of the united states in congress assembled, unless such state be actually invaded by enemies, or shall have received certain advice of a resolution being formed by some nation of Indians to invade such state, and the danger is so imminent as not to admit of a delay till the united states in congress assembled can be consulted: nor shall any state grant commissions to any ships or vessels of war, nor letters of marque or reprisal, except it be after a declaration of war by the united states in congress assembled, and then only against the kingdom or state and the subjects thereof, against which war has been so declared, and under such regulations as shall be established by the united states in congress assembled, unless such state be infested by pirates, in which case vessels of war may be fitted out for that occasion, and kept so long as the danger shall continue, or until the united states in congress assembled, shall determine otherwise.

Article VII. When land-forces are raised by any state for the common defence, all officers of or under the rank of colonel, shall be appointed by the legislature of each state respectively, by whom such forces shall be raised, or in such manner as such state shall direct, and all vacancies shall be filled up by the State which first made the appointment.

Article VIII. All charges of war, and all other expences that shall be incurred for the common defence or general welfare, and allowed by the united states in congress assembled, shall be defrayed out of a common treasury, which shall be supplied by the several states in proportion to the value of all land within each state, granted to or surveyed for any Person, as such land and the buildings and improvements thereon shall be estimated according to such mode as the united states in congress assembled, shall from time to time direct and appoint.

The taxes for paying that proportion shall be laid and levied by the authority and direction of the legislatures of the several states within the time agreed upon by the United States in Congress assembled.

Article IX. The united states in congress assembled, shall have the sole and exclusive right and power of determining on peace and war, except in the cases mentioned in the sixth article—of sending and receiving ambassadors—entering into treaties and alliances, provided that no treaty of commerce shall be made whereby the legislative power of the respective states shall be restrained from imposing such imposts and duties on foreigners as their own people are subjected to, or from prohibiting the exploration or importation of any species of goods or commodities, whatsoever—of establishing rules for deciding in all cases, what captures on land or water shall be legal, and in what manner prizes taken by land or naval forces in the service of the united states shall be divided or appropriated—of granting letters of marque and reprisal in times of peace—appointing courts for the trial of piracies and felonies commited on the high seas and establishing courts for receiving and determining finally appeals in all cases of captures, provided that no member of congress shall be appointed a judge of any of the said courts.

The united states in congress assembled shall also be the last resort on appeal in all disputes and differences now subsisting or that hereafter may arise between two or more states concerning boundary, jurisdiction or any other cause whatever; which authority shall always be exercised in the manner following. Whenever the legislative or executive authority or lawful agent of any state in controversy with another shall present a petition to congress stating the matter in question and praying for a hearing, notice thereof shall be given by order of congress to the legislative or executive authority of the other state in controversy, and a day assigned for the appearance of the parties by their lawful agents, who shall then be directed to appoint by joint consent, commissioners or judges to constitute a court for hearing and determining the matter in question: but if they cannot agree, congress shall name three persons out of each of the united states, and from the list of such persons each party shall alternately strike out one, the petitioners beginning, until the number shall be reduced to thirteen; and from that number not less than seven, nor more than nine names as congress shall direct, shall in the presence of congress be drawn out by lot, and the persons whose names shall be so drawn or any five of them, shall be commissioners or judges, to hear and finally determine the controversy, so always as a major part of the judges who shall hear the cause shall agree in the determination: and if either party shall neglect to attend at the day appointed, without showing reasons, which congress shall judge sufficient, or being present shall refuse to strike, the congress shall proceed to nominate three persons out of each state, and the secretary of congress shall strike in behalf of such party absent or refusing; and the judgment and sentence of the court to be appointed, in the manner before prescribed, shall be final and conclusive; and if any of the parties shall refuse to submit to the authority of such court, or to appear or defend their claim or cause, the court shall nevertheless proceed to pronounce sentence, or judgment, which shall in like manner be final and decisive, the judgment or sentence and other proceedings being in either case transmitted to congress, and lodged among the acts of congress for the security of the parties concerned: provided that every commissioner, before he sits in judgment, shall take an oath to be administered by one of the judges of the supreme or superior court of the state where the cause shall be tried, "well and truly to hear and determine the matter in question, according to the best of his judgment, without favour, affection or hope of reward:" provided also, that no state shall be deprived of territory for the benefit of the united states.

All controversies concerning the private right of soil claimed under different grants of two or more states, whose jurisdictions as they may respect such lands, and the states which passed such grants are adjusted, the said grants or either of them being at the same time claimed to have originated antecedent to such settlement of jurisdiction, shall on the petition of either party to the congress of the united states, be finally determined as near as may be in the same manner as is before prescribed for deciding disputes respecting territorial jurisdiction between different states.

The united states in congress assembled shall also have the sole and exclusive right and power of regulating the alloy and value of coin struck by their own authority, or by that of the respective states—fixing the standard of weights and measures throughout the united states—regulating the trade and managing all affairs with the Indians, not members of any of the states, provided that the legislative right of any state within its own limits be not infringed or violated—establishing and regulating post-offices from one state to another, throughout all the united states, and exacting such postage on the papers passing thro' the same as may be requisite to defray the expences of the said office—appointing all officers of the land forces, in the service of the united states, excepting regimental officers—appointing all the officers of the naval forces, and commissioning all officers whatever in the service of the united states—making rules for the government and regulation of the said land and naval forces, and directing their operations.

The united states in congress assembled shall have authority to appoint a committee, to sit in the recess of congress, to be denominated "A Committee of the States," and to consist of one delegate from each state; and to appoint such other committees and civil officers as may be necessary for managing the general affairs of the united states under their direction—to appoint one of their number to preside, provided that no person be allowed to serve in the office of president more than one year in any term of three years; to ascertain the necessary sums of money to be raised for the service of the united states, and to appropriate and apply the same for defraying the public expences—to borrow money, or emit bills on the credit of the united states, transmitting every half year to the respective states on account of the sums of money so borrowed or emitted,—to build and equip a navy—to agree upon the number of land forces, and to make requisitions from each state for its quota, in proportion to the number of white inhabitants in such state; which requisition shall be binding, and thereupon the legislature of each state shall appoint the regimental officers, raise the men and cloath, arm and equip them in a soldier like manner, at the expence of the united states; and the officers and men so cloathed, armed and equipped shall march to the place appointed, and within the time agreed on by the united states in congress assembled: But if the united states in congress assembled shall, on consideration of circumstances judge proper that any state should not raise men, or should raise a smaller number than its quota, and that any other state should raise a greater number of men than the quota thereof, such extra number shall be raised, officered, cloathed, armed and equipped in the same manner as the quota of such state, unless the legislature of such state shall judge that such extra number cannot be safely spared out of the same, in which case they shall raise, officer, cloath, arm and equip as many of such extra number as they judge can be safely spared. And the officers and men so cloathed, armed and equipped, shall march to the place appointed, and within the time agreed on by the united states in congress assembled.

The united states in congress assembled shall never engage in a war, nor grant letters of marque and reprisal in time of peace, nor enter into any treaties or alliances, nor coin money, nor regulate the value thereof, nor ascertain the sums and expences necessary for the defence and welfare of the united states, or any of them, nor emit bills, nor borrow money on the credit of the united states, nor appropriate money, nor agree upon the number of vessels of war, to be built or purchased, or the number of land or sea forces to be raised, nor appoint a commander in chief of the army or navy, unless nine states assent to the same: nor shall a question on any other point, except for adjourning from day to day, be determined, unless by the votes of a majority of the united states in congress assembled.

The congress of the united states shall have power to adjourn to any time within the year, and to any place within the united states, so that no period of adjournment be for a longer duration than the space of six Months, and shall publish the journal of their proceedings monthly, except such parts thereof relating to treaties, alliances or military operations, as in their judgment require secrecy; and the yeas and nays of the delegates of each state on any question shall be entered on the Journal, when it is desired by any delegate; and the delegates of a state, or any of them, at his or their request shall be furnished with a transcript of the said Journal, except such parts as are above excepted, to lay before the legislatures of the several states.

Article X. The committee of the states, or any nine of them, shall be authorized to execute, in the recess of congress, such of the powers of congress as the united states in congress assembled, by the consent of nine states, shall from time to time think expedient to vest them with; provided that no power be delegated to the said committee, for the exercise of which, by the articles of confederation, the voice of nine states in the congress of the united states assembled is requisite.

Article XI. Canada acceding to this confederation, and joining in the measures of the united states, shall be admitted into, and entitled to all the advantages of this union: but no other colony shall be admitted into the same, unless such admission be agreed to by nine states.

Article XII. All bills of credit emitted, monies borrowed and debts contracted by, or under the authority of Congress, before the assembling of the united states, in pursuance of the present confederation, shall be deemed and considered as a charge against the united states, for payment and satisfaction whereof the said united states, and the public faith are hereby solemnly pledged.

Article XIII. Every state shall abide by the determinations of the united states in congress assembled, on all questions which by this confederation are submitted to them. And the Articles of this confederation shall be inviolably observed by every state, and the union shall be perpetual; nor shall any alteration at any time hereafter be made in any of them; unless such alteration be agreed to in a congress of the united states, and be afterwards confirmed by the legislatures of every state.

And Whereas it has pleased the Great Governor of the World to incline the hearts of the legislatures we respectively represent in congress, to approve of, and to authorize us to ratify the said articles of confederation and perpetual union. Know Ye that we the undersigned delegates, by virtue of the power and authority to us given for that purpose, do by these presents, in the name and in behalf of our respective constituents, fully and entirely ratify and confirm each and every of the said articles of confederation and perpetual union, and all and singular the matters and things therein contained: And we do further solemnly plight and engage the faith of our respective constituents, that they shall abide by the determinations of the united states in congress assembled, on all questions, which by the said confederation are submitted to them. And that the articles thereof shall be inviolably observed by the states we respectively represent, and that the union shall be perpetual. In Witness whereof we have hereunto set our hands in Congress. Done at Philadelphia in the state of Pennsylvania the ninth day of July, in the year of our Lord one Thousand seven Hundred and Seventy-eight, and in the third year of the independence of America. [Names omitted]

Appendix D

The Federalist No. 10 (Madison)(1787)

TO THE PEOPLE OF THE STATE OF NEW YORK:

Among the numerous advantages promised by a well-constructed Union, none deserves to be more accurately developed than its tendency to break and control the violence of faction. The friend of popular governments never finds himself so much alarmed for their charter and fate, as when he contemplates their propensity to this dangerous vice. [The] instability, injustice, and confusion introduced into the public councils, have, in truth, been the mortal diseases under which popular governments have everywhere perished; as they continue to be the favorite and fruitful topics from which the adversaries to liberty derive their most specious declamations. [Complaints] are everywhere heard from our most considerate and virtuous citizens, equally the friends of public and private faith, and of public and personal liberty, that our governments are too unstable, that the public good is disregarded in the conflicts of rival parties, and that measures are too often decided, not according to the rules of justice and the rights of the minor party, but by the superior force of an interested and overbearing majority. However, anxiously we may wish that these complaints had no foundation, the evidence of known facts will not permit us to deny that they are in some degree true. [The] distresses under which we labor [must] be chiefly, if not wholly, effects of the unsteadiness and injustice with which a factious spirit has tainted our public administrations.

By a faction, I understand a number of citizens, whether amounting to a majority or minority of the whole, who are united and actuated by some common impulse of passion, or of interest, adverse to the rights of other citizens, or to the permanent and aggregate interests of the community.

There are two methods of curing the mischiefs of faction: the one, by removing its causes; the other, by controlling its effects.

There are again two methods of removing the causes of actions: the one by destroying the liberty which is essential to its existence; the other, by giving to every citizen the same opinions, the same passions, and the same interests.

It could never be more truly said than of the first remedy, that it was worse than the disease. Liberty is to faction what air is to fire, an aliment without which it instantly expires. But it could not be less folly to abolish liberty, which is essential to political life, because it nourishes faction, than it would be to wish the annihilation of air, which is essential to animal life, because it imparts to fire its destructive agency.

The second expedient is as impracticable as the first would be unwise. As long as the reason of man continues fallible, and he is at liberty to exercise it, different opinions will be formed. As long as the connection subsists between his reason and his self-love, his opinions and his passions will have a reciprocal influence on each other; and the former will be objects to which the latter will attach themselves. The diversity in the faculties of men, from which the rights of property originate, is not less an insuperable obstacle to a uniformity of interests. The protection of these faculties is the first object of government. From the protection of different and unequal faculties of acquiring property, the possession of different degrees and kinds of property immediately results; and from the influence of these on the sentiments and views of the respective proprietors, ensues a division of the society into different interests and parties.

The latent causes of faction are thus sown in the nature of man; and we see them everywhere brought into different degrees of activity, according to the different circumstances of civil society. A zeal for different opinions, concerning religion, concerning government, and many other points, as well as speculation as of practice; an attachment to different leaders ambitiously contending for preeminence and power; or to persons of other descriptions whose fortunes have been interesting to the human passions, have, in turn, divided mankind into parties, inflamed them with mutual animosity, and rendered them much more disposed to vex and oppress each other than to co-operate for their common good. So strong is this propensity of mankind to fall into mutual animosities, that where no substantial occasion presents itself, the most frivolous and fanciful distinctions have been sufficient to kindly their unfriendly passions and excite their most violent conflicts. But the most common and durable source of factions has been the various and unequal distribution of property. Those who hold and those who are without property have ever formed distinct interests in society. Those who are creditors, and those who are debtors, fall under a like discrimination. A landed interest, a manufacturing interest, a mercantile interest, a moneyed interest, with many lesser interests, grow up of necessity in civilized nations, and divide them into different classes, actuated by different sentiments and views. The regulation of these various and interfering interests forms the principal task of modern legislation, and involves the spirit of party and faction in the necessary and ordinary operations of the government.

No man is allowed to be a judge in his own cause, because his interest would certainly bias his judgment, and, not improbably, corrupt his integrity. With equal, nay with greater reason, a body of men are unfit to be both judges and parties at the same time; yet what are many of the most important acts of legislation, but so many judicial determinations, not indeed concerning the rights, of single persons, but concerning the rights of large bodies of citizens? And what are the different classes of legislators but advocates and parties to the cause which they determine? Is a law proposed concerning private debts? It is a question to which the creditors are parties on one side and the debtors on the other. Justice ought to hold the balance between them. Yet the parties are, and must be, themselves, the judges; and the most numerous party, or, in other words, the most powerful faction must be expected to prevail. Shall domestic manufacturers be encouraged, and in what degree, by restrictions on foreign manufactures? are questions which would be differently decided by the landed and the manufacturing classes and probably by neither with a sole regard to justice and the public good.

It is in vain to say that enlightened statesmen will be able to adjust these clashing interests, and render them all subservient to the public good. Enlightened statesmen will not always be at the helm. . . .

The inference to which we are brought is, that the *causes* of faction cannot be removed, and that relief is only to be sought in the means of controlling its *effects*.

If a faction consists of less than a majority, relief is supplied by the republican principle, which enables the majority to defeat its sinister views by regular vote. It may clog the administration, it may convulse the society; but it will be unable to execute and mask its violence under the forms of the Constitution. When a majority is included in a faction, the form of popular government, on the other hand, enables it to sacrifice to its ruling passion or interest both the public good and the rights of other citizens. To secure the public good and private rights against the danger of such a faction, and at the same time to preserve the spirit and the form of popular government, is then the great object to which our inquiries are directed. Let me add that it is the great *desideratum* by which this form of government can be rescued from the *opprobrium* under which it has so long labored, and be recommended to the esteem and adoption of mankind.

By what means is this object attainable? Evidently by one of two only. Either by the existence of the same passion or interest in a majority at the same time must be prevented, or the majority, having such coexistent passion or interest, must be rendered, by their number and local situation, unable to concert and carry into effect schemes of oppression. If the impulse and the opportunity be suffered to coincide, we well know that neither moral nor religious motives can be relied on as an adequate control. They are not found to be such on the injustice and violence of individuals, and lose their efficacy in proportion to the number combined together, that is, in proportion as their efficacy becomes needful.

From this view of the subject it may be concluded that a pure democracy, by which I mean a society consisting of a small number of citizens, who assemble and administer the government in person, can admit of no cure for the mischiefs of faction. A common passion or interest will, in almost every case, be felt by a majority of the whole; a communication and concert result from the form of government itself; and there is nothing to check the inducements to sacrifice the waker party or an obnoxious individual. Hence it is that such democracies have ever been spectacles of turbulence and contention; have ever been found incompatible with personal security or the rights of property; and have in general been as short in their lives as they have been violent in their deaths. Theoretic politicians, who have patronized this species of government, have erroneously supposed that by reducing mankind to a perfect equality in their political rights, they would, at the same time, be perfectly equalized and assimilated in their possessions, their opinion, and their passions.

A republic, by which I mean a government in which the scheme of representation takes place, opens a different prospect, and promises the cure for which we are seeking. . . .

The two great points of difference between a democracy and a republic are: first, the delegation of the government, in the latter, to a small number of citizens elected by the rest; secondly, the greater number of citizens, and greater sphere of country, over which the latter may be extended.

The effect of the first difference is, on the one hand, to refine and enlarge the public views, by passing them through the medium of a chosen body of citizens, whose wisdom may best discern the true interest of their country, and whose patriotism and love of justice will be least likely to sacrifice it to temporary or partial considerations. Under such a regulation, it may well happen that the public voice, pronounced by the representatives of the people, will be more consonant to the public good than if pronounced by the people themselves, convened for the purpose. On the other hand, the effect may be inverted. Men of factious tempers, of local prejudices, or of sinister designs, may, by intrigue, by corruption, or by other means, first obtain the suffrages, and then betray the interests of the people. The question resulting is whether small or extensive republics are more favorable to the election of proper guardians of the public weal; and it is clearly decided in favor of the latter by two obvious considerations.

In the first place, it is to be remarked that, however small the republic may be, the representatives must be raised to a certain number, in order to guard against the cabals of a few; and that, however large it may be, they must be limited to a certain number, in order to guard against the confusion of a multitude. Hence the number of representatives in the two cases not being in proportion to that of the two constituents, and being proportionally greater in the small republic, it follows that, if the proportion of fit characters be not less in the large than in the small republic, the former will present a greater option, and consequently a greater probability of a fit choice.

In the next place, as each representative will be chosen by a greater number of citizens in the large than in the small republic, it will be more difficult for unworthy candidates to practice with success the vicious arts by which elections are too often carried; and the suffrages of the people being more free, will be more likely to centre in men who possess the most attractive merit and the most diffusive and established characters.

It must be confessed that in this, as in most other cases, there is a mean, on both sides of which inconveniences will be found to lie. By enlarging too much the numbers of electors, you render the representative too little acquainted with all their local circumstances and lesser interests as by reducing it too much, you render him unduly attached to these, and too little fit to comprehend and pursue great and national objects. The federal Constitution forms a happy combination in this respect; the great and aggregate interest being referred to the national, the local and particular to the State legislatures. The other point of difference is, the greater number of citizens and extent of territory which may be brought within the compass of republican than of democratic government; and it is this circumstance principally which renders factious combinations less to be dreaded in the former than in the latter. The smaller the society, the fewer probably will be the distinct parties and interests composing it; the fewer the distinct parties and interests, the more frequently will a majority be found of the same party; and the smaller the number of individuals composing a majority, and the smaller the compass within which they are placed, the more easily will they concert and execute their plans of oppression. Extend the sphere, and you take in a greater variety of parties and interests; you make it less probable that a majority of the whole will have a common motive to invade the rights of other citizens; or if such a common motive exists, it will be more difficult for all who feel it to discover their own strength, and to act in unison with each other. Besides other impediments, it may be remarked that, where there is a consciousness of unjust or dishonorable purposes, communication is always checked by distrust in proportion to the number whose concurrence is necessary.

Hence, it clearly appears, that the same advantage which a republic has over a democracy, in controlling the effects of faction, is enjoyed by a large over a small republic,—is enjoyed by the Union over the States composing it. Does the advantage consist in the substitution of representatives whose enlightened views and virtuous sentiments render them superior to local prejudices and to schemes of injustice? It will not be denied that the representation of the Union will be most likely to possess these requisite endowments. Does it consist in the greater security afforded by a greater variety of parties, against the event of any one party being able to outnumber and oppress the rest? In an equal degree does the increased variety of parties comprised within the Union, increase this security. Does it, in fine, consist in the greater obstacles opposed to the concert and accomplishment of the secret wishes of an unjust and interested majority?Here, again, the extent of the Union gives it the most palpable advantage.

The influence of factious leaders may kindle a flame within their particular States, but will be unable to spread a general conflagration through the other States. A religious sect may degenerate into a political faction in a part of the Confederacy; but the variety of sects dispersed over the entire face of it must secure the national councils against any danger from that source. A rage for paper money, for an abolition of debts, for an equal division of property, or for any other improper or wicked project will be less apt to pervade the whole body of the Union than a particular member of it; in the same proportion as such a malady is more likely to taint a particular county or district, than an entire State.

In the extent and proper structure of the Union, therefore, we behold a republican remedy for the diseases most incident to republican government. And according to the degree of pleasure and pride we feel in being republicans, ought to be our zeal in cherishing the spirit and supporting the character of Federalists.

Publius

Appendix E

The Federalist No. 51 (Hamilton or Madison) (1788)

In order to lay a due foundation for that separate and distinct exercise of the different powers of government, which to a certain extent is admitted on all hands to be essential to the preservation of liberty, it is evident that each department should have a will of its own; and consequently should be so constituted that the members of each should have as little agency as possible in the appointment of the members of the others. Were this principle rigorously adhered to, it would require that all the appointments for the supreme executive, legislative, and judiciary magistracies should be drawn from the same fountain of authority, the people, through channels having no communication whatever with one another. [Some] difficulties, and some additional expense would attend the execution of it. Some deviations, therefore, from the principle must be admitted. In the constitution of the judiciary department in particular, it might be inexpedient to insist rigorously on the principle: first, because peculiar qualifications being essential in the members, the primary consideration ought to be to select that mode of choice which best secures these qualifications; secondly, because the permanent tenure by which the appointments are held in that department, must soon destroy all sense of dependence on the authority conferring them.

It is equally evident, that the members of each department should be as little dependent as possible on those of the others, for the *emoluments* annexed to their offices. Were the executive magistrate, or the judges, not independent of the legislature in this particular, their independence in every other would be merely nominal.

But the great security against a gradual concentration of the several powers in the same department, consists in giving to those who administer each department the necessary constitutional means and personal motives to resist encroachments of the others. The provision for defence must in this, as in all other cases, be made commensurate to the danger of attack. Ambition must be made to counteract ambition. The interest of the man must be connected with the constitutional rights of the place. It may be a reflection on human nature, that such devices should be necessary to control the abuses of government. But what is government itself, but the greatest of all reflections on human nature? If angels were to govern men, neither external nor internal controls on government would be necessary. In framing a government which is to be administered by men over men, the great difficulty lies in this: you must first enable the government to control the governed; and in the next place oblige it to control itself. A dependence on the people is, no doubt, the primary control on the government; but 4experience has taught mankind the necessity of auxiliary precautions.

This policy of supplying, by opposite and rival interests, the defect of better motives, might be traced through the whole system of human affairs, private as well as public. We see it particularly displayed in all the subordinate distributions of power, where the constant aim is to divide and arrange the several offices in such a manner as that each may be a check on the other—that the private interest of every individual may be a sentinel over the public rights. These inventions of prudence cannot be less requisite in the distribution of the supreme powers of the State.

But it is not possible to give to each department an equal power of self-defence. In republican government, the legislative authority necessarily predominates. The remedy for this inconveniency is to divide the legislature into different branches; and to render them, by different modes of election and different principles of action, as little connected with each other as the nature of their common functions and their common dependence on the society will admit. It may even be necessary to guard against dangerous encroachments by still further precautions. As the weight of the legislative authority requires that it should be thus divided, the weakness of the executive may require, on the other hand, that it should be fortified. An absolute negative on the legislature appears, at first view, to be the natural defence with which the executive magistrate should be armed. But perhaps it would be neither altogether safe nor alone sufficient. On ordinary occasions it might not be exerted with the requisite firmness, and on extraordinary occasions it might be perfidiously abused. May not this defect of an absolute negative be supplied by some qualified connection between this weaker department and the weaker branch of the stronger department, by which the latter may be led to support the constitutional rights of the former, without being too much detached from the rights of its own department?

There are, moreover, two considerations particularly applicable to the federal system of America, which place that system in a very interesting point of view.

First. In a single republic, all the power surrendered by the people is submitted to the administration of a single government; and the usurpations are guarded against by a division of the government into distinct and separate departments. In the compound republic of America, the power surrendered by the people is first divided between two distinct governments, and then the portion allotted to each subdivided among distinct and separate departments. Hence a double security arises to the rights of the people. The different governments will control each other, at the same time that each will be controlled by itself.

Second. It is of great importance in a republic not only to guard the society against the oppression of its rulers, but to guard one part of the society against the injustice of the other part. Different interests necessarily exist in different classes of citizens. If a majority be united by a common interest, the rights of the minority will be insecure. There are but two methods of providing against this evil: the one by creating a will in the community independent of the majority—that is, of the society itself; the other, by comprehending in the society so many separate descriptions of citizens as will render an unjust combination of a majority of the whole very improbable, if not impracticable. The first method [is] but a precarious security; because a power independent of the society may as well espouse the unjust views of the major, as the rightful interests of the minor party, and may possible be turned against both parties. The second method will be exemplified in the federal republic of the United States. Whilst all authority in it will be derived from and dependent on the society, the society itself will be broken into so many parts,, interests and classes of citizens, that the rights of individuals, or of the minority, will be in little danger from interested combinations of the majority. In a free government the security for civil rights must be the same as that for religious rights. It consists in the one case in the multiplicity of interests, and in the other in the multiplicity of sects. The degree of security in both cases will depend on the number of interests and sects; and this may be presumed to depend on the extent of country and number of people comprehended under the same government. This view of the subject must particularly recommend a proper federal system to all the sincere and considerate friends of republican government, since it shows that in exact proportion as the territory of the Union may be formed into more circumscribed Confederacies, or States, oppressive combinations of a majority will be facilitated; the best security, under the republican forms, for the rights of every class of citizens, will be diminished; and consequently the stability and independence of some member of the government the only other security, must be proportionally increased.

[In] a society under the forms of which the stronger faction can readily unite and oppress the weaker, anarchy may as truly be said to reign as in a state of nature, where the weaker individual is not secured against the violence of the stronger; and as, in the latter state, even the stronger individuals are prompted, by the uncertainty of their condition, to submit to a government which may protect the weak as well as themselves; so, in the former state, will the more powerful factions or parties be gradually induced, by a like motive, to wish for a government which will protect all parties, the weaker as well as the more powerful. It can be little doubted that if the State of Rhode Island was separated from the Confederacy and left to itself, the insecurity of rights under the popular form of government, within such narrow limits would be displayed by such reiterated oppressions of factious majorities that some power altogether independent of the people would soon be called for by the voice of the very factions whose misrule had proved the necessity of it. In the extended republic of the United States, and among the great variety of interests, parties, and sects which it embraces, a coalition of a majority of the whole society could seldom take place on any other principles than those of justice and the general good; whilst there being thus less danger to a minor from the will of a major party, there must be less pretext, also, to provide for the security of the former, by introducing into the government a will not dependent on the latter, or, in other words, a will independent of the society itself. It is no less certain than it is important, notwithstanding the contrary opinions which have been entertained, that the larger the society, provided it lie within a practical sphere, the more duly capable it will be of self-government. And happily for the *republican cause*, the practicable sphere may be carried to a very great extent, by a judicious modification and mixture of the *federal principle*.

Publius

Index Guide to the Constitution

PREAMBLE

ARTICLE I. The Legislative Department. Organization of Congress and terms, qualifications, appointment, and election of Senators and Representatives. Procedure in impeachment. Privileges of the two houses and of their members. Procedure in lawmaking. Powers of Congress. Limitations on Congress and on the States.

ARTICLE II. The Executive Department. Election of President and Vice President. Powers and duties of the President. Ratification of appointments and treaties. Liability of officers to impeachment.

ARTICLE III. The Judicial Department. Independence of the judiciary. Jurisdiction of national courts. Guarantee of jury trial. Definition of treason.

ARTICLE IV. Position of the States and territories.

Full faith and credit to acts and judicial proceedings. Privileges and immunities of citizens of the several States. Rendition of fugitives from justice. Control of territories by Congress. Guarantees to the States.

ARTICLE V. Method of amendment.

ARTICLE VI. Supremacy of the Constitution, laws, and treaties of the United States. Oath of office—prohibition of a religious test.

ARTICLE VII. Method of ratification of the Constitution.
AMENDMENTS

I.   Freedom of religion, speech, press and assembly; right of petition.

II.   Right to keep and bear arms.

III.   Limitations in quartering soldiers.

IV.   Protection from unreasonable searches and seizures.

V.   Due process in criminal cases. Limitation on right of eminent domain.

VI.	Right to speedy trial by jury, and other guarantees.
VII.	Trial by jury in suits at law.
VIII.	Excessive bail or unusual punishments forbidden.
IX.	Retention of certain rights by the people.
X.	Undelegated powers belong to the States or to the people.
XI.	Exemption of States from suit by individuals.
XII.	New method of electing President.
XIII.	Abolition of slavery
XIV.	Definition of citizenship.Guarantees of due process and equal protection against State action. Apportionment of Representatives in Congress. Validity of public debt.
XV.	Extension of suffrage to colored persons.
XVI.	Tax on incomes "from whatever source derived."
XVII.	Popular election of Senators.
XVIII.	Prohibition of intoxicating liquors.
XIX.	Extension of suffrage to women.
XX.	Abolition of "lame duck" session of Congress. Change in presidential and congressional terms.
XXI.	Repeal of 18th Amendment.
XXII.	Limitation of President's terms in office.
XXIII.	Extension of suffrage to District of Columbia in presidential elections.
XXIV.	Abolition of poll tax requirement in national elections.
XXV.	Presidential succession and disability provisions.
XXVI.	Extension of suffrage to 18-year olds.

Appendix F

The Constitution of The United States of America

Proposed by Convention September 17, 1787
Effective March 4, 1789
The original spelling, capitalization, and punctuation have been retained in this version.

We the People of the United States, in Order to form a more perfect Union, establish Justice, insure domestic Tranquility, provide for the common defence, promote the general Welfare, and secure the Blessings of Liberty to ourselves and our Posterity, do ordain and establish this CONSTITUTION for the United States of America.

Article I

Section 1. All legislative Powers herein granted shall be vested in a Congress of the United States, which shall consist of a Senate and House of Representatives.

Section 2. The House of Representatives shall be composed of Members chosen every second Year by the People of the several States, and the Electors in each State shall have the Qualifications requisite for Electors of the most numerous Branch of the State Legislature.

No Person shall be a Representative who shall not have attained to the Age of twenty-five Years, and been seven Years a Citizen of the United States, and who shall not, when elected, be an Inhabitant of that state in which he shall be chosen.

Representatives and direct Taxes shall be apportioned among the several States which may be included within this Union, according to their respective Numbers, which shall be determined by adding to the whole Number of free Persons, including those bound to Service for a Term of Years, and excluding Indians not taxed, three fifths of all other Persons. The actual Enumeration shall be made within three Years after the first Meeting of the Congress of the United States, and within every subsequent Term of ten Years, in such

Manner as they shall by Law direct. The Number of Representatives shall not exceed one for every thirty Thousand, but each State shall have at Least one Representative; and until such enumeration shall be made, the State of New Hampshire shall be entitled to chuse three, Massachusetts eight, Rhode-Island and Providence Plantations one, Connecticut five, New York six, New Jersey four, Pennsylvania eight, Delaware one, Maryland six, Virginia ten, North Carolina five, South Carolina five, and Georgia three.

When vacancies happen in the Representation from any State, the Executive Authority thereof shall issue Writs of Election to fill such Vacancies.

The House of Representatives shall chuse their Speaker and other Officers; and shall have the sole Power of Impeachment.

Section 3. The Senate of the United States shall be composed of two Senators from each State, chosen by the Legislature thereof, for six Years; and each Senator shall have one Vote.

Immediately after they shall be assembled in Consequence of the first Election, they shall be divided as equally as may be into three Classes. The Seats of the Senators of the first Class shall be vacated at the Expiration of the second Year, of the second Class at the Expiration of the fourth Year, and of the third Class at the Expiration of the sixth Year, so that one-third may be chosen every second Year; and if Vacancies happen by Resignation, or otherwise, during the Recess of the Legislature of any State, the Executive thereof may make temporary Appointments until the next Meeting of the Legislature, which shall then fill such Vacancies.

No Person shall be a Senator who shall not have attained to the Age of thirty Years, and been nine Years a Citizen of the United States, and who shall not, when elected, be an Inhabitant of that State for which he shall be chosen.

The Vice President of the United States shall be President of the Senate, but shall have no vote, unless they be equally divided.

The Senate shall chuse their other Officers, and also a President pro tempore, in the absence of the Vice President, or when he shall exercise the Office of the President of the United States.

The Senate shall have the sole Power to try all Impeachments. When sitting for that purpose they shall be on Oath or Affirmation. When the President of the United States is tried, the Chief Justice shall preside: And no person shall be convicted without the Concurrence of two thirds of the Members present.

Judgment in Cases of Impeachment shall not extend further than to removal from Office, and disqualification to hold and enjoy any Office of honor, Trust, or Profit under the United States: but the Party convicted shall nevertheless be liable and subject to Indictment, Trial, Judgment, and Punishment, according to Law.

Section 4. The Times, Places and Manner of holding Elections for Senators and Representatives, shall be prescribed in each State by the

Legislature thereof; but the Congress may at any time by Law make or alter such Regulations, except as to the Places of Chusing Senators.

The Congress shall assemble at least once in every Year, and such Meeting shall be on the first Monday in December, unless they shall by Law appoint a different Day.

Section 5. Each House shall be the Judge of the Elections, Returns and Qualifications of its own Members, and a Majority of each shall constitute a Quorum to do Business; but a smaller number may adjourn from day to day, and may be authorized to compel the Attendance of absent Members, in such Manner, and under such Penalties, as each House may provide.

Each House may determine the Rules of its Proceedings, punish its Members for disorderly Behaviour, and, with the Concurrence of two thirds, expel a Member.

Each House shall keep a Journal of its Proceedings, and from time to time publish the same, excepting such Parts as may in their Judgment require Secrecy; and the Yeas and Nays of the Members of either House on any question shall, at the Desire of one fifth of those Present, be entered on the Journal.

Neither House, during the Session of Congress, shall, without the Consent of the other, adjourn for more than three days, nor to any other Place than that in which the two Houses shall be sitting.

Section 6. The Senators and Representatives shall receive a Compensation for their Services, to be ascertained by Law, and paid out of the Treasury of the United States. They shall in all Cases, except Treason, Felony, and Breach of the Peace, be privileged from Arrest during their Attendance at the Session of their respective Houses, and in going to and returning from the same; and for any Speech or Debate in either House, they shall not be questioned in any other Place.

No Senator or Representative shall, during the Time for which he was elected, be appointed to any civil Office under the Authority of the United States, which shall have been created, or the Emoluments whereof shall have been increased, during such time; and no Person holding any Office under the United States shall be a Member of either House during his continuance in Office.

Section 7. All Bills for raising Revenue shall originate in the House of Representatives; but the Senate may propose or concur with Amendments as on other bills.

Every Bill which shall have passed the House of Representatives and the Senate, shall, before it become a Law, be presented to the President of the United States; If he approve he shall sign it, but if not he shall return it, with his Objections, to that House in which it shall have originated, who shall enter the objections at large on their Journal, and proceed to reconsider it. If after such Reconsideration two thirds of that House shall agree to pass the bill, it shall be sent, together with the Objections, to the other House, by which it shall likewise be reconsidered, and if approved by two thirds of that House, it shall become a Law. But in all such Cases the Votes of both Houses shall be determined by Yeas and Nays, and the Names of the Persons voting for and against the Bill shall be entered on the Journal of each House respectively. If any Bill shall not be returned by the President within ten Days (Sundays excepted) after it shall have been presented to him, the Same shall be a Law, in like Manner as if he had signed it, unless the Congress by their Adjournment prevent its Return, in which Case it shall not be a Law.

Every Order, Resolution, or Vote to which the Concurrence of the Senate and House of Representatives may be necessary (except on a question of Adjournment) shall be presented to the President of the United States; and before the Same shall take Effect, shall be approved by him, or being disapproved by him, shall be repassed by two thirds of the Senate and House of Representatives, according to the Rules and Limitations prescribed in the Case of a Bill.

Section 8. The Congress shall have Power To lay and collect Taxes, Duties, Imposts and Excises, to pay the Debts and provide for the common Defence and general Welfare of the United States; but all Duties, and Excises shall be uniform throughout the United States;

To borrow money on the credit of the United States;

To regulate Commerce with foreign Nations, and among the several States, and with the Indian Tribes;

To establish an uniform rule of Naturalization, and uniform Laws on the subject of Bankruptcies throughout the United States;

To coin Money, regulate the Value thereof, and of foreign Coin, and fix the Standard of Weights and measures;

To provide for the Punishment of counterfeiting the Securities and current Coin of the United States;

To establish Post Offices and post Roads;

To promote the Progress of Science and useful Arts, by securing for limited Times to Authors and Inventors the exclusive Right to their respective Writings and Discoveries;

To constitute Tribunals inferior to the Supreme Court;

To define and punish Piracies and Felonies committed on the high Seas, and Offenses against the Law of Nations;

To declare War, grant Letters of Marque and Reprisal, and make Rules concerning Captures on Land and Water;

To raise and support Armies, but no Appropriation of Money to that Use shall be for a longer Term than two Years;

To provide and maintain a Navy;

To make Rules for the Government and Regulation of the land and naval forces;

To provide for calling forth the Militia to execute the Laws of the Union, suppress Insurrections and repel Invasions;

To provide for organizing, arming, and disciplining the Militia, and for governing such Part of them as may be employed in Service of the United States, reserving to the States respectively, the Appointment of the Officers, and the Authority of training the Militia according to the discipline prescribed by Congress;

To exercise exclusive Legislation in all Cases whatsoever, over such District (not exceeding ten Miles square) as may, by Cession of particular States, and the acceptance of Congress, become the Seat of the Government of the United States, and to exercise like Authority over all Places purchased by the Consent of the Legislature of the State in which the Same shall be, for the Erection of Forts, Magazines, Arsenals, Dock-yards, and other needful Building;—And

To make all Laws which shall be necessary and proper for carrying into Execution the foregoing Powers, and all other Powers vested by this Constitution in the Government of the United States, or in any Department or Officer thereof.

Section 9. The Migration or Importation of such Persons as any of the States now existing shall think proper to admit, shall not be prohibited by the Congress prior to the Year one thousand eight hundred and eight, but a tax or duty may be imposed on such Importation, not exceeding ten dollars for each Person.

The privilege of the Writ of Habeas Corpus shall not be suspended, unless when in Cases of Rebellion or Invasion the public Safety may require it.

No bill of Attainder or ex post facto Law shall be passed.

No capitation, or other direct, Tax shall be laid unless in Proportion to the Census or Enumeration herein before directed to be taken.

No Tax or Duty shall be laid on Articles exported from any State.

No Preference shall be given by any Regulation of Commerce or Revenue to the Ports of one State over those of another: nor shall Vessels bound to, or from, one State, be obliged to enter, clear, or pay Duties in another.

No Money shall be drawn from the Treasury, but in Consequence of Appropriations made by Law; and a regular Statement and Account of the Receipts and Expenditures of all public Money shall be published from time to time.

No Title of Nobility shall be granted by the United States: And no Person holding any Office of Profit or Trust under them, shall, without the Consent of the Congress, accept of any present, Emolument, Office, or Title, of any kind whatever, from any King, Prince, or foreign State.

Section 10. No State shall enter into any Treaty, Alliance, or Confederation; grant Letters of Marque and Reprisal; coin Money; emit Bills of Credit;

make any Thing but gold and silver Coin a Tender in Payment of Debts; pass any Bill Attainder, ex post facto Law, or Law impairing the Obligation of Contracts, or grant any title of Nobility.

No State shall, without the Consent of the Congress, lay any Imposts or Duties on Imports or Exports, except what may be absolutely necessary for executing its inspection Laws; and the net Produce of all Duties and Imposts, laid by any State on Imports or Exports, shall be for the use of the Treasury of the United States; and all such Laws shall be subject to the Revision and Control of the Congress.

No state shall, without the Consent of Congress, lay any duty of Tonnage, keep Troops, or Ships of War in time of Peace, enter into any Agreement or Compact with another State, or with a foreign Power, or engage in War, unless actually invaded, or in such imminent Danger as will not admit of delay.

Article II

Section 1. The executive Power shall be vested in a President of the United States of America. He shall hold his Office during the Term of four years, and, together with the Vice president, chosen for the same Term, be elected, as follows:

Each State shall appoint, in such Manner as the legislature thereof may direct, a Number of Electors, equal to the whole Number of Senators and Representatives to which the State may be entitled in the Congress: but no Senator or Representative, or Person holding an Office of Trust or Profit under the United States, shall be appointed an Elector.

The Electors shall meet in their respective States, and vote by Ballot for two persons, of whom one at least shall not be an Inhabitant of the same State with themselves. And they shall make a List of all the Persons voted for, and of the Number of Votes for each; which List they shall sign and certify, and transmit sealed to the Seat of the Government of the United States, directed to the President of the Senate. The President of the Senate shall, in the Presence of the Senate and House of Representatives, open all the Certificates, and the Votes shall then be counted. The Person having the greatest Number of Votes shall be the President, if such Number be a Majority of the whole Number of Electors appointed; and if there be more than one who have such Majority, and have an equal Number of Votes, then the House of Representatives shall immediately chuse by Ballot one of them for President; and if no Person have a majority, then from the five highest on the List the said House shall in like Manner chuse the President. But in chusing the President, the Votes shall be taken by States, the Representation from each State having one Vote; a quorum for this Purpose shall consist of a Member or Members from two-thirds of the States, and a Majority of all the states shall be necessary to a Choice. In every Case, after the Choice of the President, the Person having the greatest Number of Votes of the Electors shall be the Vice President. But if there should remain two or more who have equal votes, the Senate shall chuse from them by Ballot the Vice President.

The Congress may determine the Time of chusing the Electors, and the Day on which they shall give their Votes; which Day shall be the same throughout the United States.

No person except a natural-born Citizen, or a Citizen of the United States, at the time of the Adoption of this Constitution, shall be eligible to the Office of President; neither shall any Person be eligible to that Office who shall not have attained to the Age of thirty-five Years, and been fourteen Years a Resident within the United States.

In Case of the Removal of the President from Office, or of his Death, Resignation, or Inability to discharge the Powers and Duties of the said Office, the same shall devolve on the Vice President, and the Congress may by Law provide for the Case of Removal, Death, Resignation, or Inability, both of the President and Vice President, declaring what Officer shall then act as President, and such Officer shall act accordingly, until the disability be removed or a President shall be elected.

The President shall, at stated Times, receive for his Services a Compensation, which shall neither be increased nor diminished during the Period for which he shall have been elected, and he shall not receive within that Period any other Emolument from the United States, or any of them.

Before he enter on the execution of his Office, he shall take the following Oath or Affirmation:—"I do solemnly swear (or affirm) that I will faithfully execute the Office of President of the United States, and will, to the best of my Ability, preserve, protect, and defend the Constitution of the United States."

Section 2. The President shall be Commander in Chief of the Army and Navy of the United States, and of the Militia of the several States, when called into the actual Service of the United States; he may require the Opinion, in writing, of the principal Officer in each of the executive Departments, upon any subject relating to the Duties of their respective Offices, and he shall have power to Grant Reprieves and Pardons for Offenses against the United States, except in Cases of Impeachment.

He shall have Power, by and with Advice and Consent of the Senate, to make Treaties, provided two thirds of the Senators present concur; and he shall nominate, and by and with the Advice and Consent of the Senate, shall appoint Ambassadors, other public Ministers and Consuls, Judges of the supreme Court, and all other Officers of the United States, whose Appointments are not herein otherwise provided for, and which shall be established by Law: but the Congress may by Law vest the Appointment of such inferior Officers, as they think proper, in the President alone, in the Courts of Law, or in the Heads of Departments.

The President shall have Power to fill up all Vacancies that may happen during the Recess of the Senate, by granting Commissions which shall expire at the End of their next Session.

Section 3. He shall from time to time give to the Congress Information of the State of the Union, and recommend to their Consideration such Measures as he shall judge necessary and expedient; he may, on extraordinary occasions, convene both Houses, or either of them, and in Case of Disagreement between them, with respect to the Time of Adjournment, he may adjourn them to such Time as he shall think proper; he shall receive Ambassadors and other public Ministers; he shall take care that the Laws be faithfully executed, and shall Commission all the Officers of the United States.

Section 4. The President, Vice President and all civil Officers of the United States, shall be removed from Office on Impeachment for, and Conviction of, Treason, Bribery, or other high Crimes and Misdemeanors.

Article III

Section 1. The judicial Power of the United States, shall be vested in one supreme Court, and in such inferior Courts as the Congress may from time to time ordain and establish. The Judges, both of the supreme and inferior Courts, shall hold their Offices during good Behaviour, and shall, at stated Times, receive for their Services, a Compensation, which shall not be diminished during their Continuance in Office.

Section 2. The judicial Power shall extend to all Cases, in Law and Equity, arising under this Constitution, the Laws of the United States, and Treaties made, or which shall be made, under their Authority; — to all Cases affecting Ambassadors, other public Ministers and Consuls;—to all cases of admiralty and maritime Jurisdiction;—to Controversies to which the United States shall be a Party; — to Controversies between two or more States;— between a State and Citizens of another State;—between Citizens of different States:—between Citizens of the same State claiming Land's under Grants of different States, and between a State, or the Citizens thereof, and foreign States, Citizens or Subjects.

In all Cases affecting Ambassadors, other public Ministers and Consuls, and those in which a State shall be Party, the supreme Court shall have original Jurisdiction. In all the other Cases before mentioned, the supreme Court shall have appellate Jurisdiction, both as to Law and Fact, with such Exceptions, and under such Regulations as the Congress shall make.

The trial of all Crimes, except in Cases of Impeachment, shall be by Jury; and such Trial shall be held in the State where the said Crimes shall have been committed; but when not committed within any State, the Trial shall be at such Place or Places as the Congress may by Law have directed.

Section 3. Treason against the United States, shall consist only in levying War against them, or in adhering to their Enemies, giving them Aid and Comfort. No Person shall be convicted of Treason unless on the Testimony of two Witnesses to the same overt Act, or on Confession in open Court.

The Congress shall have Power to declare the Punishment of Treason, but no Attainder of Treason shall work Corruption of Blood, or Forfeiture except during the Life of the Person attained.

Article IV

Section 1. Full Faith and Credit shall be given in each State to the public Acts, Records, and judicial Proceedings of every other State. And the Congress may by general Laws prescribe the Manner in which such Acts, Records and Proceedings shall be proved, and the Effect thereof.

Section 2. The Citizens of each State shall be entitled to all Privileges and Immunities of Citizens in the several States.

A Person charged in any State with Treason, Felony, or other Crime, who shall flee from Justice, and be found in another State, shall on demand of the executive Authority of the State from which he fled, be delivered up, to be removed to the State having Jurisdiction of the Crime.

No Person held to Service or Labour in one State, under the Laws thereof, escaping into another, shall, in Consequence of any Law or Regulation therein, be discharged from such Service or Labour, but shall be delivered up on Claim of the Party to whom such Service or Labour may be due.

Section 3. New States may be admitted by the Congress into this Union; but no new State shall be formed or erected within the Jurisdiction of any other State; nor any State be formed by the Junction of two or more States, or parts of States, without the Consent of the Legislatures of the States concerned as well as of the Congress.

The Congress shall have Power to dispose of and make all needful Rules and Regulations respecting the Territory or other Property belonging to the United States; and nothing in this Constitution shall be so construed as to Prejudice any Claims of the United States or of any particular State.

Section 4. The United States shall guarantee to every State in this union a Republican Form of Government, and shall protect each of them against Invasion; and on Application of the Legislature, or of the Executive (when the Legislature cannot be convened) against domestic Violence.

Article V

The Congress, whenever two-thirds of both Houses shall deem it necessary, shall propose Amendments to this Constitution, or, on the Application of the Legislatures of two-thirds of the several States, shall call a Convention for proposing Amendments, which, in either Case, shall be valid to all Intents and Purposes, as part of this Constitution, when ratified by the Legislatures of three-fourths of the several States, or by Conventions in three-fourths thereof, as the one or the other Mode of Ratification may be proposed by the Congress; Provided that no Amendment which may be made prior to the Year

One thousand eight hundred and eight shall in any Manner affect the first and fourth Clauses in the Ninth Section of the first Article; and that no State, without its Consent, shall be deprived of its equal Suffrage in the Senate.

Article VI

All Debts contracted and Engagements entered into, before the Adoption of this Constitution, shall be as valid against the United States under this Constitution, as under the Confederation.

This Constitution, and the Laws of the United States which shall be made in Pursuance thereof; and all Treaties made, or which shall be made, under the Authority of the United States, shall be the supreme Law of the Land; and the Judges in every State shall be bound thereby, any Thing in the Constitution or Laws of any State to the Contrary notwithstanding.

The Senators and Representatives before mentioned, and the Members of the several State Legislatures, and all executive and judicial Officers, both of the United States and of the several States, shall be bound by Oath or Affirmation to support this Constitution; but no religious Test shall ever be required as a qualification to any Office or public Trust under the United States.

Article VII

The Ratification of the Conventions of nine States shall be sufficient for the Establishment of this Constitution between the States so ratifying the same.

Done in Convention by the Unanimous Consent of the States present the Seventeenth Day of September in the Year of our Lord one thousand seven hundred and Eighty seven, and of the Independence of the United States of America the Twelfth. In Witness whereof We have hereunto subscribed our Names.

Articles in Addition to, and Amendment of, the Constitution of the United States of America, Proposed by Congress, and Ratified by the Legislatures of the Several States, Pursuant to the Fifth Article of the Original Constitution.

[The first ten amendments went into effect in 1791.]

Amendment I

Congress shall make no law respecting an establishment of religion, or prohibiting the free exercise thereof; or abridging the freedom of speech, or of the press; or the right of the people peaceably to assemble, and to petition the Government for a redress of grievances.

Amendment II

A well regulated Militia, being necessary to the security of a free State, the right of the people to keep and bear Arms shall not be infringed.

Amendment III

No Soldier shall, in time of peace, be quartered in any house, without the consent of the Owner, nor in time of War, but in a manner to be prescribed by law.

Amendment IV

The right of the people to be secure in their persons, houses, papers, and effects, against unreasonable searches and seizures, shall not be violated, and no Warrants shall issue, but upon probable cause, supported by Oath or affirmation, and particularly describing the place to be searched, and the persons or things to be seized.

Amendment V

No person shall be held to answer for a capital or otherwise infamous crime, unless on a presentment or indictment of a Grand Jury, except in cases arising in the land or naval forces, or in the Militia, when in actual service in time of War or public danger; nor shall any person be subject for the same offence to be twice put in jeopardy of life or limb; nor shall be compelled in any criminal case to be a witness against himself, nor be deprived of life, liberty, or property, without due process of law; nor shall private property be taken for public use, without just compensation.

Amendment VI

In all criminal prosecutions, the accused shall enjoy the right to a speedy and public trial, by an impartial jury of the State and district wherein the crime shall have been committed, which district shall have been previously ascertained by law, and to be informed of the nature and cause of the accusation; to be confronted with the witnesses against him; to have compulsory process for obtaining witnesses in his favour, and to have the Assistance of Counsel for defence.

Amendment VII

In suits at common law where the value in controversy shall exceed twenty dollars, the right of trial by jury, shall be preserved, and no fact tried by a jury shall be otherwise reexamined in any Court of the United States, than according to the rules of the common law.

Amendment VIII

Excessive bail shall not be required, nor excessive fines imposed, nor cruel and unusual punishments inflicted.

Amendment IX

The enumeration in the Constitution, of certain rights, shall not be construed to deny or disparage others retained by the people.

Amendment X

The powers not delegated to the United States by the Constitution, nor prohibited by it to the States, are reserved to the States respectively, or to the people.

Amendment XI (1798)

The Judicial power of the United States shall not be construed to extend to any suit in law or equity, commenced or prosecuted against one of the United States by Citizens of another State, or by Citizens or Subjects of any Foreign State.

Amendment XII (1804)

The Electors shall meet in their respective States and vote by ballot for President and Vice-President, one of whom, at least, shall not be an inhabitant of the same State with themselves; they shall name in their ballots the person voted for as President, and in distinct ballots the person voted for as Vice-President, and they shall make distinct lists of all persons voted for as President, and of all persons voted for as Vice-President, and of the number of votes for each, which lists they shall sign and certify, and transmit sealed to the seat of the government of the United States, directed to the President of the Senate;—The President of the Senate shall, in the presence of the Senate and House of Representatives, open all the certificates and the votes shall then be counted; — The person having the greatest number of votes for President, shall be the President, if such number be a majority of the whole number of Electors appointed; and if no person have such majority, then from the persons having the highest numbers not exceeding three on the list of those voted for as President, the House of Representatives shall choose immediately, by ballot, the President. But in choosing the President, the votes shall be taken by states, the representation from each state having one vote; a quorum for this purpose shall consist of a member or members from two-thirds of the states, and a majority of all the states shall be necessary to a choice. And if the House of Representatives shall not choose a President whenever the right of choice shall devolve upon them, before the fourth day of March next following, then the Vice-President shall act as President, as in the case of the death or other constitutional disability of the President.— The person having the greatest number of votes as Vice-President, shall be the Vice-President, if such number be a majority of the whole number of Electors appointed, and if no person have a majority, then from the two highest numbers on the list, the Senate shall choose the Vice-President; a quorum for the purpose shall consist of two-thirds of the whole number of Senators, and a majority of the whole number shall be necessary to a choice. But no person constitutionally ineligible to the office of President shall be eligible to that of Vice-President of the United States.

Amendment XIII (1865)

Section 1. Neither slavery nor involuntary servitude, except as a punishment for crime whereof the party shall have been duly convicted, shall exist within the United States, or any place subject to their jurisdiction.

Section 2. Congress shall have power to enforce this article by appropriate legislation.

Amendment XIV (1868)

Section 1. All persons born or naturalized in the United States, and subject to the jurisdiction thereof, are citizens of the United States and of the State wherein they reside. No State shall make or enforce any law which shall abridge the privileges or immunities of citizens of the United States; nor shall any State deprive any person of life, liberty, or property, without due process of law; nor deny to any person within its jurisdiction the equal protection of the laws.

Section 2. Representatives shall be apportioned among the several States according to their respective numbers, counting the whole number of persons in each State, excluding Indians not taxed. But when the right to vote at any election for the choice of electors for President and Vice-President of the United States, Representatives in Congress, the Executive and Judicial officers of a State, or the members of the Legislature thereof, is denied to any of the male inhabitants of such State, being twenty-one years of age, and citizens of the United States, or in any way abridged, except for participation in rebellion, or other crime, the basis of representation therein shall be reduced in the proportion which the number of such male citizens shall bear to the whole number of male citizens twenty-one years of age in such State.

Section 3. No person shall be a Senator or Representative in Congress, or elector of President and Vice-President, or hold any office, civil or military, under the United States, or under any State, who, having previously taken an oath, as a member of Congress, or as an officer of the United States, or as member of any State legislature, or as an executive or judicial officer of any State, to support the Constitution of the United States, shall have engaged in insurrection or rebellion against the same, or given aid or comfort to the enemies thereof. But Congress may by a vote of two-thirds of each House, remove such disability.

Section 4. The validity of the public debt of the United States, authorized by law, including debts incurred for payment of pensions and bounties for services in suppressing insurrection or rebellion, shall not be questioned. But neither the United States nor any State shall assume or pay any debt or obligation incurred in aid of insurrection or rebellion against the United States, or any claim for the loss or emancipation of any slave; but all such debts, obligations, and claims shall be held illegal and void.

Section 5. The Congress shall have the power to enforce, by appropriate legislation, the provisions of this article.

Amendment XV (1870)

Section 1. The right of citizens of the United States to vote shall not be denied or abridged by the United States or by any State on account of race, color, or previous condition of servitude—

Section 2. The Congress shall have power to enforce this article by appropriate legislation.

Amendment XVI (1913)

The Congress shall have power to lay and collect taxes on incomes, from whatever source derived, without apportionment among the several States, and without regard to any census or enumeration.

Amendment XVII (1913)

The Senate of the United States shall be composed of two Senators from each State, elected by the people thereof, for six years; and each Senator shall have one vote. The electors in each State shall have the qualifications requisite for electors of the most numerous branch of the State legislatures.

When vacancies happen in the representation of any State in the Senate, the executive authority of such State shall issue writs of election to fill such vacancies: *Provided,* That legislature of any State may empower the executive thereof to make temporary appointments until the people fill the vacancies by election as the legislature may direct.

This amendment shall not be so construed as to affect the election or term of any Senator chosen before it becomes valid as part of the Constitution.

Amendment XVIII (1919)

Section 1. After one year from the ratification of this article the manufacture, sale, or transportation of intoxicating liquors within, the importation thereof into, or the exportation thereof from the United States and all territory subject to the jurisdiction thereof for beverage purposes is hereby prohibited.

Section 2. The Congress and the several States shall have concurrent power to enforce this article by appropriate legislation.

Section 3. This article shall be inoperative unless it shall have been ratified as an amendment to the Constitution by the legislatures of the several States, as provided in the Constitution, within seven years from the date of the submission hereof to the States by the Congress.

Amendment XIX (1920)

The right of citizens of the United States to vote shall not be denied or abridged by the United States or by any State on account of sex.

Congress shall have power to enforce this article by appropriate legislation.

Amendment XX (1933)

Section 1. The terms of the President and Vice-President shall end at noon on the 20th day of January, and the terms of Senators and Representatives at noon on the 3d day of January, of the years in which such terms would have ended if this article had not been ratified; and the terms of their successors shall then begin.

Section 2. The Congress shall assemble at least once in every year, and such meeting shall begin at noon on the 3d day of January, unless they shall by law appoint a different day.

Section 3. If, at the time fixed for the beginning of the term of the President, the President elect shall have died, the Vice-President elect shall become President. If a President shall not have been chosen before the time fixed for the beginning of his term, or if the President elect shall have failed to qualify, then the Vice-President elect shall act as President until a President shall have qualified; and the Congress may by law provide for the case wherein neither a President elect nor a Vice-President elect shall have qualified, declaring who shall then act as President, or the manner in which one who is to act shall be selected, and such person shall act accordingly until a President or Vice-President shall have qualified.

Section 4. The Congress may by law provide for the case of the death of any of the persons from whom the House of Representatives may choose a President whenever the right of choice shall have devolved upon them, and for the case of the death of any of the persons from whom the Senate may choose a Vice-President whenever the right of choice shall have devolved upon them.

Section 5. Sections 1 and 2 shall take effect on the 15th day of October following the ratification of this article.

Section 6. This article shall be inoperative unless it shall have been ratified as an amendment to the Constitution by the legislatures of three-fourths of the several States within seven years from the date of its submission.

Amendment XXI (1933)

Section 1. The eighteenth article of amendment to the Constitution of the United States is hereby repealed.

Section 2. The transportation or importation into any State, Territory, or possession of the United States for delivery or use therein of intoxicating liquors, in violation of the laws thereof, is hereby prohibited.

Section 3. This article shall be inoperative unless it shall have been ratified as an amendment to the Constitution by conventions in the several States, as provided in the Constitution within seven years from the date of the submission hereof to the States by the Congress.

Amendment XXII (1951)

Section 1. No person shall be elected to the office of the President more than twice, and no person who has held the office of President, or acted as President, for more than two years of a term to which some other person was elected President shall be elected to the office of the President more than once.

But this Article shall not apply to any person holding the office of President when this Article was proposed by the Congress, and shall not prevent any person who may be holding the office of President, or acting as President, during the term within which this article becomes operative from holding the office of President or acting as President during the remainder of such term.

Section 2. This article shall be inoperative unless it shall have been ratified as an amendment to the Constitution by the legislatures of three-fourths of the several states within seven years from the date of its submission to the states by the Congress.

Amendment XXIII (1961)

Section 1. The District constituting the seat of Government of the United States shall appoint in such manner as the Congress may direct:

A number of electors of President and Vice-President equal to the whole number of Senators and Representatives in Congress to which the District would be entitled if it were a State, but in no event more than the least populous State; they shall be in addition to those appointed by the States, but they shall be considered, for the purposes of the election of President and Vice-President, to be electors appointed by a State; and they shall meet in the District and perform such duties as provided by the twelfth article of amendment.

Section 2. The Congress shall have power to enforce this article by appropriate legislation.

Amendment XXIV (1964)

Section 1. The right of citizens of the United States to vote in any primary or other election for President or Vice President, for electors for President or Vice President, or for Senator or Representative in Congress, shall not be denied or abridged by the United States or any other State by reason of failure to pay any poll tax or other tax.

Section 2. The Congress shall have the power to enforce this article by appropriate legislation.

Amendment XXV (1967)

Section 1. In case of the removal of the President from office or of his death or resignation, the Vice President shall become President.

Section 2. Whenever there is a vacancy in the office of the Vice President, the President shall nominate a Vice President who shall take office upon confirmation by a majority vote of both Houses of Congress.

Section 3. Whenever the President transmits to the President pro tempore of the Senate and the Speaker of the House of Representatives his written declaration that he is unable to discharge the powers and duties of his office, and until he transmits to them a written declaration to the contrary, such powers and duties shall be discharged by the Vice President as Acting President.

Section 4. Whenever the Vice President and a majority of either the principal officers of the executive departments or of such other body as Congress may by law provide, transmit to the President pro tempore of the Senate and the Speaker of the House of Representatives their written declaration that the President is unable to discharge the powers and duties of his office, the Vice President shall immediately assume the powers and duties of the office as Acting President.

Thereafter, when the President transmits to the President pro tempore of the Senate and the Speaker of the House of Representatives his written declaration that no inability exists, he shall resume the powers and duties of his office unless the Vice President and a majority of either the principal officers of the executive departments or of such other body as Congress may by law provide, transmit within four days to the President pro tempore of the Senate and the Speaker of the House of Representatives their written declaration that the President is unable to discharge the powers and duties of his office. Thereupon Congress shall decide the issue, assembling within forty-eight hours for that purpose if not in session, If the Congress, within twenty-one days after receipt of the latter written declaration, or, if Congress is not in session, within twenty-one days after Congress is required to assemble, determines by two-thirds vote of both Houses that the President is unable to discharge the powers and duties of his office, the Vice President shall continue to discharge the same as Acting President; otherwise, the President shall resume the powers and duties of his office.

Amendment XXVI (1971)

Section 1. The right of citizens of the United States, who are eighteen years of age or older, to vote shall not be denied or abridged by the United States or by any State on account of age.

Section 2. The Congress shall have the power to enforce this article by appropriate legislation.

Appendix G

The Constitution of the Confederate States of America, March 11, 1861

WE, the people of the Confederate States, each State acting in its sovereign and independent character, in order to form a permanent federal government, establish justice, insure domestic tranquility, and secure the blessings of liberty to ourselves and our posterity —invoking the favor and guidance of Almighty God do ordain and establish this Constitution for the Confederate States of America.

Article I

Section 1—All legislative powers herein delegated shall be vested in a Congress of the Confederate States, which shall consist of a Senate and House of Representatives.

Section 2. (1) The House of Representatives shall be chosen every second year by the people of the several States; and the electors in each State shall be citizens of the Confederate States, and have the qualifications requisite for electors of the most numerous branch of the State Legislature; but no person of foreign birth, not a citizen of the Confederate States, shall be allowed to vote for any officer, civil or political, State or Federal.

(2) No person shall be a Representative who shall not have attained the age of twenty-five years, and be a citizen of the Confederate States, and who shall not, when elected, be an inhabitant of that State in which he shall be chosen.

(3) Representatives and direct taxes shall be apportioned among the several States which may be included within this Confederacy, according to their respective numbers, which shall be determined by adding to the whole number of free persons, including those bound to service for a term of years, and excluding Indians not taxed, three-fifths of all slaves. The actual enumeration shall be made within three years after the first meeting of the

Congress of the Confederate States, and within every subsequent term of ten years, in such manner as they shall by law direct. The number of Representatives shall not exceed one for every fifth thousand, but each State shall have at least one Representative; and until such enumeration shall be made, the State of South Carolina shall be entitled to choose six; the State of Georgia ten; the State of Alabama nine; the State of Florida two; the State of Mississippi seven; the State of Louisiana six; and the State of Texas six.

(4) When vacancies happen in the representation of any State, the Executive authority thereof shall issue writs of election to fill such vacancies.

(5) The House of Representatives shall choose their Speaker and other officers; and shall have the sole power of impeachment; except that any judicial or other federal officer resident and acting solely within the limits of any State, may be impeached by a vote of two-thirds of both branches of the Legislature thereof.

Section 3. (1) The Senate of the Confederate States shall be composed of two Senators from each State, chosen for six years by the Legislature thereof, at the regular session next immediately preceding the commencement of the term of service; and each Senator shall have one vote.

(2) Immediately after they shall be assembled, in consequence of the first election, they shall be divided as equally as may be into three classes. The seats of the Senators of the first class shall be vacated at the expiration of the second year; of the second class at the expiration of the fourth year; and of the third class at the expiration of the sixth year; so that one- third may be chosen every second year; and if vacancies happen by resignation or otherwise during the recess of the Legislature of any State, the Executive thereof may make temporary appointments until the next meeting of the Legislature, which shall then fill such vacancies.

(3) No person shall be a Senator, who shall not have attained the age of thirty years, and be a citizen of the Confederate States; and who shall not, when elected, be an inhabitant of the State for which he shall be chosen.

(4) The Vice-President of the Confederate States shall be President of the Senate, but shall have no vote, unless they be equally divided.

(5) The Senate shall choose their other officers, and also a President *pro tempore,* in the absence of the Vice- President, or when he shall exercise the office of President of the Confederate States.

(6) The Senate shall have sole power to try all impeachments. When sitting for that purpose they shall be on oath or affirmation. When the President of the Confederate States is tried, the Chief-Justice shall preside; and no person shall be convicted without the concurrence of two-thirds of the members present.

(7) Judgment in cases of impeachment shall not extend further than removal from office and disqualification to hold and enjoy any office of honor, trust, or profit, under the Confederate States; but the party convicted

shall, nevertheless, be liable to and subject to indictment, trial, judgment, and punishment according to law.

Section 4. (1) The times, places, and manner of holding elections for Senators and Representatives, shall be prescribed in each State by the Legislature thereof, subject to the provisions of this Constitution; but the Congress may, at any time, by law, make or alter such regulations, except as to the times and places of choosing Senators.

(2) The Congress shall assemble at least once in every year; and such meeting shall be on the first Monday in December, unless they shall, by law, appoint a different day.

Section 5. (1) Each House shall be the judge of the elections, returns, and qualifications of its own members, and a majority of each shall constitute a quorum to do business; but a smaller number may adjourn from day to day, and may be authorized to compel the attendance of absent members, in such manner and under such penalties as each House may provide.

(2) Each House may determine the rules of its proceedings, punish its members for disorderly behavior, and, with the concurrence of two-thirds of the whole number, expel a member.

(3) Each House shall keep a journal of its proceedings, and from time to time publish the same, excepting such part as may in its judgment require secrecy, and the ayes and nays of the members of either House, on any question, shall, at the desire of one-fifth of those present, be entered on the journal.

(4) Neither House, during the session of Congress, shall, without the consent, of the other, adjourn for more than three days, nor to any other place than that in which the two Houses shall be sitting.

Section 6. (1) The Senators and Representatives shall receive a compensation for their services, to be ascertained by law, and paid out of the Treasury of the Confederate States. They shall, in all cases except treason and breach of the peace, be privileged from arrest during their attendance at the session of their respective Houses, and in going to and returning from the same; and for any speech or debate in either House, they shall not be questioned in any other place.

(2) No Senator or Representative shall, during the time for which he was elected, be appointed to any civil office under the authority of the Confederate States, which shall have been created, or the emoluments whereof shall have been increased during such time; and no person holding any office under the Confederate States shall be a member of either House during his continuance in office. But Congress may, by law, grant to the principal officer in each of the Executive Departments a seat upon the floor of either House, with the privilege of discussing any measure appertaining to his department.

Section 7. (1) All bills for raising revenues shall originate in the House of Representatives; but the Senate may propose or concur with amendments as on other bills.

(2) Every bill which shall have passed both Houses shall, before it becomes a law, be presented to the President of the Confederate States; if he approve he shall sign it; but if not, he shall return it with his objections to that House in which it shall have originated, who shall enter the objections at large on their journal, and proceed to reconsider it. If, after such reconsideration, two-thirds of that House shall agree to pass the bill, it shall be sent, together with the objections, to the other House, by which it shall likewise be reconsidered, and if approved by a two-thirds of that House, it shall become a law. But in all such cases, the votes of both Houses shall be determined by yeas and nays, and the names of the persons voting for and against the bill shall be entered on the journal of each House respectively. If any bill shall not be returned by the President within ten days (Sundays excepted) after it shall have been presented to him, the same shall be a law in like manner as if he had signed it, unless the Congress, by their adjournment, prevent its return; in which case it shall not be a law. The President may approve any appropriation and disapprove any other appropriation in the same bill. In such case he shall, in signing the bill, designate the appropriations disapproved; and shall return a copy of such appropriations, with his objections, to the House in which the bill shall have originated; and the same proceedings shall then be had as in case of other bills disapproved by the President.

(3) Every order, resolution, or vote, to which the concurrence of both Houses may be necessary (except on question of adjournment) shall be presented to the President of the Confederate States; and before the same shall take effect shall be approved by him; or being disapproved by him, may be repassed by two-thirds of both Houses according to the rules and limitations prescribed in case of a bill.

Section 8. The Congress shall have power —

(1) To lay and collect taxes, duties, imposts, and excises, for revenue necessary to pay the debts, provide for the common defence, and carry on the Government of the Confederate States; but no bounties shall be granted from the treasury; nor shall any duties or taxes on importations from foreign nations be laid to promote or foster any branch of industry; and all duties, imposts, and excises shall be uniform throughout the Confederate States.

(2) To borrow money on the credit of the Confederate States.

(3) To regulate commerce with foreign nations, and among the several States, and with the Indian tribes; but neither this, nor any other clause contained in the Constitution shall be construed to delegate the power to Congress to appropriate money for any internal improvement intended to facilitate commerce; except for the purpose of furnishing lights, beacons, and

buoys, and other aids to navigation upon the coasts, and the improvement of harbors, and the removing of obstructions in river navigation, in all which cases, such duties shall be laid on the navigation facilitated thereby, as may be necessary to pay the costs and expenses thereof.

(4) To establish uniform laws of naturalization, and uniform laws on the subject of bankruptcies throughout the Confederate States, but no law of Congress shall discharge any debt contracted before the passage of the same.

(5) To coin money, regulate the value thereof, and of foreign coin, and fix the standard of weights and measures.

(6) To provide for the punishment of counterfeiting the securities and current coin of the Confederate States.

(7) To establish post-offices and post-routes; but the expenses of the Post-office Department, after the first day of March, in the year of our Lord eighteen hundred and sixty-three, shall be paid out of its own revenues.

(8) To promote the progress of science and useful arts, by securing for limited times to authors and inventors the exclusive right to their respective writings and discoveries.

(9) To constitute tribunals inferior to the Supreme Court.

(10) To define and punish piracies and felonies committed on the high seas, and offences against the law of nations.

(11) To declare war, grant letters of marque and reprisal, and make rules concerning captures on land and water.

(12) To raise and support armies; but no appropriation of money to that use shall be for a longer term than two years.

(13) To provide and maintain a navy.

(14) To make rules for government and regulation of the land and naval forces.

(15) To provide for calling forth the militia to execute the laws of the Confederate States; suppress insurrections, and repel invasions.

(16) To provide for organizing, arming, and disciplining the militia, and for governing such part of them as may be employed in the service of the Confederate States; reserving to the States, respectively, the appointment of the officers, and the authority of training the militia according to the discipline prescribed by Congress.

(17) To exercise exclusive legislation, in all cases whatsoever, over such district (not exceeding ten miles square) as may, by cession of one or more States, and the acceptance of Congress, become the seat of the Government of the Confederate States; and to exercise a like authority over all places purchased by the consent of the Legislature of the State in which the same shall be, for the erection of forts, magazines, arsenals, dock-yards, and other needful buildings, and

(18) To make all laws which shall be necessary and proper for carrying into execution the foregoing powers, and all other powers vested by this

Constitution in the Government of the Confederate States, or in any department or officer thereof.

Section 9. (1) The importation of negroes of the African race, from any foreign country, other than the slaveholding States or Territories f the United States of America, is hereby forbidden; and Congress is required to pass such laws as shall effectually prevent the same.

(2) Congress shall also have power to prohibit the introduction of slaves from any State not a member of, or Territory not belonging to, this Confederacy.

(3) The privilege of the writ of *habeas corpus* shall not be suspended, unless when in cases of rebellion or invasion the public safety may require it.

(4) No bill of attainder, or *ex post facto* law, or law denying or impairing the right of property in negro slaves shall be passed.

(5) No capitation or other direct tax shall be laid unless in proportion to the census or enumeration hereinbefore directed to be taken.

(6) No tax or duty shall be laid on articles exported from any State, except by a vote of two-thirds of both Houses.

(7) No preference shall be given by any regulation of commerce or revenue to the ports of one State over those of another.

(8) No money shall be drawn from the treasury but in consequence of appropriations made by law; and a regular statement and account of the receipts and expenditures of all public money shall be published from time to time.

(9) Congress shall appropriate no money from the treasury except by a vote of two-thirds of both Houses, taken by yeas and nays, unless it be asked and estimated for by some one of the heads of departments, and submitted to Congress by the President; or for the purpose of paying its own expenses and contingencies; or for the payment of claims against the Confederate States, the justice of which shall have been judicially declared by a tribunal for the investigation of claims against the Government, which it is hereby made the duty of Congress to establish.

(10) All bills appropriating money shall specify in federal currency the exact amount of each appropriation and the purposes for which it is made; and Congress shall grant no extra compensation to any public contractor, officer, agent, or servant, after such contract shall have been made or such service rendered.

(11) No title of nobility shall be granted by the Confederate States; and no person holding any office of profit or trust under them shall, without the consent of the Congress, accept of any present, emoluments, office, or title of any kind whatever, from any king prince, or foreign state.

(12) Congress shall make no law respecting an establishment of religion, or prohibiting the free exercise thereof; or abridging the freedom of speech

or of the press; or the right of the people peaceably to assemble and petition the Government for a redress of grievances.

(13) A well-regulated militia being necessary to the security of a free State, the right of the people to keep and bear arms shall not be infringed.

(14) No soldier shall, in time of peace, be quartered in any house without the consent of the owner; nor in time of war, but in a manner prescribed by law.

(15) The right of the people to be secure in their persons, houses, papers, and against unreasonable searches and seizures, shall not be violated; and no warrant shall issue but upon probable cause, supported by oath or affirmation, and particularly describing the place to be searched, and the person or things to be seized.

(16) No person shall be held to answer for a capital or otherwise infamous crime, unless on a presentment or indictment of a grand jury, except in cases arising in the land or naval forces, or in the militia, when in actual service, in time of war, or public danger; nor shall any person be subject for the same offence to be twice put in jeopardy of life or limb; nor be compelled in any criminal case to be a witness against himself; nor be deprived of life, liberty, or property, without due process of law; nor shall any private property be taken for public use without just compensation.

(17) In all criminal prosecutions the accused shall enjoy the right to a speedy and public trial, by an impartial jury of the State and district wherein the crime shall have been committed, which district shall have been previously ascertained by law, and to be informed of the nature and cause of the accusation; to be confronted with the witnesses against him, to have compulsory process for obtaining witnesses in his favor; and to have the assistance of counsel for his defence.

(18) In suits in common law, where the value in controversy shall exceed twenty dollars, the right of trial by jury shall be preserved; and no one so tried by a jury shall be otherwise remained in any court of the Confederacy, that according to the rules of the common law.

(19) Excessive bail shall not be required, nor excessive fines imposed, nor cruel or unusual punishment inflicted.

(20) Every law or resolution having the force of law, shall relate to but one subject, and that shall be expressed in the title.

Section 10. (1) No State shall enter into any treaty, alliance or confederation; grant letters of marque and reprisals; coin money; make any thing but gold and silver coin a tender in payment of debts; pass any bill of attainder, or *ex post facto* law, or law impairing the obligation of contracts; or grant any title of nobility.

(2) No State shall, without the consent of Congress, lay any imposts or duties on imports or exports except what may be absolutely necessary for executing its inspection laws; and the net produce of all duties and imposts,

laid by any State on imports or exports, shall be for the use of the Treasury of the Confederate States; and all such laws shall be subject to the revision and control of Congress.

(3) No State shall, without the consent of Congress, lay any duty of tonnage, except on sea-going vessels for the improvement of its rivers and harbors navigated by the said vessels; but such duties shall not conflict with any treaties of the Confederate States with foreign nations; and any surplus of revenue, thus derived, shall after making such improvement, be paid into the common treasury; nor shall any State keep troops or ships of war in time of peace, enter into any agreement or compact with another State, or with a foreign power or engage in war, unless actually invaded or in such imminent danger as will not admit of delay. But when any river divides or flows through two or more States, they may enter into compacts with each other to improve the navigation thereof.

Article II

Section 1. (1) The Executive power shall be vested in a President of the Confederate States of America . He and the Vice-President shall hold their offices for the term of six years; but the President shall not be reeligible. The President and Vice-President shall be elected as follows:

(2) Each State shall appoint in such manner as the Legislature thereof may direct, a number of electors equal to the whole number of Senators and Representatives to which the State may be entitled in Congress; but no Senator or Representative, or person holding an office of trust or profit under the Confederate States shall be appointed an elector.

(3) The electors shall meet in their respective States, and vote by ballot for President and Vice-President, one of whom at least, shall not be an inhabitant of the same State with themselves; they shall name in their ballots the person voted for as President, and in distinct ballots the person voted for as Vice-President and they shall make distinct lists of all persons voted for as President, and of all persons voted for as Vice-President, and of the number of votes for each; which list they shall sign and certify, and transmit, sealed, to the Government of the Confederate States, directed to the President of the Senate. The President of the Senate shall, in the presence of the Senate and House of Representatives, open all the certificates, and the votes shall then be counted; the person having the greatest number of votes for President shall be the President, if such number be a majority of the whole number of electors appointed; and if no person shall have such a majority, then, from the persons having the highest numbers not exceeding three, on the list of those voted for as President, the House of Representatives shall choose immediately, by ballot the President. But, in choosing the President the votes shall be taken by States, the Representative from each State having one vote; a quorum for this purpose shall consist of a member or members from

two-thirds of the States, and a majority of all the States shall be necessary to a choice. And if the House of Representatives shall not choose a President, whenever the right of choice shall devolve upon them, before the fourth day of March next following, then the Vice-President shall act as President, as in case of the death, or other constitutional disability of the President.

(4) The person having the greatest number of votes as Vice- President shall be the Vice-President, if such number be a majority of the whole number of electors appointed; and if no person have a majority, then from the two highest numbers on the list, the Senate shall choose the Vice- President; a quorum for the purpose shall consist of two- thirds of the whole number of Senators, and a majority of the whole number shall be necessary for a choice.

(5) But no person constitutionally ineligible to the office of President shall be eligible to that of Vice-President of the Confederate States.

(6) The Congress may determine the time of choosing the electors, and the day on which they shall give their votes; which day shall be the same throughout the Confederate States.

(7) No person except a natural born citizen of the Confederate States, or a citizen thereof, at the time of the adoption of this Constitution, or a citizen thereof born in the United States prior to the 20th December, 1860, shall be eligible to the office of President; neither shall any person be eligible to that office who shall not have attained the age of thirty-five years, and been fourteen years a resident within the limits of the Confederate States, as they may exist at the time of his election.

(8) In case of the removal of the President from office or of his death, resignation, or inability to discharge the powers and duties of the said office, the same shall devolve on the Vice-President; and the Congress may, by law, provide for the case of the removal, death, resignation or inability both of the President and the Vice-President, declaring what officer shall then act as President, and such officer shall then act accordingly until the disability be removed or a President shall be elected.

(9) The President shall, at stated times, receive for his services a compensation, which shall neither be increased nor diminished during the period for which he shall have been elected; and he shall not receive within that period any other emolument from the Confederate States, or any of them.

(10) Before he enters on the execution of the duties of his office he shall take the following oath or affirmation:

> "I do solemnly swear (or affirm) that I will faithfully execute the office of President of the Confederate States, and will, to the best of my ability, preserve, protect, and defend the Constitution thereof."

Section 2. (1) The President shall be commander-in-chief of the army and navy of the Confederate States, and of the militia of the several States, when called into the actual service of the Confederate States; he may require the opinion, in writing, of the principal officer in each of the Executive Departments, upon any subject relating to the duties of their respective offices; and he shall have power to grant reprieves and pardons for offences against the Confederate States, except in cases of impeachment.

(2) He shall have power, by and with the advice and consent of the Senate, to make treaties, provided two-thirds of the Senators present concur; and he shall nominate, and by and with the advice and consent of the Senate, shall appoint ambassadors, other public ministers, and consuls, Judges of the Supreme Court, and all other officers of the Confederate States, whose appointments are not herein otherwise provided for, and which shall be established by law; but the Congress may by law vest the appointment of such inferior officers, as they think proper, in the President alone, in the courts of law, or in the heads of departments.

(3) The principal officer in each of the Executive Departments, and all persons connected with the diplomatic service, may be removed from office at the pleasure of the President. All other civil officers of the Executive Department may be removed at any time by the President, or other appointing power, when their services are unnecessary, or for dishonesty, incapacity, inefficiency, misconduct, or neglect of duty; and when so removed, the removal shall be reported to the Senate, together with the reasons therefor.

(4) The President shall have power to fill all vacancies that may happen during the recess of the Senate, by granting commissions which shall expire at the end of the next session, but no person rejected by the Senate shall be reappointed to the same office during their ensuing recess.

Section 3. (1) The President shall, from time to time, give the Congress information of the state of the Confederacy, and recommend to their consideration such measures as he shall judge necessary and expedient; he may, on extraordinary occasions, convene both Houses, or either of them; and, in case of disagreement between them, with respect to the time of adjournment he may adjourn them to such time as he shall think proper; he shall receive ambassadors and other public ministers; he shall take care that the laws be faithfully executed, and shall commission all the officers of the Confederate States.

Section 4. (1) The President and Vice-President, and all civil officers of the Confederate States, shall be removed from office on impeachment for, or conviction of, treason, bribery, or other high crimes and misdemeanors.

Article III

Section 1. (1) The judicial power of the Confederate States shall be vested in one Superior Court, and in such inferior courts as the Congress may from time to time ordain and establish. The judges, both of the Supreme and inferior courts, shall hold their offices during good behavior, and shall, at stated times, receive for their services a compensation, which shall not be diminished during their continuance in office.

Section 2. (1) The judicial power shall extend to all cases arising under the Constitution, the laws of the Confederate States, or treaties made or which shall be made under their authority; to all cases affecting ambassadors, other public ministers, and consuls; to all cases of admiralty or maritime jurisdiction; to controversies to which the Confederate States shall be a a party; to controversies between two or more States; between a State and citizens of another State, where the State is plaintiff; between citizens claiming lands under grants of different States, and between a State or the citizens thereof, and foreign States, citizens, or subjects; but no State shall be sued by a citizen or subject of any foreign State.

(2) In all cases affecting ambassadors, other public ministers, and consuls, and those in which a State shall be a party, the Supreme Court shall have original jurisdiction. In all the other cases before mentioned, the Supreme Court shall have appellate jurisdiction, both as to law and fact, with such exceptions, and under such regulations as the Congress shall make.

(3) The trial of all crimes, except in cases of impeachment, shall be by jury, and such trial shall be held in the State where the said crimes shall have been committed; but when not committed within any State, the trial shall be at such place or places as the Congress may by law have directed.

Section 3. (1) Treason against the Confederate States shall consist only in levying war against them, or in adhering to their enemies, giving them aid and comfort. No person shall be convicted of treason unless on the testimony of two witnesses to the same overt act, or on confession in open court.

(2) The Congress shall have power to declare the punishment of treason but no attainder of treason shall work corruption of blood, or forfeiture, except during the life of the person attainted.

Article IV

Section 1. (1) Full faith and credit shall be given in each State to the public acts, records, and judicial proceedings of every other State. And the Congress may, by general laws, prescribe the manner in which such acts, records, and proceedings shall be proved, and the effect thereof.

Section 2 (1) The citizens of each State shall be entitled to all the privileges and immunities of citizens of the several States, and shall have the right of transit and sojourn in any State of this Confederacy, with their slaves and other property; and the right of property in said slaves shall not be thereby impaired.

(2) A person charged in any State with treason, felony, or other crime against the laws of such State, who shall flee from justice, and be found in another State, shall, on demand of the executive authority of the State from

which he fled, be delivered up to be removed to the State having jurisdiction of the crime.

(3) No slave or other person held to service or labor in any State or Territory of the Confederate States, under the laws thereof, escaping or unlawfully carried into another, shall, in consequence of any law or regulation therein, be discharged from such service or labor; but shall be delivered up on claim of the party to whom such slave belongs, or to whom such service or labor may be due.

Section 3. (1) Other States may be admitted into this Confederacy by a vote of two-thirds of the whole House of Representatives, and two-thirds of the Senate, the Senate voting by States; but no new State shall be formed or erected within the jurisdiction of any other State; nor any State be formed by the junction of two or more States, or parts of States, without the consent of the Legislatures of the States concerned as well as of the Congress.

(2) The Congress shall have power to dispose of and make all needful rules and regulations concerning the property of the Confederate States, including the lands thereof.

(3) The Confederate States may acquire new territory; and Congress shall have power to legislate and provide governments for the inhabitants of all territory belonging to the Confederate States, lying without the limits of the several States, and may permit them, at such times, and in such manner as it may by law provide, to form States to be admitted into the Confederacy. In all such territory, the institution of negro slavery, as it now exists in the Confederate States, shall be recognized and protected by Congress and by the territorial government; and the inhabitants of the several Confederate States and Territories shall have the right to take to such territory any slaves lawfully held by them in any of the States or Territories of the Confederate States.

(4) The Confederate States shall guarantee to every State that now is or hereafter may become a member of this Confederacy, a Republican form of Government, and shall protect each of them against invasion; and on application of the Legislature, (or of the Executive when the Legislature is not in session,) against domestic violence.

Article V

Section 1. (1) Upon the demand of any three States, legally assembled in their several Conventions, the Congress shall summon a Convention of all the States, to take into consideration such amendments to the Constitution as the said States shall concur in suggesting at the time when the said demand is made; and should any of the proposed amendments to the Constitution be agreed on by the said Convention—voting by States—and the same be ratified by the Legislatures of two-thirds of the several States, or by conventions in two-thirds thereof—as the one or the other mode of ratification may be proposed by the general convention—they shall thenceforward form a part of this Constitution. But no State shall, without its consent, be deprived of its equal representation in the Senate.

Article VI

1. —The Government established by this Constitution is the successor of the Provisional Government of the Confederate States of America, and all the laws passed by the latter shall continue in force until the same shall be repealed or modified; and all the officers appointed by the same shall remain in office until their successors are appointed and qualified, or the offices abolished.

2. All debts contracted and engagements entered into before the adoption of this Constitution shall be as valid against the Confederate States under this Constitution as under the Provisional Government.

3. This Constitution, and the laws of the Confederate States, made in pursuance thereof, and all treaties made, or which shall be made, under the authority of the Confederate States, shall be the supreme law of the land; and the judges in every State shall be bound thereby, any thing in the Constitution or laws of any State to the contrary notwithstanding.

4. The Senators and Representatives before mentioned, and the members of the several State Legislatures, and all executive and judicial offices, both of the Confederate States and of the several States, shall be bound by oath or affirmation, to support this Constitution; but no religious test shall ever be required as a qualification to any office or public trust under the Confederate States.

5. The enumeration, in the Constitution of certain rights, shall not be construed to deny or disparage others retained by the people of the several States.

6. The powers not delegated to the Confederate States by the Constitution, nor prohibited by it to the States, are reserved to the States, respectively, or to the people thereof.

Article VII

1. —The ratification of the conventions of five States shall be sufficient for the establishment of this Constitution between the States so ratifying the same.

2. When five States shall have ratified this Constitution in the manner before specified, the Congress, under the provisional Constitution, shall prescribe the time for holding the election of President and Vice-President, and for the meeting of the electoral college, and for counting the votes and inaugurating the President. They shall also prescribe the time for holding the first election of members of Congress under this Constitution, and the time for assembling the same. Until the assembling of such Congress, the Con-

gress under the provisional Constitution shall continue to exercise the legislative powers granted them; not extending beyond the time limited by the Constitution of the Provisional Government.

Adopted unanimously by the Congress of the Confederate States of South Carolina, Georgia, Florida, Alabama, Mississippi, Louisiana, and Texas, sitting in convention at the capitol, in the city of Montgomery, Ala. on the eleventh day of March, in the year eighteen hundred and sixty-one.

Howell Cobb
President of the Congress.
[Signatures]

Index